Cisco Network Admission Control, Volume I:

NAC Framework Architecture and Design

Denise Helfrich, Lou Ronnau, Jason Frazier, Paul Forbes

Cisco Press

Cisco Press
800 East 96th Street
Indianapolis, IN 46240 USA

Cisco Network Admission Control, Volume I
NAC Framework Architecture and Design

Denise Helfrich, Lou Ronnau, Jason Frazier, Paul Forbes

Copyright© 2007 Cisco Systems, Inc.

Published by:
Cisco Press
800 East 96th Street
Indianapolis, IN 46240 USA

Printed in the United States of America 1 2 3 4 5 6 7 8 9 0

First Printing   December 2006

Library of Congress Cataloging-in-Publication Number: 2005923482

ISBN: 1-58705-241-5

Warning and Disclaimer

This book is designed to provide information about Network Admission Control Framework Release 2 components and identifies steps to prepare, plan, and design NAC Framework. Every effort has been made to make this book as complete and as accurate as possible, but no warranty or fitness is implied.

The information is provided on an "as is" basis. The authors, Cisco Press, and Cisco Systems, Inc. shall have neither liability nor responsibility to any person or entity with respect to any loss or damages arising from the information contained in this book or from the use of the discs or programs that may accompany it.

The opinions expressed in this book belong to the author and are not necessarily those of Cisco Systems, Inc.

Feedback Information

At Cisco Press, our goal is to create in-depth technical books of the highest quality and value. Each book is crafted with care and precision, undergoing rigorous development that involves the unique expertise of members from the professional technical community.

Readers' feedback is a natural continuation of this process. If you have any comments regarding how we could improve the quality of this book, or otherwise alter it to better suit your needs, you can contact us through email at feedback@ciscopress.com. Please make sure to include the book title and ISBN in your message.

We greatly appreciate your assistance.

Trademark Acknowledgments

All terms mentioned in this book that are known to be trademarks or service marks have been appropriately capitalized. Cisco Press or Cisco Systems, Inc. cannot attest to the accuracy of this information. Use of a term in this book should not be regarded as affecting the validity of any trademark or service mark.

Corporate and Government Sales

Cisco Press offers excellent discounts on this book when ordered in quantity for bulk purchases or special sales.

For more information, please contact: U.S. Corporate and Government Sales 1-800-382-3419 corpsales@pearsontechgroup.com

For sales outside the U.S., please contact: International Sales international@pearsoned.com

Publisher	Paul Boger
Cisco Representative	Anthony Wolfenden
Cisco Press Program Manager	Jeff Brady
Executive Editor	Brett Bartow
Production Manager	Patrick Kanouse
Development Editor	Andrew Cupp
Project Editor	Jennifer Gallant
Copy Editor	John Edwards
Technical Editors	David Anderson
	Darrin Miller
	Ramakrishnan Rajamoni
Publishing Coordinator	Vanessa Evans
Book and Cover Designer	Louisa Adair
Composition	Mark Shirar
Indexer	Tim Wright
Proofreader	Water Crest Publishing, Inc.

Americas Headquarters
Cisco Systems, Inc.
170 West Tasman Drive
San Jose, CA 95134-1706
USA
www.cisco.com
Tel: 408 526-4000
800 553-NETS (6387)
Fax: 408 527-0883

Asia Pacific Headquarters
Cisco Systems, Inc.
168 Robinson Road
#28-01 Capital Tower
Singapore 068912
www.cisco.com
Tel: +65 6317 7777
Fax: +65 6317 7799

Europe Headquarters
Cisco Systems International BV
Haarlerbergpark
Haarlerbergweg 13-19
1101 CH Amsterdam
The Netherlands
www.europe.cisco.com
Tel: +31 0 800 020 0791
Fax: +31 0 20 357 1100

Cisco has more than 200 offices worldwide. Addresses, phone numbers, and fax numbers are listed on the Cisco Website at **www.cisco.com/go/offices.**

About the Authors

Denise Helfrich is currently a technical program sales engineer developing and supporting global online labs for the Worldwide Sales Force Delivery. For the previous six years, she was a technical marketing engineer in the Access Router group, focusing on security for Cisco Systems. She is the author of many Cisco training courses, including Network Admission Control. She has been active in the voice/networking industry for over 20 years.

Lou Ronnau, CCIE No. 1536, is currently a technical leader in the Applied Intelligence group of the Customer Assurance Security Practice at Cisco Systems. He is the author of many Cisco solution guides along with *Implementing Network Admission Control: Phase One Configuration and Deployment.* He has been active in the networking industry for over 20 years, the last 12 years with Cisco Systems.

Jason Frazier is a technical leader in the Technology Systems Engineering group for Cisco Systems. He is a systems architect and one of the founders of Cisco's Identity-Based Networking Services (IBNS) strategy. Jason has authored many Cisco solution guides and often participates in industry forums such as Cisco Networkers. He has been involved with network design and security for seven years.

Paul Forbes is a technical marketing engineer in the Office of the CTO, within the Security Technology Group. His primary focus is on the NAC Partner Program, optimizing the integration between vendor applications and Cisco networking infrastructure. He is also active in other security architecture initiatives within the Office of the CTO. He has been active in the networking industry for ten years, as both a customer and working for Cisco.

About the Technical Reviewers

David Anderson, CCIE No. 7660, is an engineer in Cisco's Security Technology CTO Group. In his current role, he is working on next-generation security solutions for identity management, admission control, and security policy enforcement. He has worked on a variety of products and solutions during his seven years at Cisco. This work has included dial-access, disaster recovery, business continuance, application optimization, data center design, security architectures, and network admission control. David has authored and contributed to multiple design guides and white papers on these subjects. He has also presented these topics at conferences and forums in multiple countries. David currently holds both CCIE and CISSP certifications.

Darrin Miller is an engineer in Cisco's security technology group. Darrin is responsible for system-level security architecture. Darrin has worked primarily on policy-based admission and incident response programs within Cisco. Previous to that, Darrin has conducted security research in the areas of IPv6, SCADA, incident response, and trust models. This work has included protocol security analysis and security architectures for next-generation networks. Darrin has authored and contributed to several books and white papers on the subject of network security. Darrin has also spoken around the world at leading network security conferences on a variety of topics. Prior to his eight years at Cisco, Darrin held various positions in the network security community.

Ramakrishnan (Ramki) Rajamoni, CCIE No. 9016, is an engineer in Cisco's NSITE solution testing group. He has been associated with the Network Admission Control program since 2004. Previous to that, Ramki was involved with Cisco's IPsec and MPLS solutions. Prior to Cisco, Ramki held various positions in networking and customer support. In addition, Ramki has also authored and contributed to numerous works, and presented at various conferences on computer architecture.

Acknowledgments

The authors would like to give special recognition to Russell Rice for his vision, leadership, and drive to bring NAC from a concept into a real, viable solution across many Cisco product lines and technologies. Also many thanks to our technical editors David Anderson, Darrin Miller, and Ramki Rajamoni for providing their expert technical knowledge and precious time editing the book.

Denise Helfrich: I would like to thank Russell Rice for the opportunity to work on the initial NAC team to develop training for Cisco's global sales force. A special thanks to Steve Acheson, Lou Ronnau, Thomas Howard, David Anderson, Darrin Miller, Jon Woolwine, and Bob Gleichauf. These experts helped by sharing their knowledge and expertise, which allowed me to put their experiences to words that many could benefit from. Lastly but most importantly, thanks to my husband David for being supportive during the years of working many hours on NAC and writing chapters for this book.

Lou Ronnau: I would like to thank Steve, Denise, Jason, David, Thomas, Darrin, Paul, Brian, and Mits; working with these folks was one of the most enjoyable experiences of my time at Cisco. I also thank Russell Rice and Bob Gleichauf for the NAC vision and for listening to us, Susan Churillo for keeping us straight in the early days, and the entire team of NAC developers. I'd also like to thank my wife Veronica and son Benjamin for putting up with the long hours and travel this project took. Now it's time to spend some of those frequent-flier miles!

Jason Frazier: I would like to thank my wife Christy; you are the source of all that has and ever will be achievable for me. Your love and care have made all our successes possible. Our love will endure all things, and we will continue this journey together forever, sweetheart. From the bottom of my heart, thank you; I love you baby. IPPWRS. To my son Davis, I love you more than you will ever know. Your mother and I are the luckiest parents in the world. We are truly blessed. As you move through your life, know that we will always be there for you.

Finally, to my friends and colleagues at Cisco, I have benefited from your continued support, guidance, and dedication. There are too many of you to list, and I truly thank you.

Paul Forbes: I would like to thank my coauthors, especially Denise for her patience and determination, as well as my immediate colleagues (Jason, Thomas, Darrin, David, Mits, Brian, Lou, and Russell) for their experience, talent, vision, and most of all, passion for the technology. I'd also like to thank my wife Kristen for her unwavering devotion and love. Lastly, I'd like to thank my parents for their contributions of wisdom and opportunities over the many years of my life.

Contents at a Glance

Contents

Command Syntax Conventions

The conventions used to present command syntax in this book are the same conventions used in the IOS Command Reference. The Command Reference describes these conventions as follows:

- **Boldface** indicates commands and keywords that are entered literally as shown. In actual configuration examples and output (not general command syntax), boldface indicates commands that are manually input by the user (such as a **show** command).

- *Italics* indicate arguments for which you supply actual values.

- Vertical bars (|) separate alternative, mutually exclusive elements.

- Square brackets [ ] indicate optional elements.

- Braces { } indicate a required choice.

- Braces within brackets [{ }] indicate a required choice within an optional element.

Introduction

Computers affect our lives every day. We use them daily to communicate in the form of e-mail and instant messaging, to surf the Internet to research a topic, to manage our personal business like banking, and to seek entertainment such as downloading music and online shopping. Computers are also used when we check out at the grocery store, withdraw cash from an automated teller machine, and talk on our mobile phones.

What do all of these have in common? They connect to a network that likely interconnects to the Internet. Connecting to the Internet exposes a computing device to malicious activity, even if it is connected just briefly. Most malicious activity comes in the form of software that is intended to harm, disable, or pull data from host computers. This software is referred to as *malware*. Today common malware includes worms, viruses, Trojans, spyware, data leakage, and identity theft. These common threats initially targeted desktop computers and servers, especially their software applications. Even the computer novice knows the benefits of using antivirus software.

A surge in malware is predicted to start targeting other devices besides servers and desktop computers. Reports are starting to surface about viruses affecting handheld devices such as personal digital assistants (PDAs), mobile phones, and wireless networks. Recent news reported that embedded computers in some automobiles are being infected. It makes you wonder what the next target will be.

Businesses need to change from the inherent IP connectivity paradigm to an admission control model such as that offered by the Cisco Systems Network Admission Control technology.

Security Challenges

Today, a variety of security challenges affect all businesses, regardless of size and location.

These businesses face ongoing challenges in combating malware and ensuring compliance. Deploying firewalls and antivirus scanners alone can't stop the malicious software from getting inside a corporate network. One challenge is that today's workers are mobile, using technology to work anytime from anywhere. Home workers frequently do not stay up to date with operating system patches or antivirus updates, and many don't use a personal firewall. They are a likely source of spreading infections after they have logged in to the corporate network.

Another challenge is to provide the latest security updates and patches quickly to all host computers on a network. And even when these are distributed, there is no guarantee that users install the new software immediately (or at all). To provide a secure network, you need to enforce compliance uniformly among all hosts. When updates are provided, you can't assume that all users load the new software immediately or within a short period of time.

As a result, malware continues to disrupt business, causing downtime and continual patching. Noncompliant servers and desktops are far too common and are difficult to detect and contain. Locating and isolating infected computers are time-consuming and resource-intensive tasks.

The challenges worsen when security updates also involve different types of handheld devices and IP phones.

What Can Security IT Do?

Cisco has a self-defending network strategy that works with a defense-in-depth philosophy, with no dependence on any one technology. Malicious activity comes in many forms and from outside and inside your network. A single defensive technology is not sufficient for today's environment. For example, a knight preparing for battle uses many defensive elements to increase the likelihood of defeating his foe. In addition to relying on just a sword, the knight uses body armor, a helmet, and a shield.

Security risks are inherent in any network, but you can reduce your exposure by deploying overlapping and complementary security solutions within your infrastructure. A self-defending network should be intelligent and able to identify threats, prevent the threat from occurring, and ultimately adapt to threats by self-learning with no human intervention.

Security should be integrated throughout the network devices inside the LAN and WAN as well as at the endpoint devices. A self-defending network should include the following technologies:

- **Threat defense**—Prevents and provides pervasive response against attacks and threats. Examples include firewalls, network intrusion prevention systems (IPSs), and endpoint security such as host intrusion prevention systems (HIPSs) and antivirus scanning.

- **Secure connectivity**—Provides secure end-to-end network connectivity by transporting information in a confidential manner regardless of the traffic. Virtual private networks (VPNs) are common with businesses, using technologies such as Secure Sockets Layer (SSL) and IPsec VPNs.

- **Admission control**—Allows the network to intelligently control who is on your network, where they can go, and what they can do; it also tracks what they did. Examples include authentication, authorization, and accounting (AAA) for users and devices, Identity-Based Networking Services (IBNS), 802.1X, and Network Admission Control (NAC).

A self-defending network must be able to provide updates quickly and easily to prevent new or existing malware from affecting endpoints. Examples include security updates such as antivirus protection to endpoint devices, operating system patches, and anomaly detection.

This self-defending network strategy continues to evolve, and you should expect new technologies to be created. For example, the next likely new technology will be infection containment, where networks adapt to contain the infection and even remediate and clean an endpoint device automatically. To stay up to date with Cisco's strategy or to learn more, refer to http://www.cisco.com/go/selfdefend.

Goals of This Book

The purpose of this book is to focus on one of the many technologies that are part of the Cisco self-defending network strategy—Network Admission Control.

This book is the first volume of *Cisco Network Admission Control*. It describes the NAC Framework architecture and provides a technical description for each of the NAC Framework components offered by Cisco.

This book also identifies important tasks that help you prepare, plan, design, implement, operate, and optimize a NAC Framework solution. You have many things to consider before deploying NAC into your network. If not carefully planned and designed, when implemented, the deployment could cause more disruption to your users than that from the malicious activity you are intending to protect them from.

This book is intended to provide the prerequisite knowledge for the second volume of *Cisco Network Admission Control,* which covers NAC deployment and troubleshooting. The second volume describes the process of successfully deploying and troubleshooting each component as well as the overall solution. It provides step-by-step instructions through the individual component configurations.

Who Should Read This Book

The primary audience consists of security and network personnel. Roles include the following:

- Network and security architects, designers, and engineers
- Networking and security technical assistance engineers
- Computer security experts
- IT staff responsible for installing and maintaining desktops and servers

The secondary audience can include the following consultants, management, and desktop administrators:

- Anyone who wants to understand what NAC is and how it can benefit an organization
- Networking-proficient people who want to understand NAC and the various implementations at a technical level

The level of reader experience can vary and can include a networking novice with a solid understanding of desktop/server operation or a networking professional with an intermediate or higher level of understanding. We assume that the reader has an understanding of the Cisco SAFE Blueprint (which you can find at http://www.cisco.com/go/safe) and is familiar with Cisco security point products and security technologies.

How This Book Is Organized

This book is designed to be read beginning with Chapter 1 and in order, because concepts and terms described in the first two chapters are assumed in later chapters. Chapter and appendix summaries are as follows:

- **Chapter 1, "Network Admission Control Overview"**—This chapter describes the Cisco Network Admission Control solution, identifies its benefits, describes the main components of NAC Framework, and covers how they work together to defend your network.

- **Chapter 2, "Understanding NAC Framework"**—This chapter provides a deeper description of how NAC operates and identifies the types of information NAC Framework uses to make its admission decisions. NAC uses different modes of operation that are based on the network access device that the host connects to. The packet flow processes and protocols involved differ by the mode used. Also, this chapter identifies special considerations for hosts and endpoints that do not use NAC protocols but still need to be able to use the network, bypassing the NAC process.

- **Chapter 3, "Posture Agents"**—This chapter examines the role of hosts in NAC Framework and describes how Cisco Trust Agent and NAC-enabled applications interoperate.

- **Chapter 4, "Posture Validation Server"**—This chapter describes the process a policy server goes through to determine and enforce a policy. It also explains how rules are created and how actions are assigned.

- **Chapter 5, "NAC Layer 2 Operations"**—This chapter describes how NAC works when implemented using NAC-L2-802.1X. The chapter begins by describing the 802.1X technology and explains how, when combined with NAC, it provides additional identity checking along with posturing.

- **Chapter 6, "NAC Layer 3 Operations"**—This chapter describes how NAC works when implemented using NAC-L3-IP and NAC-L2-IP. This chapter begins by describing the Extensible Authentication Protocol over User Datagram Protocol (EAPoUDP) framework, which is fundamental to triggering the NAC posturing process.

- **Chapter 7, "Planning and Designing for Network Admission Control Framework"**—This chapter identifies important tasks that help you prepare, plan, design, implement, operate, and optimize a Network Admission Control Framework solution. Included are sample worksheets to help gather and organize requirements for designing NAC Framework.

- **Chapter 8, "NAC Now and Future Proof for Tomorrow"**—This chapter describes additional capabilities that businesses might want to include with their future admission policies, such as requiring the network infrastructure to use learned information about a host computer or user to determine rights and privileges that dictate resource authorization or access to certain applications or data. Examples of possible future applications for NAC enforcement are discussed.

- **Appendix A, "Answers to Review Questions"**—This appendix contains answers to the review questions at the end of each chapter.

This chapter covers the following topics:

- What is Network Admission Control?
- NAC benefits
- NAC Framework components
- NAC Framework requirements
- NAC Framework operational overview
- NAC Framework deployment scenarios

CHAPTER 1

Network Admission Control Overview

Network Admission Control (NAC) is a technology framework sponsored by Cisco Systems, working in collaboration with many leading security vendors, that includes antivirus, remediation, and desktop management. Their focus is to work together to create solutions that limit damage from emerging security threats from malware such as worms, viruses, Trojan horses, and spyware.

This chapter describes Cisco's NAC solutions, identifies its benefits, and describes the main components of NAC Framework and how they work together to defend your network.

What Is Network Admission Control?

With NAC, a business can use the network infrastructure to enforce security policy compliance to endpoints such as PCs, servers, and personal digital assistants (PDAs). This compliance is based on an endpoint's posture, which is a security state determined by the endpoint's level of conformity to the network admission policy. A typical compliance check for an endpoint occurs against the operating system and associated applications.

An endpoint that is NAC-enabled contains a NAC posture agent that has the capability to obtain host credentials, which contain information gathered from NAC-enabled applications. Host credentials vary by application. Common examples of host credentials include confirmation that the application is installed and running, that the host has a personal firewall enabled, and that the host has the correct software version. The date of the most recent update is another example.

NAC allows network access only to compliant and trusted endpoints, which are referred to as *healthy hosts.*

NAC can also identify noncompliant endpoints and deny them access to the network or give them access to only an isolated zone so that they do not to infect compliant or healthy hosts. This isolation area is referred to as a *quarantine zone* where noncompliant endpoints are placed which typically allows access only to computing resources so that they can obtain the necessary software updates to conform to the network admission policy. This compliance update process is referred to as *remediation.*

Endpoints that are not NAC-enabled cannot be evaluated for compliance; they can be denied access or can optionally be exempt from the NAC process through several techniques discussed later in this chapter. Devices that are not NAC-enabled are referred to as *NAC agentless hosts (NAHs)*. NAH examples include printers, IP phones, or devices not managed by the business, such as a guest laptop computer.

As the Cisco NAC technology evolves, look for more endpoints to be added to this compliance check, including IP phones and other devices that connect to the network.

NAC is one of the technologies of the Cisco Self-Defending Network. When NAC is combined with other network security technologies, the two can collectively react quickly to an outbreak with little to no human intervention. Refer to "Core Elements of the Cisco Self-Defending Network Strategy" at http://www.cisco.com for more information on this topic.

Cisco NAC Technology Progression

Cisco continues to expand its NAC capabilities and offerings. The following describes major Cisco NAC events:

- NAC Framework release 1.0 (formerly referred to as Phase One) became available from Cisco Systems in June 2004 with many Layer 3 Cisco network access devices (NADs). Examples of release 1.0 NADs are Cisco routers and Cisco VPN concentrators. Cisco Secure Access Control Server (ACS) version 3.3 and a posture agent called Cisco Trust Agent were also required framework components. Cisco also partnered with many security and management vendors to provide NAC-enabled applications and management tools. Together, Cisco and vendors provide a solution that can detect, enforce, and monitor software compliance throughout a business's network.

- In October 2004, Cisco acquired Perfigo CleanMachines and added it to the NAC technology options. This technology was renamed Cisco Clean Access and then NAC Appliance in 2005. This technology provides a rapid and less difficult NAC deployment using an all-in-one approach with a self-contained endpoint assessment, policy management, and remediation services. It provides similar operating system compliance checks and policy enforcement, but can operate on a multivendor network infrastructure. NAC Appliance does not require Cisco Secure ACS and, at the time of this writing, works in a non-802.1X LAN environment. Another big difference is that NAC Appliance currently does not work with security and management vendors like NAC Framework. NAC Framework allows the vast types of posture information to be used for compliance checks and enforcements.

- In November 2005, NAC Framework release 2.0 became available and added even more features, including more NADs that work at Layer 2, more protocols, and the ability to scan NAHs to determine their security posture. Upgrading ACS to version 4.0 is a requirement to take advantage of the NAC Framework release 2.0 features.

Looking toward the future, it is reasonable to assume that both NAC technologies (NAC Framework and NAC Appliance) will continue to add functionality and provide more checks and enforcements for network admission. It is our opinion that NAC Framework and NAC Appliance functionality will eventually merge into a single NAC technology managed by a centralized common console versus the two approaches offered at the time of this writing. If the merged NAC occurs, it will most likely use the strengths that each offers for a new NAC phase.

This book focuses on NAC Framework release 2.0 technology. The book does not focus on NAC Appliance. While the end result of NAC Appliance is similar, the configuration and deployment models are different than that of NAC Framework.

The next section describes how hosts can gain access to a network that does not implement NAC and the problems this access can create. Then, you learn the fundamentals of how NAC can mitigate, remediate, and manage security threats.

Accessing a Network That Does Not Implement NAC

Prior to NAC, when a host computer connected to the network, it was given free access regardless of its posture, or in some instances, only its identity was checked to identify the machine or user. In this situation, current security compliance of the host itself is typically unknown.

Even if a network had been purged of known threats, the entry of a noncompliant computer could once again make that network vulnerable to attacks. Figure 1-1 shows a noncompliant host computer attempting to access a network.

Figure 1-1   *Noncompliant Host Enters Network Without Network Admission Control*

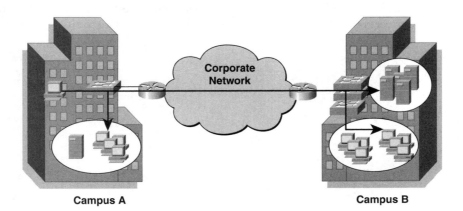

(1) Noncompliant host attempts access   (2) Access permitted anywhere   (3) Malware spreads; all endpoints exposed

Campus A   Campus B

In Figure 1-1, the following process occurs:

1 A noncompliant host attempts to connect to the network. The host computer might be using an older operating system service pack and hot fix or might not be running the latest antivirus software, but no method exists to deny such hosts. This common scenario takes advantage of a vulnerability within your trusted network.

2 The network allows noncompliant devices to access the entire corporate network.

   This permits access to noncompliant devices within your trusted network and allows malware such as a worm to propagate throughout the corporate network and even to others, such as business partners outside your network. Other noncompliant hosts are potentially infected.

Besides spreading malicious code, the previous scenario also consumes network resources when propagating malware. Another dilemma is when a noncompliant host needs patching or virus signature updates, it must first be connected to the network to get the needed updates. In the past, no way existed to isolate the noncompliant hosts to a specific area of the network where they could receive the updates while also preventing other network activity until they are compliant.

Complications such as this are one of the reasons that malware continues to propagate after a fix has been released and applied. The more time that elapses before all endpoints are brought into compliance increases the risk. And that's the problem—time itself. People cannot react quickly enough to ensure that all these safeguards are in place. An automated system is needed.

Accessing a NAC Network

Cisco NAC technology provides an automated mechanism to detect and enforce the network security policy. With NAC, the network can detect endpoints that are out of policy compliance before network access is granted. Figure 1-2 shows a network that utilizes NAC.

Figure 1-2   *Network Admission Control Detects Noncompliant Host*

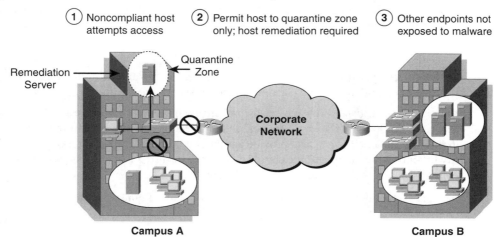

In Figure 1-2, the following process occurs:

1   A noncompliant host computer at the branch attempts network access. The network detects that the host computer is out of compliance. The network infrastructure can deny the host network access altogether or quarantine it so that remedial action can be taken without impacting other hosts on the network. The action is under the system administrator's control by means of admission and security policies that are defined by the administrator.

2   The noncompliant host is quarantined and not allowed to access the entire network; rather, it is redirected to a quarantine subnet, where a remediation server exists.

3   The spread of malware is circumvented, and other endpoints are not exposed.

By preventing noncompliant endpoints from joining the community at large, a potentially dangerous new threat is avoided. For noncompliant users, resistance is futile; prepare to be remediated!

NAC Benefits

NAC offers the following benefits to businesses:

- **Protects corporate assets**—NAC enforces the corporate security software compliance policy for endpoints.

- **Protects against business disruptions**—This applies to productivity in the infrastructure and employees. Starting your day with an infected computer and dealing with the loss of precious data are frustrating and require time to recover from. NAC limits this disruption by minimizing the occurrence of infections in the network.

- **Provides a return on investment (ROI)**—NAC Framework increases the value of existing Cisco network infrastructure by using what is already in place; in many cases, upgrading the software adds new security features like NAC. Another ROI for NAC Framework is ensuring that network computers are using the existing security applications, such as antivirus, and are compliant with the latest update.

- **Reduces operating costs**—NAC frees technical staff from the firefighting mode of containing infections and cleaning endpoint devices one by one.

In summary, NAC benefits businesses by proactively protecting corporate assets, reducing business interruptions from malware, and freeing desktop services staff from reacting in a firefighting mode. NAC can also provide a return on investment by using existing Cisco network infrastructure to enforce compliance, while ensuring that existing NAC vendor security applications are being used accordingly.

The next section describes the major components of NAC Framework.

NAC Framework Components

NAC allows network infrastructure components, known as NADs, to permit or deny hosts access to the network based on the software compliance of the host. This process is referred to as *posture validation*.

The main NAC Framework components of the posture validation process are shown in Figure 1-3.

Figure 1-3   *NAC Framework Components*

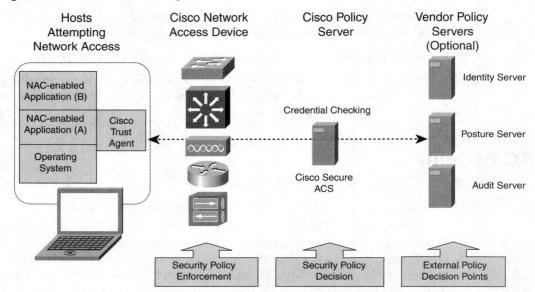

The main components of NAC Framework include the following:

- **Cisco Trust Agent**—Software that resides on a host computer. The trust agent acts as middleware, collecting security state information from multiple NAC-enabled application clients, such as antivirus clients. It communicates this information in the form of host credentials, which are ultimately routed to the policy server, where compliance is checked and the security posture is determined. Cisco Trust Agent can also determine the operating system patch and hot fix information of a host.

  Optionally, businesses can add NAC-enabled security application software on a host computer to provide additional protection capabilities that depend on the application. Examples of security application software are host-based intrusion prevention systems (HIPS), antivirus programs, personal firewalls, and other host security functions. Cisco Security Agent (CSA) is a HIPS example offered by Cisco Systems. An additional benefit that CSA provides with NAC is that it can proactively detect and inform of host event changes through asynchronous status queries.

  NAC partner vendors provide NAC-enabled applications that communicate their credentials and state with Cisco Trust Agent. Many provide antivirus scanners, and some provide additional identity-based services. For a list of NAC program partners, refer to the "Cisco Network Admission Control Program" link at http://www.cisco.com/go/nac.

  Cisco has licensed the trust agent technology to its NAC partner vendors so that it can be integrated with their security software client products. The trust agent technology is free and integrates with the CSA.

- **Network access devices (NADs)**—Network devices that enforce admission control policy include Cisco routers, switches, wireless access points, and security appliances. These devices demand host security credentials and relay this information to policy servers, where network admission control decisions are made. Based on customer-defined policy, the network can enforce the appropriate admission control decision for each endpoint: permit network access, deny network access, redirect to a quarantine zone, or restrict from specific subnets.

- **Policy server**—Server that evaluates the endpoint security information relayed from NADs and determines the appropriate admission policy for them to enforce. The Cisco Secure ACS is the Cisco policy server, which is the foundation of the policy server system and is a requirement for NAC Framework. Optionally, ACS works in concert with NAC-supported vendor policy servers to provide deeper credential validation capabilities, such as identity servers (for example, a directory server database) and posture servers (for example, antivirus policy servers). The vendor policy server communicates the vendor's credential compliance status to Cisco Secure ACS, which makes the final determination regarding the admission policy for the endpoint. Another optional policy server is an audit server. A NAC-compatible audit server can determine the posture credentials of an NAH, removing reliance on a posture agent being present on the host. This audit server is especially useful for evaluating endpoints that are not managed by the business and those devices that are not NAC compatible that need access to the network.

In addition to the required NAC components, a management system is recommended to manage and monitor the various devices. Reporting tools are available to operation personnel to identify which devices are compliant and, most importantly, which devices are not compliant.

NAC Framework Requirements

At the time of this writing, the mandatory requirements for the NAC Framework solution are Cisco Secure ACS, NAC-enabled NADs, and Cisco Trust Agent.

ACS is the only authentication, authorization, and accounting (AAA) server that has the necessary logic to handle the NAC posture validation process. NAC support began with ACS version 3.3.

The hosts should have Cisco Trust Agent installed to fully participate in the NAC Framework solution, and a network device must be capable of supporting NAC acting as a NAD.

Optional pieces of the NAC Framework solution include many different NAC-enabled applications installed on a host, external policy servers that can integrate with the application-specific software, and external audit servers. Each of these optional pieces round out the NAC Framework solution and make it more manageable and capable.

The following sections identify hardware and software requirements for NAC Framework components.

NAD Requirements

NAC introduced new memory and CPU requirements on network access hardware platforms. For this reason, some older hardware platforms do not support NAC Framework. For the most current information, refer to http://www.cisco.com and search on "Feature Navigator" to confirm NAC support requirements for platform, memory, software version, and software image.

The following sections summarize the platform support.

Router Support

NAC was first introduced on Cisco IOS router platforms using security images beginning with IOS Release 12.3(8)T. The following are supported:

- Cisco 800 series 831, 836, 837, 871, 876, 877, and 878.
- Cisco 2600XM series (non-XM 2600 series do not support NAC).
- Cisco 3640 and 3660-ENT.
- Cisco 1700 series 1701, 1711, 1721, 1751, and 1760. The 1710, 1720, and 1750 models are not supported.
- Cisco 1800 series.
- Cisco 2800 series.
- Cisco 3700 and 3800 series.
- Cisco 7200, 7301, and 7500 series.

The release of IOS Release 12.4(6)T security images added auditing support in router platforms as well as several other new features. For more information, consult the IOS 12.4T Release notes at http://www.cisco.com in the Documentation area.

Switch Support

Cisco Catalyst switch support began with NAC release 2.0. The following Cisco switch platforms are supported:

- Cisco Catalyst 2940, 2950, 2955, 2960, and 2970 switches running IOS Release 12.2(25)SED or later.
- Cisco Catalyst 3550, 3560, and 3750 switches running IOS Release 12.2(25)SED or later.
- Cisco Catalyst 4500 and 4900 switches running IOS Release 12.2(25)SG or later.
- Cisco Catalyst 6500 switches with a supervisor 2 or better running CatOS version 8.5.1 or later.

VPN Concentrator Support

Cisco VPN 3000 Series Concentrators also support NAC over their remote-access virtual private network (VPN) solutions running version 4.7 with IPsec only.

Wireless Support

Support for Cisco wireless access points, service modules, and client devices include the following:

- Cisco Aironet access points deployed autonomously in standalone or Wireless Domain Services (WDS) mode—Cisco Aironet 1100, 1130AG, 1200, 1230AG, 1240AG, and 1300 series access points running Cisco IOS Release 12.3(7)JA or later.

- Cisco Aironet lightweight access points deployed with a Cisco Wireless LAN Controller (Cisco Aironet 1000, 1130AG, 1200, 1230AG, 1240AG, and 1500 series access points and Cisco 2000, 4100, or 4400 series Wireless LAN Controllers as well as the Cisco Catalyst 6500 series WiSM and Cisco Wireless LAN Controller Module for Integrated Services Routers) running Cisco Unified Wireless Network Software Release 3.1 or later.

- Cisco Catalyst 6500 series Wireless LAN Services Module (WLSM) deployed as a WDS device running Cisco IOS Release 1.4.1 or later.

- Any 802.11 Wi-Fi client devices with an IEEE 802.1X supplicant that supports NAC. (Note: Cisco-supplied supplicant is for Ethernet adapter only, not WLAN adapter):

  — Cisco Aironet client device with third-party NAC supplicant from Funk Odyssey or Meeting House AEGIS client.

  — Wi-Fi client device from third-party NAC supplicant providers such as Funk Odyssey or Meeting House AEGIS client.

  — Cisco Compatible client devices running version 4.0 or later. (Version 4.0 of Cisco Compatible includes the required NAC supplicant.)

Cisco Secure ACS Requirements

Support for NAC release 1.0 began with ACS version 3.3, which supported NAC polices for posture enforcement on endpoints. NAD enforcement was supported only on Cisco routers and VPN concentrators with version 3.3.

NAC release 2.0 support begins with ACS version 4.0. This release began support for network admission policies for posture and identity enforcement. NAD enforcement is supported on Cisco routers, VPN concentrators, and Catalyst switches and Cisco wireless access points, wireless controllers, wireless service modules, and wireless clients. Version 4.0 also supports the use of audit servers to be part of the NAC policy decision.

Cisco Trust Agent Requirements

Cisco Trust Agent 1.0 became available with NAC release 1.0. Initially it supported some Microsoft operating systems.

With Cisco Trust Agent 2.0, many features were added, including the following:

- The ability to determine the operating system, patch, and hot fix information of a host
- Additional host operating system support that includes the following:
  - Microsoft Windows NT 4.0
  - Microsoft Windows 2000 Professional and Server
  - Microsoft Windows XP Professional
  - Microsoft Windows 2003
  - Red Hat Linux Enterprise Linux 3.0

NOTE	The MAC Operating System is planned to be supported in the next Cisco Trust Agent version. Refer to the latest CTA datasheet for the most current list of operating system support.

Summary of Requirements

New features will continue to become available that will increment the software versions listed previously. Refer to the Cisco Feature Navigator at http://www.cisco.com to stay current with the platform support, minimum hardware, and required software that support NAC and other framework complementary features.

NAC Framework Operational Overview

This section describes how the NAC components function together to enforce a security admission policy. Figure 1-4 shows a schematic of the NAC process.

Figure 1-4 *NAC Software Compliance Enforcement Process*

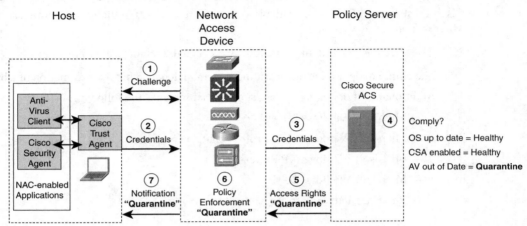

A simple NAC example is shown in Figure 1-4 that uses only the required NAC components. This NAC process involves enforcing a software compliance policy and has the following seven major steps:

1 A NAC-enabled host attempts network access. The NAD initiates posture validation with Cisco Trust Agent.

NOTE   What triggers the process depends on the NAD, its capabilities, and its configuration. Chapter 2, "Understanding NAC Framework," describes the different processes based on the trigger mechanism and NAD used for network access.

---

2 Cisco Trust Agent collects security state information in the form of host credentials from each of the NAC-enabled security applications. In this example, CSA and the antivirus application send their own set of host credentials. All the requested host credentials are communicated to the NAD.

3 The NAD securely relays the host credentials to Cisco Secure ACS.

4 Cisco Secure ACS looks at the host credentials from each NAC-enabled security application: a set of credentials from Cisco Trust Agent, a set from CSA, and a set from the antivirus application.

Cisco Secure ACS looks through its policies and compares them against the host credentials received:

— From Cisco Trust Agent, the credentials for the host operating system (OS) are compliant. The posture assigned is healthy.

— From CSA, the credentials show that the application is enabled. The posture assigned is healthy.

— From the antivirus software, the credentials show it is out of date. The posture assigned is quarantine.

ACS takes action on the posture with the most restrictive result. In this example, the antivirus has the most restrictive posture, which is quarantine. Hence, the enforcement action is to quarantine the host.

NOTE	Administrators can program the desired authorization policy for a specific posture. These include network access assignment, message to the user, URL redirect where ACS sends a URL to automatically redirect an Internet browser to a remediation server, NAC timers, or other actions.

In this example, the quarantine policy allows access to the subnet for the remediation server, provides a message to the user stating that he must update now, and a URL redirect to the remediation server, and rechecks the host credentials in 3 minutes.

5 Cisco Secure ACS sends access instructions to the NAD for enforcement of a host that is to be quarantined.

6 The NAD receives instructions from Cisco Secure ACS and enforces the policy on the interface for that host that only permits network access to the remediation server subnet. The 3-minute timer for that host has started.

7 The NAD sends Cisco Trust Agent the message notification to display to the user. The user sees the message appear on his display and has a choice to either follow the instructions to become compliant or do nothing and be unable to gain network access (except to the remediation server).

This process takes little time to complete. Depending on the network activity and the Cisco Secure ACS policy, it could take milliseconds from the time the user initiates network access until he gets access or receives a message stating why he doesn't have access.

In this scenario, the user opens the browser and is automatically redirected to the remediation server to update the antivirus software. After the 3-minute timer expires, the host is rechecked to make sure that it is the same host and to determine whether it is compliant. The process starts over; this time, the host is considered "healthy," and full network access is granted.

In addition to the initial network access request (that is, the beginning of a workday), the NAD periodically polls the Cisco Trust Agent with a status query (SQ) to make sure that it is still the same host at the same IP address. SQ also makes sure that nothing has changed with the client's posture since the last poll (for example, whether CSA or antivirus is turned off). This timer is configurable.

The NAD also performs a full validation periodically to verify that the device is still compliant with the admission policies in the event a new one was added after the host initially validated. This timer is also configurable.

An endpoint should not go through the admission process in some situations, such as the following:

- Known host that uses an operating system that does not support Cisco Trust Agent
- Guest PC, such as a visitor, that needs Internet access
- Printer
- IP phone

In these cases, hosts do not have Cisco Trust Agent because either it is not supported for that device or it is not installed. These devices are considered NAHs. Provisioning for NAHs is available to administrators by either manually configuring specific devices to be exempt or by using an NAH auditing server to scan the host and determine its level of compliance. The NAH audit component became available in NAC release 2 and allows the audit server to determine whether an NAH is compliant automatically compared to the previous manual identification and configuration technique. Both of these NAH techniques are discussed further in Chapter 2.

NAC Framework Deployment Scenarios

By now, you should realize that NAC Framework is extremely flexible, providing enforcement to a connected endpoint regardless of the network access method being used. As shown in Figure 1-5, NAC operates across all access methods, including campus switching, wireless, router WAN and LAN links, IPsec connections, and remote-access links.

The first NAC deployment rule is to use a NAC-enabled NAD closest to the hosts for checking compliance. The second rule is that compliance checking for a host should occur at one NAD (closest to the host), not throughout the network. The NAD closest to the endpoint might not be capable of performing compliance checks or enforcing the admission policy. Examples are non-Cisco devices or an older NAD that does not support NAC. As a result, NAC deployments can vary.

Figure 1-5   *NAC Deployment Scenarios*

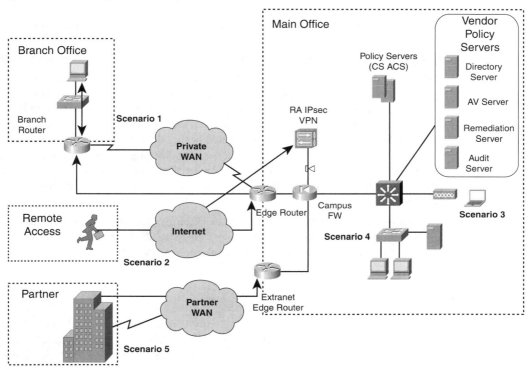

The following are common NAC deployment scenarios, as depicted in Figure 1-5:

- **Branch office compliance**—As shown in scenario 1, NAC can be deployed at a branch office to ensure that hosts comply with the latest antivirus and operating system patches before allowing them access to WAN or Internet connections to the corporate network. Alternatively, compliance checks can be performed at the main office before access is granted to the main corporate network.

- **Remote-access compliance**—Scenario 2 shows that NAC helps to ensure that remote and mobile worker hosts have the latest antivirus and operating system patches before allowing them to access company resources through dialup, IPsec, and other VPN connections.

- **Wireless campus protection**—In scenario 3, NAC checks wireless hosts connecting to the network to ensure that they are properly patched. The 802.1X protocol is used in combination with device and user authentication to perform this validation.

- **Campus access and data center protection**—Scenario 4 shows that NAC monitors desktops and servers within the office, helping to ensure that these devices comply with corporate antivirus and operating system patch policies before granting them LAN access. This reduces the risk of malware, such as worm and virus infections, spreading through an organization by expanding admission control to Layer 2 switches.

- **Extranet compliance**—In scenario 5, NAC can check the compliance of every computer system trying to obtain network access, not just those managed by IT. Managed and unmanaged hosts, including contractor and partner systems, can be checked for compliance with antivirus and operating system policies. If the Cisco Trust Agent is not present on the interrogated host, a default access policy can be enforced limiting the host to a specific subnet, thus limiting its ability to infect other devices on the entire network. Another option for unmanaged hosts is to use an audit server to scan for software compliance; the appropriate access can then be determined and enforced.

NAC Framework is extremely flexible where network admission policy enforcement can be deployed at branch offices, remote-access network entry points, wireless access points, LAN access points, and guest and contractor access points.

Summary

NAC Framework is a leading solution, working with its many partners to enforce organizational security policies to network endpoints. NAC is part of the Cisco Self-Defending Network strategy targeted at fighting the war against malware, such as worms, viruses, Trojans, and spyware.

NAC Framework consists of the following required components: Cisco Trust Agent, network access devices, and Cisco Secure ACS. Optional components that add more capabilities include vendor policy servers, NAC-enabled applications, audit servers, and management and reporting tools.

Not all NADs are NAC capable. Minimum hardware and software requirements exist. The Feature Navigator at http://www.cisco.com is a good tool for determining whether the NAD can support NAC.

NAC allows network access only to compliant and trusted endpoint devices such as PCs, servers, and PDAs. NAC can also identify noncompliant endpoints and deny them access, place them in a quarantine area for remediation, or give them restricted access to computing resources.

Endpoints that are not NAC enabled cannot be evaluated for compliance; they can be denied access or can optionally be excluded from the NAC process. Techniques available include manually configuring the endpoint to be exempt from the NAC process or using an audit server to automatically scan the endpoint and determine compliance. NAC operates across all network access methods, including campus switching; wireless, router WAN, and LAN links; IPsec connections; and remote access.

The next chapter dives deeper into the technical details of how NAC operates.

Resources

"Cisco NAC: The Development of the Self-Defending Network," http://www.cisco.com/warp/public/779/largeent/nac/CSDNI_WP_v11.pdf.

"Cisco Network Admission Control for Wireless LANs," http://www.cisco.com/en/US/products/ps6521/prod_brochure0900aecd80355b2f.html.

"Cisco Trust Agent Datasheet," http://wwwin.cisco.com/stg/nac/pdf/cta_datasheet.pdf.

"Network Admission Control Switching Solutions," http://www.cisco.com/en/US/netsol/ns628/networking_solutions_package.html.

"Release Notes for Network Admission Control, Release 1.0," http://www.cisco.com/en/US/netsol/ns617/networking_solutions_release_note09186a0080270825.html#wp44545.

"Training, NAC Lesson 1—Technical Overview," http://wwwin-tools.cisco.com/cmn/jsp/index.jsp?id=34348.

Review Questions

You can find the answers to the review questions in Appendix A.

1 Which NAC component(s) act(s) as the policy enforcement point? Choose all that apply.

    a NAC-enabled Cisco router

    b NAC-enabled Cisco switch

    c NAC-enabled software application

    d Cisco Trust Agent

    e Cisco Secure ACS

2 Which NAC component(s) operate(s) as the policy decision point? Choose all that apply.

   a NAC-enabled Cisco router

   b NAC-enabled Cisco switch

   c Cisco Secure ACS

   d CiscoWorks VMS

   e Supported NAC partner antivirus or identity server

3 Which NAC component(s) communicate(s) host credentials to the NAD? Choose all that apply.

   a Cisco Secure ACS

   b Cisco Trust Agent

   c Cisco Security Agent

   d NAC-enabled software application

4 What type of actions can the Cisco policy server specify to enforce on the device? Choose all that apply.

   a Display a message to the user

   b Redirect users to a remediation server

   c Permit or deny network access

   d Notify an administrator

   e Send a lock to the host computer

5 Guests frequent the campus and routinely use the public conference rooms. Many of the guest vendors use the Internet in meetings to demonstrate their services. You are responsible for enforcing the company security policy, which requires specific updates to an antivirus application and to host operating systems. What options do you have for guests that allow them access to the Internet while maintaining the security policy? Choose all that apply.

    a Use an audit server to scan hosts and determine their compliance state for policy enforcement. Guest network access can be determined by the compliance outcome.

    b No exceptions exist for nonconforming guests; network access is not allowed.

    c Configure a default access policy that only allows access to the Internet on the NAD supporting those conference rooms.

    d Have the conference room NADs provide a pool of IPs that are assigned to a guest DHCP pool and configure those IP addresses to be exempted on the NAD.

    e All of the above.

    f Options a. and c.

This chapter covers the following topics:

- NAC Framework authorization process
- Posture token types
- Using information from the host for the admission decision
- Dealing with hosts that are not NAC capable
- NAC modes of operation
- NAC communication protocols
- NAC-L3-IP and NAC-L2-IP posture validation and enforcement process
- NAC-L2-802.1X identity with posture validation and enforcement process
- NAC agentless host auditing process
- Authorization and enforcement methods
- NAC agentless host and exception handling

CHAPTER 2

Understanding NAC Framework

Network Admission Control (NAC) Framework is a flexible but complex solution involving many parts of your network. This chapter begins with a deeper description of how NAC operates and identifies the types of information that make its admission decisions. NAC uses different modes of operation that are based on the network access device (NAD) that the host connects to. The packet flow processes and protocols involved can differ by the mode used. Hosts and endpoints that do not use NAC protocols but still need to be able to use the network, bypassing the NAC process, require special consideration.

This chapter discusses the following topics:

- NAC communication modes and when they are used
- How host credentials are used in a policy to determine levels of compliance
- Techniques that allow network admission for endpoints and hosts that are not NAC enabled
- Application posture tokens, system posture tokens, and six predefined posture token states
- Enforcement actions available for noncompliant hosts
- Different access control methods used by various Cisco network access devices
- Exempting devices attempting network access that are not NAC capable from the validation and enforcement process

NAC Framework Authorization Process

NAC operates by requesting a set of credentials from a host attempting network access.

It is important to understand the different modes and how they operate differently before proceeding to the later chapters. Figure 2-1 describes the authorization process, this time at a deeper level than the previous chapter. In this example, both identity and host compliance are determined at the same time.

Figure 2-1 *NAC Posture Validation Flow*

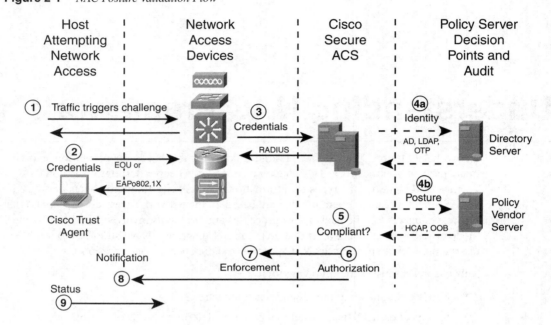

As shown in Figure 2-1, this more complex NAC example has the following nine major steps:

 1 The host attempts network access, and its access attempt triggers the NAC process. This causes the NAD to initiate an Extensible Authentication Protocol (EAP) exchange with the Cisco Trust Agent running on the host. The host's identity is requested as part of EAP, and this identity is passed to the back-end authentication, authorization, and accounting (AAA) server, a Cisco Secure Access Control Server (ACS). The Cisco Secure ACS initiates an EAP session with the host. During the Cisco Secure ACS–to–Cisco Trust Agent EAP session, the NAD acts only as a pass-through device, performing reencapsulation of EAP packets.

 2 The Cisco Secure ACS negotiates a secure tunnel with the client as part of the EAP session setup. Cisco Secure ACS then requests posture validation credentials from the host's security applications by way of their associated posture plug-ins. Each NAC-enabled application communicates its credentials to Cisco Trust Agent. These credentials can contain one or more attributes that have values associated with them that pertain to the state of the security applications communicating with the NAC solution on the host.

3 The NAD passes the credentials and identity from Cisco Trust Agent to ACS using a protected Transport Layer Security (TLS) tunnel, where the NAD never sees them. Depending on the support for NAC in the security application, ACS can be optionally configured to pass the entire credential from a posture plug-in to a partner's external validation server(s).

4 In this example, multiple external servers validate the user identity as well as the host posture. ACS sends both servers only the information they need to make a decision about their specific credentials.

   a ACS receives identity information about the user logged on to the host. ACS has been configured to pass this identity information to an external user database such as an Active Directory server, Lightweight Directory Access Protocol server, One Time Password server, or another type of user store. This is an optional step; however, it relieves ACS from the responsibility for maintaining usernames and user identity credentials. Note that identity information is only present in the Extensible Authentication Protocol over 802.1X (EAPo802.1X) flows.

   b Meanwhile, ACS also receives host posture credentials from a NAC-enabled vendor's application on the host. ACS can optionally send posture credentials to a separate vendor's posture validation server (PVS). Doing this can reduce the load on the ACS server while providing more centralized automatic policy updates by the security vendor's external PVS. In this scenario, the policy evaluation responsibility is passed to the security vendor's PVS, which reports the evaluation results to ACS.

5 Each external PVS performs its individual posture check from the received credentials and sends its own posture decision results back to ACS. ACS looks at all the decisions to make a final decision on whether the host is compliant. The decision is based on the most restrictive result. Because identity is a required part of the NAC-L2-802.1X session, if the identity authentication fails when operating in NAC-L2-802.1X mode, the entire session will fail and the authorization process will not perform the posture check.

6 ACS makes the final decision and determines the authorization level. It assigns the appropriate enforcement and action for this user or host. Part of the enforcement actions Cisco Secure ACS sends to the NAD can include timers that can specify how long a NAD can grant access to the host without reposturing that host. When operating in NAC-L2-IP or NAC-L3-IP mode, the enforcement action can also include how often a NAD must check the status of the host.

7 The NAD receives the appropriate network access policy from ACS for the host and enforces the decision. If the host is compliant with network admission policies and valid machine or user credentials exist in NAC-L2-802.1X sessions, network access is granted.

8 A message is also sent back to Cisco Trust Agent running on the host. Optionally, it can inform the end user by way of a notification pop-up message.

9 Because a host cannot be Layer 2 adjacent to the NAD in either the NAC-L2-IP or NAC-L3-IP modes, a status query takes place between the NAD and the Cisco Trust Agent during regular intervals to ensure that the user/host status has not changed since the last validation process. If a status change occurs with a host operating in NAC-L2-802.1X mode, the posture plug-ins signal the 802.1X supplicant operating on that host to initiate the EAP.

Posture Token Types

Prior to NAC, the concept of the network enforcing access policies based on a host's health status was not imaginable. Now NAC can classify hosts into one of several different states that represent the host's relative health on the network. Each individual security application can have a health token associated with it. These tokens are called application posture tokens (APTs). The worst or most restrictive of these APTs becomes the system posture token (SPT). The SPT represents that particular host's health from a network admissions policy standpoint. The following keywords have been reserved for this classification purpose. These keywords are ordered from least restrictive to most restrictive:

- **Healthy**—A host is compliant with the admission policy because no updates are available. Examples include the operating system (OS), personal firewall policies, and up-to-date antivirus files. No updates to this host are required or available.

NOTE   Even if updates are available, an administrator might determine that the host is healthy as long as it has an update version greater than a predetermined version number. The determination of what is acceptable is left to the discretion of the administrator. The latest updates available by a vendor might not always be the preferred ones by the administrator.

- **Checkup**—A host does not have the required antivirus signatures, operating system patches, or firewall policies installed, but it is not so far out of date that network access for that host needs to be restricted. A pop-up window displayed from Cisco Trust Agent should notify the user that security updates are available and recommended.

- **Transition**—This token is used for two different conditions:
  - The first condition is when a partially booted host does not have all necessary services running that allow a healthy posture check. In this scenario, the host would be put into the transition state and the revalidation timer would be set for a short period of time to allow the host to finish its boot process and the necessary services to start.
  - The second condition is where a transition token is used for an auditing process for a host that is not NAC enabled. In this scenario, the health of the host is not known until the audit completes. This allows the NAD to grant temporary (and perhaps limited) network access for the auditing to successfully complete as well as to provide a URL redirection if required.

  The transition token is not meant to be an assigned token the way that the other tokens are assigned. Transition merely means that the posture validation process has not completed and that a token will be assigned at the conclusion of the posture process.

- **Quarantine**—A host is out of policy with the network admission requirements. A pop-up notification informs the user that her host is out of compliance, and normal network access is denied until compliance is detected. Instructions should also inform the user of the necessary steps to become compliant to regain normal network access. ACS can also be configured for a Cisco Trust Agent action to automatically launch a browser to the specified remediation server needed to update the user's host. In NAC-L2-IP or NAC-L3-IP modes, the NAD can be configured to perform URL redirection on web requests for the host to a remediation server.

- **Infected**—An active virus infection has been detected on that host or the antivirus or personal firewall services have been disabled, assuming an infection has already occurred. This state typically has the greatest restrictions imposed to prevent the host from contacting any network resources except for remediation servers. In some cases, the host can be isolated from gaining access to the network. A pop-up window displayed by Cisco Trust Agent should be configured to notify the user of the actions taken and the reasons behind those actions.

- **Unknown**—A host type cannot be determined, and some access might be permitted. An example is allowing a guest user or other host that is not NAC enabled to have limited network access such as accessing the Internet only or other accordance with the business's network access policy.

Healthy is considered the best state. Checkup, transition, and quarantine are ranked by sequence. Infected is the worse state.

Using Information from the Host for the Admission Decision

Information is gathered from the host and passed to Cisco Trust Agent. Cisco Trust Agent communicates this information to the NAC policy server ACS. Optionally, ACS can send the vendor-specific information to the vendor's PVS to determine compliance with the admission policy.

The following two forms of data can be collected from the host:

- Host credential information is collected from NAC-enabled application agents.
- Optional arbitrary information can be collected by Cisco Trust Agent using custom scripting.

Host Credential Information

The NAC Framework solution uses credentials provided by the Cisco Trust Agent and any other security applications to inform the policy server about the health of those applications. Each credential contains one or more attributes with data associated with those attributes.

As shown in Table 2-1, different data types and operations can be performed on the received attributes for a given policy.

Table 2-1 *Credentials and Attributes*

Application	Vendor	App-Type	Attributes
Cisco Trust Agent	Cisco	Posture agent	PA-Name
			PA-Version
			OS-Type
			OS-Version
			OS-Release
			OS-Kernel-Version
			Machine-Posture-State
		Host	ServicePacks
			HotFixes
			HostFQDN
Cisco Security Agent	Cisco	Host intrusion prevention	CSAMCName
			CSAOperationalState
			CSAStates
			CSAVersion
			TimeSinceLastSuccessfulPoll

Table 2-1 *Credentials and Attributes (Continued)*

Application	Vendor	App-Type	Attributes
Other	Third-party NAC partners	Antivirus, personal firewall, patch management	Software-Name Software-ID Software-Version Scan-Engine-Version DAT-Version DAT-Date Protection-Enabled PFW-policy-version

The top row in this table represents attributes from Cisco Trust Agent that can be collected and analyzed. The second row represents Cisco Security Agent (CSA) attributes, and the last row represents other NAC-enabled applications offered by vendors. Vendor attributes vary and can be imported and used by ACS for policy evaluation.

NAC policies use credentials and attributes that represent a variety of different conditions on the host, such as the antivirus signature file version, particular patches or service packs that have been installed on that host, or values associated with the host itself, such as a fully qualified domain name. These attribute values are then tested against specific policies configured in ACS.

For example, a Cisco Trust Agent policy can use the following attributes to check on a specific OS service pack:

- Application: Cisco Trust Agent
- Vendor: Cisco
- App Type: Host
- Attributes: Service Packs

An operation is also assigned to the different attribute value types that are included with different policies in ACS. Table 2-2 shows the different value types.

Table 2-2 *Credential and Attribute Operations*

Octet Array	Integer32	Unsigned32	String (UTF-8)	IPv4Addr	IPv6Addr	Time (4 octets)	Version (4-x-2-octet sets)
=, !=	=, <, >, !=, >=, <=	=, <, >, !=, >=, <=	=, !=, contains, starts with, regex	wildcards and mask	wildcards and mask	=, <, >, !=, >=, <=	=, <, >, !=, >=, <=

NOTE	The credential and attribute fields allow an almost limitless definition of a credential. For example, a string can be used to perform a registry check.

Operations vary based on the attribute. Operation choices include the following:

- =
- <
- >=
- starts with
- contains

For example, the following operation and value is assigned to the Service Pack attribute:

Service Pack >= 3

In this example, >= is the attribute operation. To comply with this policy, the host service pack must be greater than or equal to 3. Otherwise, it is not compliant with the Cisco Trust Agent host policy.

Typically, multiple attributes are assigned in a policy, where all attributes must be met for compliance. For example, the following must be met for the host to be considered healthy in this scenario:

Service Pack >=3
HotFix = KB888302
HotFix = KB890047

Creating policies with host credentials and attributes are discussed in greater detail in Chapter 4, "Posture Validation Servers."

Arbitrary Information Collection with Cisco Trust Agent Scripting

You might want to collect arbitrary data from your hosts that might not be provided by a posture plug-in associated with a vendor's security application. This data can include version information from non-NAC-participating vendors and windows registry keys. Cisco has provided a method of collecting and using this data with the Cisco Trust Agent scripting interface. The Cisco Trust Agent scripting interface makes use of text files that your custom application creates containing the specific information you want to include in your NAC implementation.

Dealing with Hosts That Are Not NAC Capable

Figure 2-1 describes a high-level operation of NAC with the Cisco Trust Agent installed on a host attempting network access. In some situations, the hosts or other types of endpoints on your network might not be capable of running Cisco Trust Agent, which means they cannot communicate with NAC Framework. If NAC cannot communicate with the host or endpoint, authentication fails and no network access is granted. This might not be desirable.

Hosts that are not NAC capable are referred to as *NAC agentless hosts (NAHs)*. Provisioning for NAHs is available and can be configured by using a variety of static exemption techniques or by using an NAH auditing process.

Static Exemptions for NAH

NAHs can be exempted from the NAC process by creating an exception list that identifies the host's or endpoint's unique static IP address or the MAC address. You can create an exemption list on a NAD; this exempts the hosts listed from the NAC process. As an alternative, the MAC addresses can be entered into specific sections of ACS software for use on a network-wide scale, where the host can be mobile.

NOTE   Centralized IP whitelisting is no longer possible in ACS 4.0.

In addition to the IP or MAC address, you can also use a device type to create an exception. An example of this would be a Cisco IP Phone, where that phone is connected to a Cisco switch port and communicates with the switch using Cisco Discovery Protocol (CDP). The switch learns about the device type and dynamically exempts that specific device from the NAC process by placing it into the voice VLAN.

NAC Agentless Auditing

Another method of dealing with an NAH is by using an auditing process, as shown in Figure 2-2.

Figure 2-2 *NAC Agentless Host Audit Flow*

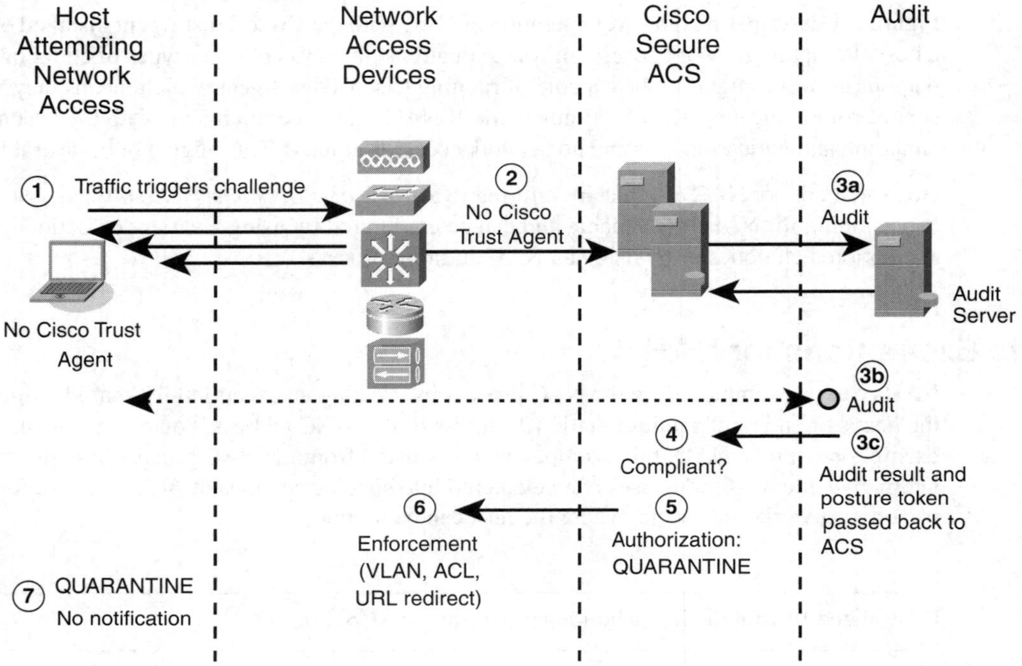

The following process describes the audit flow shown in Figure 2-2:

1. After triggering the NAC process, the NAD attempts to initiate an EAP session with the host.

2. After three unsuccessful EAP hello attempts occur, the NAD and ACS are configured to trigger the NAH audit process in either NAC-L2-IP or NAC-L3-IP mode.

3. The following three steps occur:

   a. ACS contacts an audit server using the Generic Authorization Message Exchange (GAME) protocol.

   b. The audit server initiates the auditing process. This audit process can take one of two forms: (a) an active audit, where the audit server contacts the host out-of-band of the NAC process and attempts to assess the condition of the host that triggered the audit using a network-scanning technique or (b) Cisco Secure ACS configures the NAD to perform a URL redirection on HTTP requests from the host. This action would trigger an auditing applet from the audit server.

   c. The result of the audit is a posture token that the audit server sends back to ACS.

4 ACS then looks at the posture token to determine an appropriate action. In this example, because Cisco Trust Agent is not installed and running on the host, the audit server has assigned a quarantine token to the host. ACS has assigned a quarantine SPT to the host because that is the most restrictive APT.

5 ACS informs the NAD of the enforcement quarantine policy.

6 The NAD enforces network admission by means of a restrictive access control list (ACL) or a URL redirect to a remediation server.

7 The device is quarantined, but because the host does not have a Cisco Trust Agent, a pop-up message does not appear. Instead, the user sees a quarantine web page from his browser if the host has had a URL redirection assigned as part of the enforcement action.

For hosts that do not have Cisco Trust Agent installed, you have the following choices:

- Redirect the NAH to an audit server to scan and determine whether the host is compliant. Then communicate the decision to ACS to determine the admission policy and actions the NAD should enforce on the host. This is an option when operating in NAC-L2-IP or NAC-L3-IP mode.

- Do no provisioning for hosts or endpoints without Cisco Trust Agent. The result is that the NAH fails authentication and network access is denied.

NAC Modes of Operation

NAC operates in at least one of the following modes:

- NAC-L3-IP
- NAC-L2-IP
- NAC-L2-802.1X

Generally, the first part of these terms (L*x*) refers not to the protocol used by NAC for communication, but to the type of network port that is communicating with the host undergoing the posture validation procedure. In this manner, L3 refers to a router port working at Layer 3, and L2 is a switch port working at Layer 2.

The final part of the term refers to the protocol that carries the EAP packet between the host undergoing posture validation and the NAD. IP refers to the EAP over UDP (EoU) implementation, and 802.1X refers to the EAP over 802.1X method, which can also carry identity information for a user, a host, or both. Each of these modes has different triggering methods, capabilities, and access enforcement methods.

NAC-L3-IP and NAC-L2-IP Overview

NAC-L2-IP and NAC-L3-IP both use the Internet Protocol (IP) to carry the authentication packets from the host undergoing NAC to the network. Because IP is used for this communication, these hosts do not need to be directly connected to the devices acting as a NAD, but can be several IP subnet hops away. This introduces a problem where the NAD might not know that a host's status has changed. For example, a host completes posture validation into a healthy state. That same host disconnects from the network. Now a different host connects and is assigned the previously used IP address by way of DHCP. The NAD would not see a change in the host IP address or MAC address, assuming that host was connected to a nonlocal network. To prevent this type of problem from occurring, a status query protocol exists and checks back with the host at configurable intervals to make sure that nothing has changed since it last looked.

The discovery of the host varies by the type of NAD port that the host connects through. In the case of a switch port, with NAC-L2-IP, the discovery of the new host is done by DHCP snooping or by Address Resolution Protocol (ARP) inspection. In the case where a host is connected through a router port performing NAC, with NAC-L3-IP, a packet sent by the host that is forwarded through the router triggers the NAC process. Both of these discovery processes are traffic based, meaning that traffic transmitted by the host is required to trigger the NAC process. NAC-L2-IP and NAC-L3-IP work with either static or dynamic network address translation (NAT) but are incompatible with NAT overload or port address translation (PAT). This is because NAC-L2-IP and NAC-L3-IP maintain a session with each individual IP address. PAT hides multiple hosts behind a single IP address and does not permit individual sessions between the host and the NAD.

NAC-L2-802.1X Overview

The IEEE 802.1X protocol is a data-link layer protocol. This implies that the host must be directly connected to the switch port that is performing the NAC process. NAC-L2-802.1X is the NAC mode that combines the 802.1X protocol with NAC for machine and user identity checking along with posturing for endpoint authentication.

Because the host is directly connected to the switch port performing NAC, an Ethernet linkup signal from the host is enough to trigger EAP and the NAC process. The host can also send an EAP over LAN (EAPoL) start packet to trigger this process in certain circumstances while the Ethernet link is maintained. In either case, the NADs begin the actual EAP protocol with the client.

NAC Communication Protocols

Prior to jumping into the detailed operation of NAC, it is helpful to understand the protocols that are used for communications in the NAC solution. NAC uses EAP extensively, both as an established standard and as a proprietary prestandard (at the time of this writing).

EAP Primer

The Extensible Authentication Protocol (EAP) provides a flexible framework for authentication, with support for multiple internal authentication methods. EAP can run directly over a data-link layer protocol, such as IEEE 802, or over a transport layer protocol, such as User Datagram Protocol (UDP). While an in-depth knowledge of EAP is not necessary for administration of a NAC-enabled network, some knowledge of EAP operation is helpful during troubleshooting operations.

EAP is a request/response protocol, where the authenticator makes a request and the peer responds to that request. The EAP authenticator can act as a pass-through device for a back-end authentication server. Because EAP is a request/response protocol, only a single packet can be outstanding at a time. For each request sent by the server/authenticator, a response must be received by the peer. EAP attempts a small number of retransmissions but provides no provisioning for reordering of packets, so the lower-layer protocol must not change the packet order. EAP also does not provide reassembly of fragmented packets. This means that the message size is limited to the maximum transmission unit (MTU) of the network medium.

EAP sessions are always initiated by the authenticator or by a back-end server. EAP packets can be one of four types:

- Request
- Response
- Success
- Failure

The receipt of an EAP success packet does not mean that the NAC authentication permits the peer onto the network, only that the EAP authentication protocol completed successfully. The network admission decision is based on the hosts' compliance with network policies. More information regarding EAP can be found in RFC 3748.

Client-Side Front-End Protocols

EAP carries the necessary information from the hosts undergoing admission into the network that is performing NAC. The EAP conversation is started by the NAD after discovery of a new host connected through an interface or traversing a NAD with NAC configured. This works slightly differently depending on whether the network interface is a switch port or a router port and whether the underlying protocol carrying the EAP packet is UDP/IP or IEEE 802.1X.

EAP over UDP (EoU)

In NAC modes where EAP is carried over IP, UDP is used as the transport protocol. It uses a default port of 21862, or 5566 in hexadecimal; this can be changed on both the NAD and the hosts participating in NAC. This was the initial NAC mode introduced by routers at Layer 3. This also works on Layer 3–capable switches that support NAC.

EAP over 802.1X (EAPo802.1X)

In this implementation, the EAP packet is carried from the host to the switch port by an IEEE 802.1X MAC frame. Part of this encapsulation includes the Flexible Authentication with Secure Tunneling (FAST or EAP-FAST) protocol. EAP-FAST allows multiple credential types, such as user identity and posture credentials, to be chained together in a single authentication packet. This allows NAC-L2-802.1X to perform both user and machine identity authentication as well as posture validation. The switch performs the reencapsulation to EAP over RADIUS necessary for transmission of the EAP packet to ACS.

RADIUS and EAP over RADIUS

For communications between the NAD and ACS, the EAP packet is encapsulated into a RADIUS packet by the NAD. These packets follow the same request/respond communication defined by the EAP protocol, with a separate EAP session for each host participating in the NAC solution.

Server-Side Protocols

The following sections describe Cisco-proprietary protocols that are licensed to NAC partners for interoperability between ACS and vendor servers for NAC policy validation and auditing functions. These protocols are the Host Credentials Authorization Protocol (HCAP) and GAME.

Host Credential Authorization Protocol (HCAP)

Administration of a AAA server becomes increasing complex with each additional credential and the associated attributes received from hosts with posture agents. A more efficient method of allowing an external PVS to conduct the evaluation of attributes exists by using HCAP. HCAP is a request/response protocol that is used for communication between the AAA policy server (ACS) and PVS. The AAA server sends an HCAP request to an external PVS along with forwarded credential(s) pertaining to the PVS. The PVS then evaluates the attributes contained in the credential(s) and returns results to the AAA server. HCAP is based on HTTP and can be protected with encryption for additional security.

Generic Authorization Message Exchange (GAME)

ACS uses a specific implementation of Security Assertion Markup Language (SAML) called Generic Authorization Message Exchange (GAME) for its communication with an audit server that is part of NAC. GAME is a request/response protocol that ACS uses to send the audit request to an audit server and then uses to check the progress of an audit session. The GAME protocol also has its roots in HTTP and can be encrypted for additional security.

Vendor-Specific Out-of-Band Protocols

In addition to the previously mentioned protocols, several security application vendors use out-of-band protocols to enable communication between that vendor's server and the security agents that have been deployed on hosts. These protocols are sometimes proprietary and are not part of a standard NAC solution. However, they must be permitted by any enforcement action whenever they are used during the remediation process.

NAC-L3-IP and NAC-L2-IP Posture Validation and Enforcement Process

As described in the "NAC Framework Authorization Process" section, earlier in this chapter, the posture validation process begins with the discovery of a new host attempting to gain access to the network. Figure 2-3 identifies the protocol flows of NAC-L3-IP and NAC-L2-IP posture validation.

Figure 2-3   *NAC-L3-IP and NAC-L2-IP Posture Validation Flow*

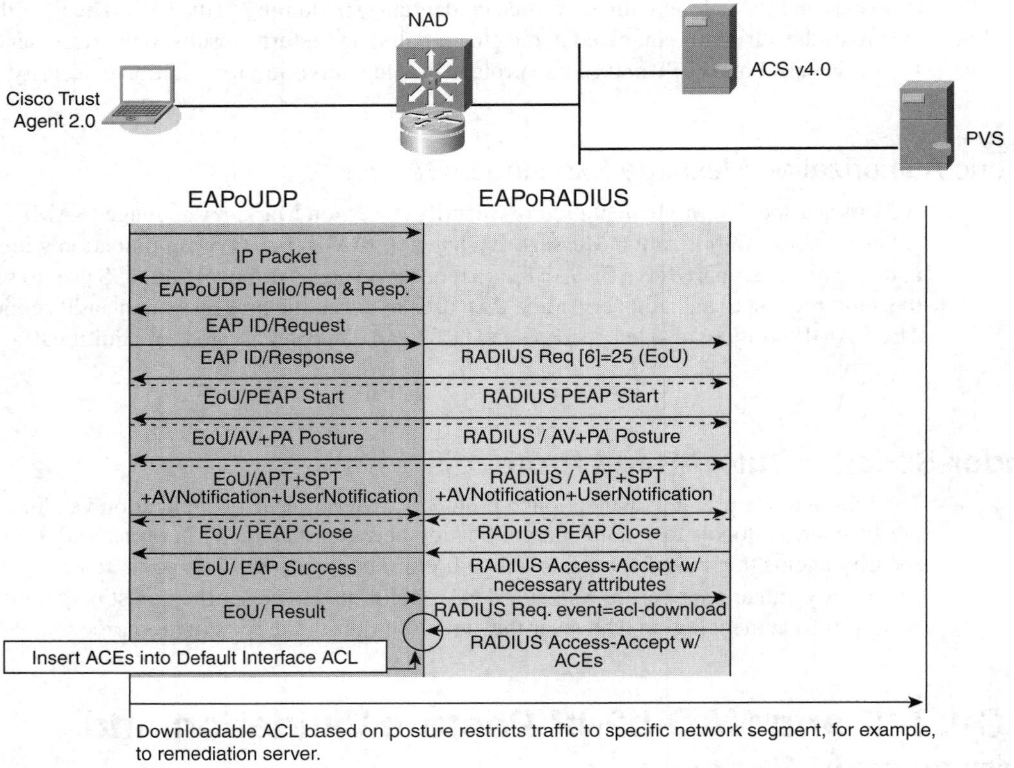

Downloadable ACL based on posture restricts traffic to specific network segment, for example, to remediation server.

As shown in Figure 2-3, the NAD initiates an EAP session with the host by sending an EAP hello request. The host then responds with an EAP hello response. The NAD sends an EAP identity request that is followed by an EAP identity response from the host. At this point, the NAD initiates a RADIUS request to ACS that includes the identity and address information about the host. ACS then initiates a Protected EAP (PEAP) session with the host. At this point, the NAD acts as a pass-through device only, reencapsulating the EoU packets from the host into EAP over RADIUS packets to be sent to ACS. Part of the PEAP initiation consists of the ACS sending its server certificate to the host. The host then verifies the trust of the ACS server. After the PEAP session has been established, a protected tunnel exists between the host and the ACS server. ACS then requests the host credentials necessary for the policy checks that have been configured. The received credentials and attribute information is compared against locally configured policies and any credentials configured to be sent to an external policy validation server are now sent.

In this example, the host posture is out of compliance and determined to be a quarantine posture, ACS send the NAD quarantine enforcement instructions for the noncompliant host. These enforcement instructions include both Internet Engineering Task Force (IETF) RADIUS standard attributes and Cisco vendor-specific RADIUS attributes. These attributes include the name and access control entry information for ACLs applied, the status query timer value, the revalidation timer value, a text string that contains the SPT for the host, and a URL redirection target URL for the host.

NAC-L3-IP and NAC-L2-IP Status Query

Because the host can be several hops away from the NAD configured for NAC enforcement, a protocol to sense any changes in the host is needed. Figure 2-4 describes the status query protocol.

Figure 2-4   *NAC-L3-IP and NAC-L2-IP Status Query*

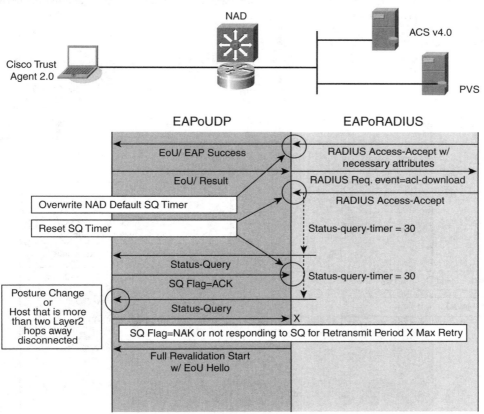

After a host's posture is successfully checked, a status query timer is configured on the NAD as part of the enforcement process shown in Figure 2-4. The value of the timer in seconds can vary depending on the posture token that was set as part of the validation process. When the status query timer expires, a status query challenge is sent from the NAD to the host. If the host responds correctly, the status query timer is reset and no further action is taken. During a status query, the ACS server is not contacted. If the host does not respond correctly or cannot respond correctly because of a host change, the full posture validation process is initiated again, including validation of the host credentials by ACS.

NAC-L3-IP and NAC-L2-IP Revalidation

During normal NAC operation, ACS is only involved during the initial validation of a host. After a host has been validated, it has access rights that might not expire. There is no notification from ACS to a NAD or a host that the policy for network admission has changed. An example of a policy change can be a new mandatory operating system hot fix or an antivirus signature update has become available. To remedy this situation, a revalidation timer is configured to periodically check a host's posture against the network access policy, as shown in Figure 2-5.

Figure 2-5 *NAC-L3-IP and NAC-L2-IP Revalidation*

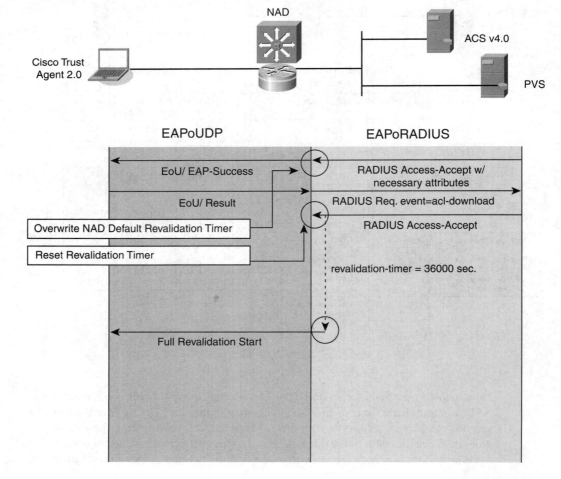

Figure 2-5 describes the NAC revalidation process. This process assures compliance when the policy itself changes as a result of an additional immediate security patch.

NOTE   Revalidation timers can be configured in the NAD and ACS.

When the revalidation timer expires, the NAD initiates a posture validation session with the host. The difference between an initial validation and a revalidation is that during revalidation, the host has already obtained some set of access rights and those access rights are not removed or changed unless the results of the revalidation process are different from the initial validation.

NAC-L2-802.1X Identity with Posture Validation and Enforcement Process

The previous sections dealt with posture validation communication occurring over IP. This section describes a method of posture validation that can include identity information in the admission decision. The EAP packets can be carried over MAC frames from a host that has not yet received an IP address.

Figure 2-6 describes the L2-802.1X posture validation process that includes checking and enforcement for both device compliance as well as user identity and machine identity.

In addition to transporting posture credentials, NAC-L2-802.1X can include identity credentials as part of the decision-making process. NAC-L2-802.1X uses EAP-FAST as a tunneling protocol, which allows authentication credentials to be chained together. As shown in Figure 2-6, the posture session begins when the NAD observes a linkup or the NAD receives an EAPoL start packet from the host. This triggers the initial EAP identity request, which is followed by an EAP identity response from the host. At this point, the NAD reencapsulates the host's identity into an EAP over RADIUS packet that is sent to the ACS. This triggers an EAP session initiated by ACS to the host, with the NAD acting as a pass-through device, similar to the method used in a NAC-L2-IP or NAC-L3-IP session. The host and ACS complete the EAP-FAST tunnel negotiation, which includes an encryption method. The ACS server then requests the identity and posture credentials from the host. Both the posture credentials and any machine identity credentials or user credentials are used in the posture decision process. After a host posture has been determined, the results are passed back to the host. The appropriate access rights and enforcement action are then sent to the NAD.

Figure 2-6 *NAC-L2-802.1X Identity with Posture Validation Flow*

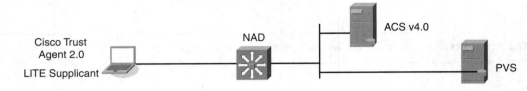

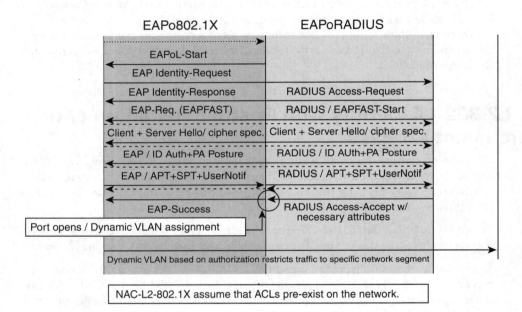

NOTE   If identity fails, no posture credentials are checked.

One of the enforcement actions available with NAC-L2-802.1X is dynamic VLAN assignment.

Figure 2-7 describes how the VLAN assignment is derived from ACS and used by the NAD to enforce access to the network.

Figure 2-7   *NAC-L2-802.1X Dynamic VLAN Assignment*

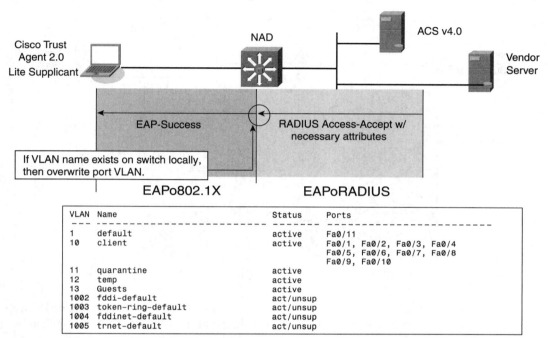

```
VLAN Name                            Status    Ports
---- -------------------------       -------   -------------------------
1    default                         active    Fa0/11
10   client                          active    Fa0/1, Fa0/2, Fa0/3, Fa0/4
                                               Fa0/5, Fa0/6, Fa0/7, Fa0/8
                                               Fa0/9, Fa0/10
11   quarantine                      active
12   temp                            active
13   Guests                          active
1002 fddi-default                    act/unsup
1003 token-ring-default              act/unsup
1004 fddinet-default                 act/unsup
1005 trnet-default                   act/unsup
```

A VLAN assignment is sent to the NAD from ACS as part of the enforcement process after a completed validation. This message uses IETF standard RADIUS attributes to carry the VLAN type, tunnel type, and VLAN name. The VLAN must have been preconfigured on the switch acting as the NAD for this to be successful. NAC-L2-802.1X also has a revalidation mechanism that is available to cover the situation where the network admission policy has changed after a host has completed the validation process. This is configured with the IETF session timeout RADIUS attribute and the terminate-action RADIUS attribute.

In this example, ACS decides the posture token is quarantine for the authenticating device. The switch is instructed to assign a VLAN with the name of quarantine.

As shown in Figure 2-8, after successful authentication, a revalidation timer initiates.

Figure 2-8 *NAC-L2-802.1X Reauthentication Process*

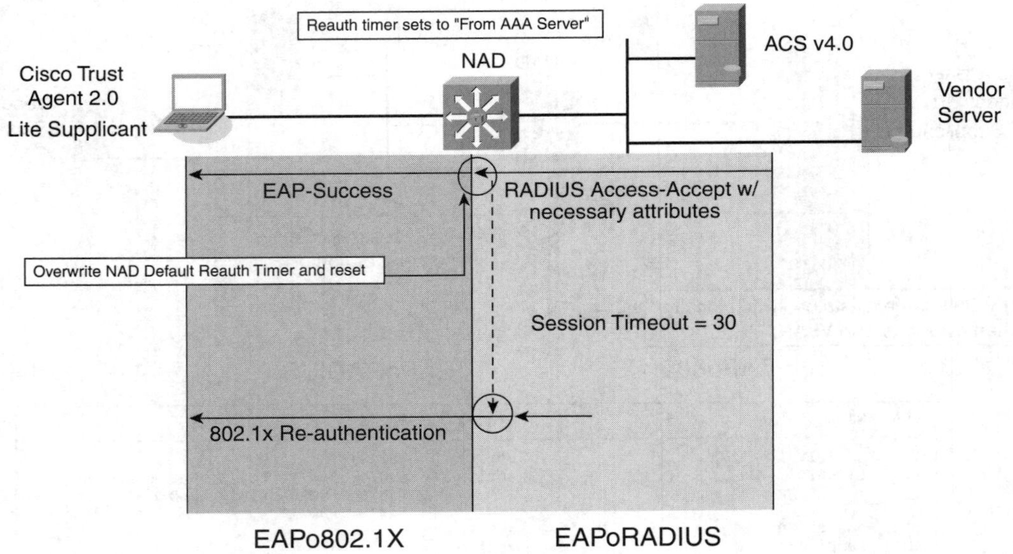

Each host is assigned a revalidation timer as part of the NAC-L2-802.1X validation process. The timer can vary based on the posture. As in this example, where the host is quarantined, the timer is set shorter than a posture of healthy. Upon expiration of this timer, the NAD initiates an EAPoL session with the host by sending an EAPoL identity request packet to the host. As with the NAC-L2-IP mode, the host's access rights remain in place during the validation process. If any change in access rights occurs as a result of a change in the posture revalidation, those changes are applied after the revalidation process completes.

NOTE   Revalidation timers can be configured in the NAD and ACS.

An additional feature of the NAC-L2-802.1X mode is an asynchronous status query. If the status of the host changes (for example, a user disables the antivirus program or the antivirus program updates itself), the host can initiate a revalidation by the transmission of an EAPoL start packet.

NAC Agentless Host Auditing Process

A NAC agentless host (NAH) refers to a host that does not have a posture agent installed. These hosts cannot fully participate in the NAC solution. If the NAC solution cannot communicate with the host or no exception is made, the host cannot access the network when attempting to connect to NAC-enabled NADs. If your network has been configured for NAC-L2-IP or NAC-L3-IP mode with an auditing solution, NAC might be able to use agentless auditing in situations where an IP host does not, or cannot, run a NAC posture agent. As of this writing, only NAC-L2-IP and NAC-L3-IP modes support agentless auditing because auditing can only take place over an IP session. Auditing of a host can take place using two separate methods: an active network scan and a URL redirection.

As shown in Figure 2-9, an audit server can be part of the NAC posture evaluation process.

Figure 2-9   *Audit Server Network Scanning*

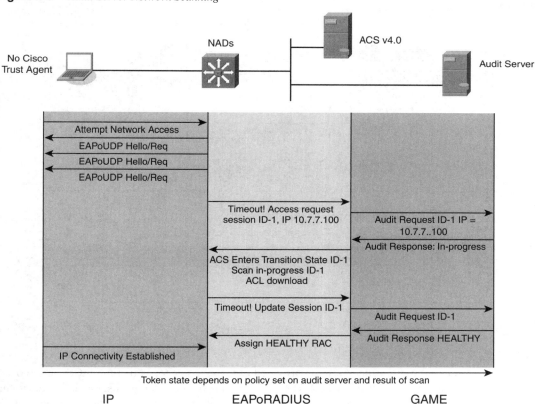

Audit of a host attempting network access using the network-scanning method begins after three unanswered EoU hello request packet attempts from the NAD. The NAD then sends an agentless request to ACS that triggers an audit request to the audit server. ACS periodically checks the audit server to determine the state of the audit session. When the audit is complete, the audit server responds with a token that represents the condition of the host. At that time, ACS sends the appropriate access rights and any enforcement necessary to the NAD.

As shown in Figure 2-10, the auditing process can also be triggered by the host being assigned a URL redirect to the auditing server.

Figure 2-10 *Audit Server URL Redirection and Applet Load*

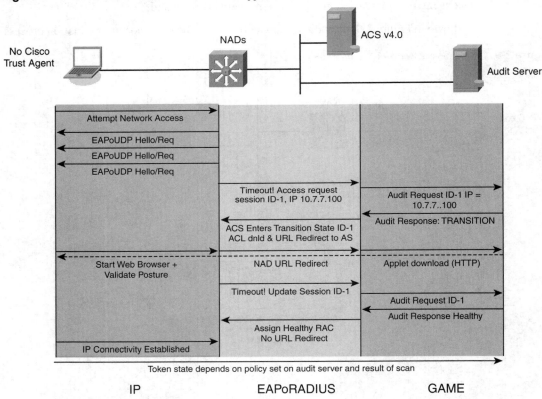

Again, after three successive unanswered EOU hello packets, this time, ACS can send a URL redirection action to the NAD. After opening the browser, the user is redirected to the audit scanner's page, where an applet download occurs and the scanning takes place. ACS temporarily assigns a transition token to the host and configures the NAD to permit audit server access only to the host. The user must manually open his browser to complete the scanning in this scenario because Cisco Trust Agent is not present on the host. ACS checks the progress of the audit in a similar fashion as the network-scanning method. After the scan completes, ACS uses the results to enforce the appropriate access policy.

Authorization and Enforcement Methods

As a result of a successful validation, NAC takes some type of enforcement action. A successful validation is one where the validation process has completed. This does not mean that the host was validated into a healthy state, only that some state was returned to the host and to the NAD and that the EAP session completed successfully. This successful EAP session is known as a *successful authentication* and is logged in the ACS successful authentication logs, regardless of posture.

The enforcement action is necessary if the host is to have access rights other than what are provided to the host by default. In many cases, the host can be isolated until some access right or enforcement action is sent to the NAD. These enforcement actions vary depending on the mode in which NAC is operating. Although this might change in the future, at the time of this writing, NAC enforcement is implemented in the following ways:

- For IP mode either NAC-L2-IP or NAC-L3-IP, the enforcement action consists of a downloadable ACL to the NAD and optionally a URL redirection.
- For NAC-L2-802.1X mode, VLAN assignment is used as an enforcement action.

The following sections describe each of these enforcement actions.

ACL Types

One of the primary enforcement methods that NAC uses is that of an ACL on a specific host as a result of a validation. The enforcement action uses a downloadable ACL from ACS to limit IP addresses through the NAD interface that services the host. The ACLs differ in name depending on where they are placed as well as the type of port that is used.

An ACL can consist of one of the following two types in NAC:

- **Standard ACL**—Includes a destination address only.
- **Extended ACL**—Includes a source address, optional source ports, and destination address and destination ports. In NAC Framework, the extended ACL is most often used in the enforcement action.

The following sections describe the different types of ACLs used by NAC Framework.

PACL

A port access control list (PACL) is an ACL that has been applied on the port of a switch. This switch port can be operating as a network layer interface or as a normal switch port. PACLs work the same as ACLs on router ports.

RACL

A router access control list (RACL) is a specific name for an ACL applied on a router interface. When an ACL is applied on a router interface as a result of enforcement action by the NAC solution, the router replaces the source address in the ACL entries with the source address of the host that this ACL is being applied against. This customizes the enforcement action for that host (and that host only).

VACL

A VLAN access control list (VACL) is an ACL that has been applied on a VLAN in a switch acting as a NAD. Because VLAN ACLs are applied to traffic entering as well as exiting the VLAN, these ACLs need to be written to permit traffic bidirectionally. An example would be to permit a host of 10.1.1.1 as the source address in an ACL entry and also as the destination is a separate entry in the same ACL.

VLANs and Policy-Based ACLs (PBACLs)

Specific to NAC-L2-802.1X mode employing the Catalyst 6500 platform as a NAD, VLAN assignment with assignment to a security policy group can be taken. A security policy group, also called a policy-based ACL (PBACL), is an access list that uses a group as part of the ACL entry. An example would be "permit group quarantine 10.1.1.1." This security policy group assignment uses a Cisco vendor-specific RADIUS attribute "sec:pg" for assignment. When combined with a VLAN assignment, the PBACL can further limit the network resources available to a host. Note that provisioning for bidirectionality must be made for PBACLs just as it has been made for VLAN ACLs.

Cisco Trust Agent and Posture Plug-in Actions

An action can also be taken by the posture agent (Cisco Trust Agent) or posture plug-ins as a result of a validation. As part of the enforcement configuration, Cisco Trust Agent can receive instructions to display a message as part of a completed validation; it can also receive a notification string. This causes Cisco Trust Agent to start the default browser on the host and open it to the page listed in the notification string. This URL could be the page of a remediation server or a page giving the user more instructions about how she should complete the remediation process necessary on her host. Various posture plug-ins have specific actions that are unique to their capabilities and vary by NAC vendors. Some examples of actions are to initiate scanning of the files on a host and to initiate an upgrade of files for that particular posture plug-in.

NAH and Exception Handling

You learned about the network auditing method for handling NAHs earlier in this chapter in the "NAC Agentless Host Auditing Process" section.

Several other methods exist that can handle hosts with no ability to participate in the NAC Framework solution. One of these is the use of a static exception. A *static exception* is simply the presence of the IP address, the MAC address, or the device type in a NAD configuration. This exempts those particular hosts from participating in NAC. Part of the configuration for a static exception includes the specific access rights for the exempted hosts.

Agentless hosts can also be handled with MAC Authentication Bypass (MAB). MAB consists of a list of MAC addresses that have been configured in ACS that should not be subject to the NAC validation and enforcement process. The operational details and a configuration description for MAB is covered in Chapter 5, "NAC Layer 2 Operations."

Summary

NAC Framework is a solution that allows a network administrator to leverage the investment already made in a network infrastructure to provide additional protection and enforcement of network security policies. Compliance of network endpoints is validated prior to allowing those endpoints to communicate with network resources.

The three NAC Framework modes of operations are NAC-L3-IP, NAC-L2-IP, and NAC-L2-802.1X. The type of port on a network device determines the mode available as well as the NAC triggering process, types of protocol, and enforcement method used.

A posture token classifies hosts into one of several different states that represent the host's relative health on the network. Policy servers can check more than one attribute, resulting in an application posture token being assigned. The worst, or most restrictive, of all the application posture tokens becomes the system posture token.

Hosts that are not in compliance with the network access policy can be forced to complete the remediation process through a variety of enforcement methods.

Hosts that do not have Cisco Trust Agent installed are called NAC agentless hosts. You have choices as to how to handle them, as follows:

- You can configure the NAD to exempt the host from the NAC process by means of a static IP address if operating in NAC-L2-IP or NAC-L3-IP mode or by device type.

- You can configure the ACS to exempt the host from the NAC process by means of a MAC address if operating in NAC-L2-802.1X mode.

- You can redirect the NAH to an audit server to scan and determine whether the host is compliant. Then communicate the decision to ACS to determine the admission policy and actions the NAD will enforce on the host. This is an option when operating in NAC-L2-IP or NAC-L3-IP mode.

- You can do no provisioning for hosts or endpoints without Cisco Trust Agent. The result is that the NAH fails authorization and network access is denied.

Resource

"All About NAC" from Networkers 2005, http://wwwin.cisco.com/Mkt/events/nw/2005/post/presos/docs/TECSEC-112.ppt.

Review Questions

You can find the answers to the review questions in Appendix A.

1 Match the NAC protocol to its function:

   a EoU

   b HCAP

   c GAME

   d EAPo802.1X

   __ Uses IEEE MAC frame

   __ Uses port 21862

   __ Queries the PVS

   __ Queries an audit server

2 Which of the following are EAP packets types? Choose all that apply.

   a Request and response

   b Hello and acknowledge

   c Request and acknowledge

   d Success and failure

3 Which protocol is available for communication of the host credentials to security vendor policy validation servers?

   a GAME

   b HCAP

   c ACS

   d RADIUS

4 Which Cisco Trust Agent:Cisco:Host credential attributes can be evaluated by a NAC policy? Choose all that apply.

   a Service packs

   b Hot fixes

   c OS-Version

   d Protection-Enabled

5 Which of the following methods can trigger the NAC process for a host connecting to a NAD that uses the NAC-L2-802.1X mode? Choose all that apply.

   a Any IP traffic

   b DHCP snooping

   c EAPoL-Start

   d Ethernet linkup signal from the host

   e Dynamic ARP inspection

6 Which two methods can trigger the NAC process for a host connecting to a NAD that uses the NAC-L2-IP mode?

   a Any IP traffic

   b DHCP snooping

   c EAPoL-Start

   d Ethernet linkup signal from the host

   e ARP inspection

7 Which method can trigger the NAC process for a host connecting to a NAD that uses the NAC-L3-IP mode?

  a Any IP traffic

  b DHCP snooping

  c EAPoL-Start

  d Ethernet linkup signal from the host

  e Dynamic ARP inspection

8 Which of the following defines the situation where the NAD challenges a host to make sure that nothing has changed since the validation process?

  a Revalidation

  b Status query

  c Posture validation

  d EAP identity response

9 Which techniques can be used to permit a network printer onto a NAC-protected subnet, even though it is not NAC capable? Choose all that apply.

  a Include the printer's MAC in the NAD exception table.

  b Include the printer's static IP address in the NAD exception table.

  c Include the printer's device type "printer" in the NAD or ACS NAC exception table.

  d Use an audit server to scan and validate the printer.

10 Which posture token is assigned to a host when it has not fully booted up and some services have not yet started?

  a Checkup

  b Unknown

  c Transition

  d Quarantine

11 Which of the following APTs does ACS decide to use as the SPT and take action against?

Quarantine—Cisco Trust Agent host from local ACS check

Healthy—Cisco Trust Agent PA from local ACS check

Checkup—CSA from local ACS check

Checkup—Antivirus client from vendor PVS

  a Both checkup and quarantine actions

  b Checkup actions, because two exist

  c Quarantine action only

  d ACS defers action to antivirus client's PVS

12 Which two methods can be used to audit an agentless host?

  a Exception table

  b MAC Authentication Bypass

  c Network scan

  d URL redirection to an audit server

13 Which NAC Framework component causes a user's browser to pop up with the URL redirect from the notification string?

  a Posture plug-in agent

  b NAD

  c Cisco Trust Agent

  d Audit server

14 Which of the following ACLs is used for enforcement by routers serving as NADs?

  a VACL

  b PACL

  c RACL

  d PBACL

This chapter covers the following topics:

- Posture agent overview
- Cisco Trust Agent architecture
- Posture plug-in functionality
- Vendor application example: Cisco Security Agent

CHAPTER 3

Posture Agents

For Network Admission Control (NAC)–enabled hosts to be able to communicate their posture credentials to the posture server, a posture agent must exist on the host.

Cisco Trust Agent is the posture agent. It communicates with various NAC-enabled host applications by way of their posture plug-ins. NAC third-party vendors must build their own posture plug-ins to communicate their credentials to the policy decision points. Each vendor is identified by a unique vendor ID that identifies the vendor's application type (for example, antivirus) and attributes (for example, version).

Cisco Trust Agent aggregates host posture credentials from all the NAC-enabled application plug-ins and communicates them to the network.

This chapter examines the role of hosts in NAC and describes how Cisco Trust Agent and NAC-enabled applications interoperate.

This chapter describes the following items:

- The two major functions of the NAC posture agent
- The process for posture validation
- The process for identity and posture validation
- Posture plug-ins and the vendor namespace format
- The posture plug-in contents of .dll and .inf files
- The Cisco Trust Agent–supported host operating systems
- Four benefits of using Cisco Security Agent (CSA) with NAC Framework implementations

Posture Agent Overview

As shown in Figure 3-1, three distinct roles exist within a NAC Framework solution:

- Hosts connecting to the network
- Network access devices (NADs) that serve as the policy enforcement point (PEP)
- Policy servers that act as the policy decision point (PDP)

Figure 3-1 *Network Admission Control Logical Roles*

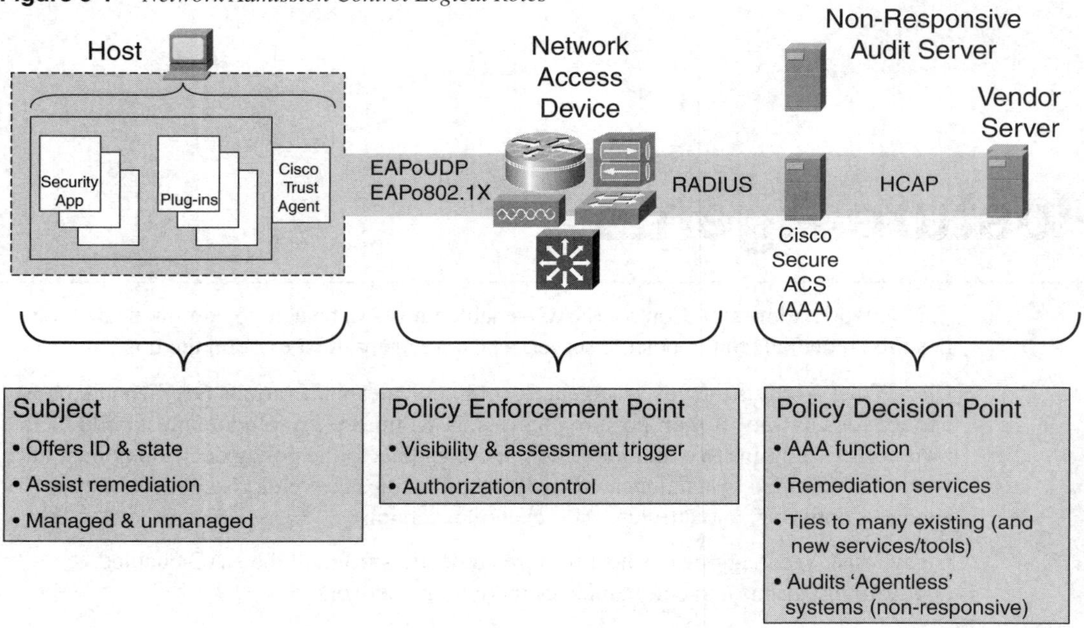

Posture is the term that describes the collection of credentials and attributes that define the state or health of a user's computer and the applications on that computer, which this book refers to as the *host*.

With NAC, a posture agent is required and resides on the host, or *subject,* and communicates information such as device operating system and application-level information, in the form of *credentials.*

The NAD forwards the host credentials for validation against the policy decision points (PDPs) of the NAC Framework solution. A policy decision is made and network enforcement instructions are sent by the Cisco Secure Access Control Server (ACS) to be enforced by the NAD.

The posture agent also performs a variety of functions, such as informing the user by a custom configurable message notification that is sent to the user describing the posture condition of his host. The following is a notification example for a noncompliant host: "Your computer is lacking the necessary updates and therefore is not granted access to the network. In order to resume normal network access, please update your computer now at the following location." In addition to the message notification, a notification string, such as a URL entry, can also be configured by administrators that automatically send a noncompliant host to a remediation server.

Additional actions exist and vary by vendor applications.

Cisco Trust Agent Architecture

The following sections describe these components of Cisco Trust Agent:

- Posture agent plug-in file, which defines the host posture credential attributes
- Cisco Trust Agent log file and the type of events captured, which are useful for troubleshooting host problems with NAC

These sections also identify the operating systems that are supported by Cisco Trust Agent.

First, we walk you through the architecture of posture agents, beginning with the mandatory component, Cisco Trust Agent, as shown in Figure 3-2.

Figure 3-2   *Cisco Trust Agent Architecture*

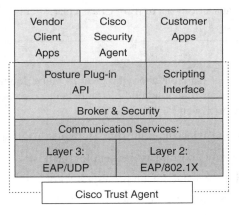

Cisco Trust Agent resides on the host and runs in the background as a service. Services exist and vary by Cisco Trust Agent version. These services should be automatically started and running; they include the following:

- Cisco Trust Agent (prior to Cisco Trust Agent version 2.0)
- Cisco Trust Agent Event Logging Service (prior to Cisco Trust Agent version 2.0)
- Cisco Posture Server Daemon (Cisco Trust Agent version 2.0)
- Cisco Systems, Inc. Cisco Trust Agent Posture State Daemon (Cisco Trust Agent version 2.0)
- Cisco Trust Agent EoU Daemon (Cisco Trust Agent version 2.0)
- Cisco Trust Agent Logger Daemon (Cisco Trust Agent version 2.0)

If 802.1X is included, the following additional services should be running:

- Cisco Trust Agent 802.1X Wired Client (Cisco Trust Agent version 2.0)
- Cisco Trust Agent 802.1X Wired Client Log (Cisco Trust Agent version 2.0)

Cisco Trust Agent provides the following two major functions:

- Cisco Trust Agent can collect information regarding the host operating system through internal posture plug-ins and acts as a broker by collecting credentials from third-party host application posture plug-ins.

- Cisco Trust Agent communicates to the NAD upstream with one of following protocols: Extensible Authentication Protocol over User Datagram Protocol (EAP over UDP, EAPoUDP, or EoU) and EAP over LAN (EAPoL), otherwise known as 802.1X.

NOTE   For 802.1X implementations, Cisco Trust Agent does not communicate directly to the NAD. All EAP transactions occur from Cisco Trust Agent to the supplicant and to the NAD, and vice versa.

Cisco Trust Agent is available at no charge and can be downloaded by any registered user at http://cisco.com/cgi-bin/tablebuild.pl/cta. It can also come bundled with CSA as well as some third-party NAC vendor applications.

Cisco Trust Agent also has the following additional features:

- Operating system posture assessment for the host
- Client notification and default browser integration
- Cisco Trust Agent Scripting Interface (CTASI)

Cisco Trust Agent includes two posture plug-ins of its own: one to report the status of the posture agent itself and one to report some basic information about the host that it's running on. Each of these posture plug-ins returns a credential as part of the validation process.

Cisco Trust Agent can also launch a web browser at the conclusion of the validation process. This is enabled by placing a URL in the notification string of the corresponding ACS configuration for posture validation. A pop-up message might also be displayed by Cisco Trust Agent or other applications that have this functionality by populating the PA Message section of the Posture Validation section in the Network Access Profiles setup on ACS.

When arbitrary information about a host is needed to make a complete posture assessment, the CTASI can be used. A user script can write a formatted file that CTASI can read into Cisco Trust Agent's internal database. This database is then sent as an additional credential for the posture decision-making process.

Cisco Trust Agent has two primary versions: one with an 802.1X supplicant and one without the supplicant.

Beginning with the core mandatory functionality, Cisco Trust Agent can operate solely for posture assessment using EoU with either version. By default, Cisco Trust Agent uses UDP port number 21862 for EoU communications. This port can be changed by editing the ctad.ini configuration file, which is described later in this section. Note that whichever UDP port is used, any host personal firewall must be modified to permit incoming traffic to this UDP port. Otherwise, Cisco Trust Agent will be unable to communicate NAC requests to the NAD, resulting in the host failing to authenticate and thereby receiving restricted access to the network.

Cisco Trust Agent can also gather identity and posture credentials simultaneously using the embedded, wired-only 802.1X supplicant.

NOTE   Cisco Trust Agent includes an 802.1X supplicant for wired interfaces only. For wired *and* wireless support, a third-party supplicant vendor can be engaged (such as Meetinghouse Data Communications, http://www.mtghouse.com).

With the NAC-L2-IP (EoU) method, the NAD detects a new host by way of DHCP or Address Resolution Protocol (ARP), where it queries the host, and if installed, Cisco Trust Agent responds to this query. At this point, the NAD signals the Cisco Secure ACS that it has a new host to be admitted to the network.

ACS and Cisco Trust Agent build a secure tunnel using Protected EAP (PEAP). PEAP requires the use of digital certificates. The PEAP tunnel is secured by way of a certificate presented by ACS during the establishment of the session. Because Cisco Trust Agent is installed with a root or intermediate root certificate, it trusts ACS and therefore builds a secure tunnel.

NOTE   For more information on the PEAP process, refer to the "NAC-L3-IP and NAC-L2-IP Posture Validation and Enforcement Process" section in Chapter 2, "Understanding NAC Framework."

NOTE   When Cisco Trust Agent is installed, it must have either the ACS server's certificate or a certificate in the chain of authority, either the root or an intermediate root certificate. For more information on installing and using digital certificates with Cisco Trust Agent, refer to the *Cisco Trust Agent Administrator Guide* located at http://www.cisco.com.

In cases where you want to evaluate user and/or device identity and posture credentials, you should use 802.1X.

The 802.1X technology can be used either with the embedded wired-only supplicant or a third-party supplicant. In this scenario, the Extensible Authentication Protocol–Flexible Authentication via Secure Tunneling (EAP-FAST) method must be used as the outer authentication method (at the time of this writing). The ability to handle multiple authentication types, for example, both user and machine identity and posture validation, in one authentication request is called *credential chaining*. EAP-FAST is currently the only EAP tunneling method that allows credential chaining. EAP-FAST is similar to PEAP in that it's also a tunneled protocol that supports a variety of authentication methods. What's different is that EAP-FAST does not require digital certificates like PEAP; it's designed to run on nearly every host device and preferred by some customers who don't want to use digital certificates.

Inner EAP types that can be used for identity authentication include the following:

- **EAP–Microsoft Challenge Handshake Authentication Protocol (MSCHAP) v2:** Used for Microsoft Active Directory based on username and password credentials.
- **EAP–Transport Layer Security (TLS):** Used with machine and/or user certificates.
- **EAP–Generic Token Card (GTC):** Used with Lightweight Directory Access Protocol (LDAP) or one-time passwords like Rivest, Shamir, and Adelman (RSA) SecurID tokens for identity information and include the relevant posture information as type-length values (TLVs) in the exchange with the ACSs.

For more on EAP-FAST, refer to http://www.ietf.org/internet-drafts/draft-cam-winget-eap-fast-03.txt.

In addition, user notifications are expressed by way of Cisco Trust Agent notification pop-ups, as shown in Figure 3-3, as well as by opening the host's default browser to a URL.

Figure 3-3 *User Notification Example of a Quarantine Condition*

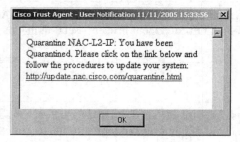

All of this information is expressed in the admission control policy, as configured in ACS.

In summary, the Cisco Trust Agent performs the following two mandatory functions:

- Communication with the NAD by either EAPoUDP or EAPoL (802.1X)
- Communication with NAC-capable applications on the host

Posture Agent Plug-in Files

Cisco Trust Agent includes two posture assessment capabilities: gathering its own posture information and gathering posture details from the host, such as operating system information through internal posture plug-ins.

The following is an example of an .inf file from Cisco Trust Agent's posture plug-in, or ctapp.inf, file:

```
[main]
PluginName=ctapp.dll
VendorID=9
VendorIDName=Cisco Systems
AppList=pa

[pa]
AppType=1
AppTypeName=CtaEoU
AttributeList=attr1,attr2,attr3,attr4,attr5,attr6,attr7,attr8
attr1=1,notify,AppPostureResult
attr2=2,notify,SysPostureResult
attr3=3,string,AppName
attr4=4,version,AppVersion
attr5=5,string,OSName
attr6=6,version,OSVersion
attr7=11,Unsigned32,CTAState
attr8=7,notify,UserNotify
```

The following is an example of Cisco Trust Agent's host posture plug-in, or CiscoHostPP.inf, file:

```
[main]
PluginName=CiscoHostPP.dll
VendorID=9
VendorIDName=Cisco Systems
AppList=CiscoHost

[CiscoHost]
AppType=2
AppTypeName=Host Posture Plugin
AttributeList=attr6,attr7,attr8
attr6=6,string,ServicePack
attr7=7,string,HotFixes
attr8=8,string,SystemName
```

You can see the attributes or credentials that these Cisco Trust Agent plug-ins gather for evaluation. Other NAC posture plug-ins are similar in how they are organized. However, the specific attributes differ by application.

A posture plug-in can also act on messages received from ACS at the conclusion of the posture validation process. These messages take two forms. One is a pop-up message that is displayed on the host's screen, informing the user of the posture validation results and optionally including an active URL. The second is a notification string that can be sent as a result of the validation process. This notification string can launch the default web browser on the host or can trigger the posture plug-in to begin a remediation process such as the update of an antivirus signature file. The actions triggered by the notification string vary according to the specific security application that the posture plug-in is associated with.

Cisco Trust Agent Logging

Cisco Trust Agent has logging capabilities that are extremely useful for troubleshooting NAC events. However, they are disabled by default (at the time of this writing).

To enable logging, go to the Cisco Trust Agent configuration directory on the host where Cisco Trust Agent is installed. The Cisco Trust Agent log file is located by default at C:\Documents and Settings\All Users\Application Data\Cisco Systems\CiscoTrustAgent\.

Rename the ctalogd.tmp file to ctalogd.ini. The log file is then created in the Logs subdirectory as soon as the Cisco Trust Agent receives the next EAPoUDP/EAPoL request. If the log file is not created, either you didn't rename the file correctly or the Cisco Trust Agent is not receiving EAPoUDP/EAPoL requests, which can be caused by a personal firewall blocking the requests or Cisco Trust Agent port from the NAD. Logging can also be enabled and configured through the command-line program clogcli.exe.

At the time of this writing, the default maximum log size is 4 MB and can be changed by editing the ctalogd.ini file. When the maximum log size is reached, a new log file is created. Over time, an unlimited number of files are created.

For information about log files or how to customize them, refer to the "Cisco Trust Agent Event Logging" section of the *Cisco Trust Agent Administrator Guide* located at http://www.cisco.com.

Operating System Support

As of this writing, Cisco Trust Agent supports the Windows and Red Hat Linux (Enterprise, Advanced, and Workstation, versions 3.*x* and 4.*x*) operating systems. Additional platform support for Microsoft Windows Mobile 5 and Windows XP Tablet, Sun Solaris, and Apple Macintosh OS X is anticipated.

As you saw from the two plug-ins described earlier (ctapp.inf and CiscoHostPP.inf), Cisco Trust Agent can gather the following information on a Windows NT 4.0, Windows 2000, or Windows XP system:

- Operating system name (for example, Windows XP Professional)
- Operating system version (for example, Version 2002)

- Operating system service pack (for example, Service Pack 2)
- Operating system hot fixes (for example, KB123456, KB234567, and so on)
- Machine name (for example, the host Fully Qualified Domain Name [FQDN])
- Cisco Trust Agent information:
  - Posture agent name (for example, Cisco Trust Agent)
  - Posture agent version (for example, 2.0.0.30)
  - Machine posture state (for example, booting versus logged in)

For Red Hat Linux, Cisco Trust Agent can collect the following information:

- Selected Red Hat Package Manager (RPM) versions
- Operating system type (for example, Red Hat Enterprise Linux ES)
- Operating system (OS) release (includes OS kernel name, version, and hardware platform)
- Kernel version (same as output of **uname –r**)
- Cisco Trust Agent information:
  - Posture agent name (for example, Cisco Trust Agent)
  - Posture agent version (for example, 2.0.0.30)
  - Machine posture state (for example, booting versus logged in)

The Linux host posture plug-in can retrieve the version number of certain packages, but these packages *must* be predefined in the ACS policy. Be aware that the Linux RPM version format is inconsistent when requested as a string or an octet. The following are examples of how the version number can appear. Cisco Trust Agent returns a package version number using a special format.

The first example is a posture validation rule configured in ACS that requests the version number of the OpenSSL package. When requested as a string, the version number is returned as a combination of numbers and letters, such as 0.9.7a.

The second example is when requested as a 4-octet number; the version number returned might be 0.9.7.97.

NOTE   Cisco Trust Agent for Linux does *not* support the retrieval of the host's FQDN.

Cisco Trust Agent, in combination with posture plug-ins and, optionally, with various third-party host applications, can deliver a deep view into the security policy compliance of a business's fleet of hosts.

Posture Plug-in Functionality

Posture plug-ins gather data from various security applications or host operating systems in a format that is acceptable for transmission to the posture agent, Cisco Trust Agent.

A critically significant aspect of the NAC Framework approach is its ability to intelligently integrate into third-party applications. As part of the Cisco NAC Partner Program (more information is available at http://www.cisco.com/en/US/partners/pr46/nac/partners.html), vendors of host antivirus, endpoint security, compliance and audit, and remediation and patch management products use Cisco Trust Agent to deliver credentials specific to their solution for validation against a comprehensive access control policy. Third-party security and compliance solutions can now use the ubiquitous presence of the network as a powerful enforcement point, and thereby deliver a significant extension on the customer's existing capital and operational investment in that application.

Each NAC vendor's posture plug-in is assigned a vendor ID by way of Internet Assigned Numbers Authority (IANA). A list of IANA assignments can be found at http://www.iana.org/assignments/enterprise-numbers.

Within that identifier, the vendor can implement a per-application type, followed by the various attributes that the vendor would like evaluated for admission control policy validation. The NAC vendor must follow a specific format or namespace as follows:

Vendor:Application-Type:Attribute

Refer to Table 3-1 for a list of credentials available from the host at the time of this writing. The list can vary depending on the installed posture agents.

Table 3-1 *Credential Attributes*

Application	Vendor	Application Type	Attributes
Cisco Trust Agent	Cisco	Posture agent (PA)	PA-Name
			PA-Version
			OS-Type
			OS-Version
			OS-Release
			OS-Kernel-Version
			Machine PostureState
Cisco Trust Agent	Cisco	Host	Service Packs
			HotFixes
			HostFQDN

Table 3-1   *Credential Attributes (Continued)*

Application	Vendor	Application Type	Attributes
CSA	Cisco	Host-based intrusion prevention system (HIPS)	CSAMCName CSAOperationalState CSAStates CSAVersion TimeSinceLast Successful Poll
Other	Various	Antivirus, personal firewall (PFW), and so on	Software-Name Software-ID Software-Version Scan-Engine-Version DAT-Version DAT-Date Protection-Enabled PFW-policy-version

In Windows versions, every Cisco NAC vendor must create the following two files that interoperate with Cisco Trust Agent:

- **.dll**—Links Cisco Trust Agent and the host application that in effect makes it a posture agent. The .dll file contains the application code for its specific plug-in actions that works with the application's notification string.

- **.inf**—Describes the various attributes available from the vendors plug-in. These are typically located in one of the following host directories:

  — For Cisco Trust Agent v1: C:\Program Files\Cisco Systems

  — For Cisco Trust Agent v2 or greater: C:\Program Files\Common Files\PostureAgent\Plugins

When a NAC vendor's credential is sent from the host to ACS, ACS must be capable of understanding it. To accomplish this, ACS must contain the partner attribute definition files (ADFs) that are specific to that NAC vendor. These ADFs can be imported into the ACS dictionary by using the CS-Util tool. Refer to version 4.0 of the *Cisco Secure ACS Configuration Guide,* located at http://www.cisco.com, Technical Documents for Cisco Security. An additional function of posture plug-ins is status change notification. When the associated security application completes a remediation process, such as receiving an updated signature file for an antivirus program, the posture plug-in can signal Cisco Trust Agent that a status change has occurred. When Cisco Trust Agent has been installed with a supplicant in NAC-L2-802.1X mode, Cisco Trust Agent can signal the supplicant to send an EAPoL start packet to the NAD. This triggers the initiation of a normal authentication sequence by the NAD. This feature is currently only available with a supplicant operating in NAC-L2-802.1X mode and is called *asynchronous status query*. When operating in NAC-L2-IP or NAC-L3-IP mode, the host must wait to receive a status query before triggering a revalidation.

Vendor Application Example: Cisco Security Agent

Many NAC-enabled vendor applications provide capabilities that can interoperate with NAC, thus extending the value of the existing application investment into a wider range of solutions. An example is Cisco Security Agent (CSA). CSA contains its own posture plug-in files, enabling it to send a credential to the NAC solution.

CSA provides the following four benefits to complement a NAC Framework solution:

- Cisco Trust Agent protection
- NAC state awareness
- Trusted quality of service
- Efficient mass deployment of Cisco Trust Agent

Cisco Trust Agent Protection

CSA is a behavioral-based host intrusion prevention product. It focuses on protecting the host asset and the intellectual property that resides on that asset, per its configured security policy.

In CSA versions 4.5.1 and 5.0, prebuilt rules exist that focus on two important functions: permitting Cisco Trust Agent to function as intended and protecting Cisco Trust Agent from outside interference. This interference could be caused by either a user mistake, such as uninstalling Cisco Trust Agent, or by intention, such as a worm attempting to spoof credentials. As shown in Figure 3-4, CSA has rules that permit Cisco Trust Agent to communicate with the network, open notification messages on the user's desktop, and open the default browser and pass a URL for remediation. CSA also has a rule that prevents modification of the Cisco Trust Agent files and the posture plug-in file folder.

Figure 3-4 *CSA Management Center: Cisco Trust Agent Rule Module*

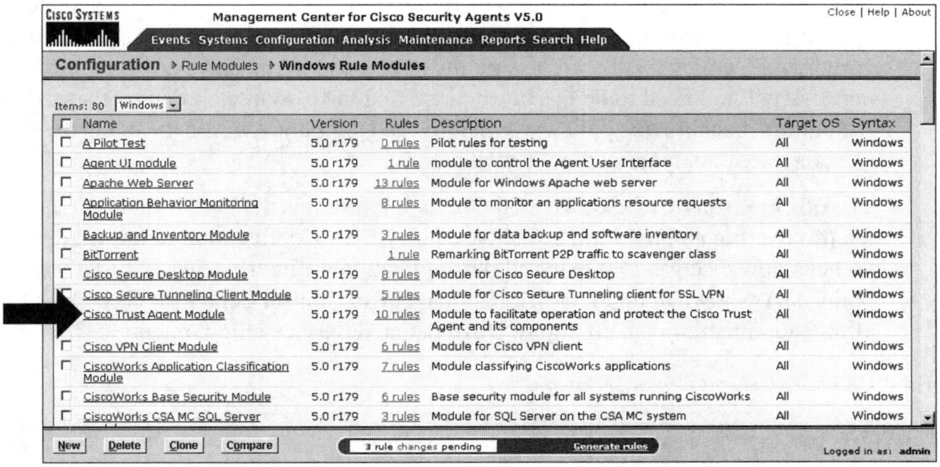

NAC State Awareness

Because Cisco Trust Agent and CSA can be installed on a host together, in this case, CSA also serves as a posture agent. As part of the integration, CSA can also see the system posture token (SPT) that is passed to Cisco Trust Agent from ACS. This allows CSA to dynamically change its specific host security policy in accordance with the admission control assessment.

Integrating host security functionality and port-based access control gives IT operations the capability to implement a policy that locks down noncompliant hosts so that only specified applications are allowed to run, and to only contact specific resources on the network. For example, IT operations can implement a policy that only permits remediation processes to run and only permits the default web browser to go to a narrow list of internal web resources.

Trusted Quality of Service

Providing a policy enforcement agent on the endpoint allows businesses to intelligently shift the trust boundary of the network into the host. This trust boundary depends on the admission control result. This type of solution is called Cisco Trusted Quality of Service (QoS).

Cisco Trusted QoS is valuable for two reasons. Because CSA can identify and secure known applications, it can properly mark the traffic from those applications with the appropriate Differentiated Services Code Point (DSCP) values (in accordance with corporate IT policy). This can be significant because traffic egressing onto the wide-area network will not need to be inspected, lessening the resource burden on the edge devices. In addition, because this policy is dynamic, the QoS policy within the company in question can adapt extremely quickly to new demands.

The other reason that Cisco Trusted QoS is important is that by virtue of the fact that you are discovering and marking traffic based on CSA's identification of known applications, you can now discover and mark all the application traffic that *does not conform* to your policies. As shown in Figure 3-5, the Management Control Center for Cisco Security Agent allows administrators to configure Differentiated Service enforcements.

Figure 3-5   *CSA Management Center: Trusted QoS*

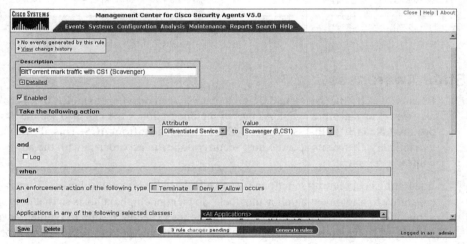

As shown here, the administrator marks certain traffic to be a Scavenger class (Differentiated Service Scavenger (8,CS1)) and selectively drops it if it exceeds a certain rate. Even more interestingly, questionable traffic can selectively be routed through upstream security devices by using other routing and switching functions, such as policy-based routing, virtual routing and forwarding (VRF), or Cisco Optimized Edge Routing (OER). This can greatly decrease the utilization on these security devices, because they would only be inspecting and enforcing questionable traffic versus all traffic.

For more information on Trusted QoS, refer to the Cisco Security Agent Management Center (CSA MC) documentation located at http://www.cisco.com/univercd/cc/td/doc/product/vpn/ciscosec/csa/csa50/trqos.pdf.

Bundling Cisco Trust Agent for Deployment

A final CSA benefit is to use the CSA MC to import and install the Cisco Trust Agent along with CSA onto hosts automatically. This can be done by associating installation options such as a silent install with the supplicant and the required certificate into the CSA build kit process. This allows the operator to *bundle* and even update Cisco Trust Agent on any host that has CSA installed. An example of how to select this bundling option in CSA MC is shown in Figure 3-6.

Figure 3-6   *CSA Management Center: Cisco Trust Agent Bundling*

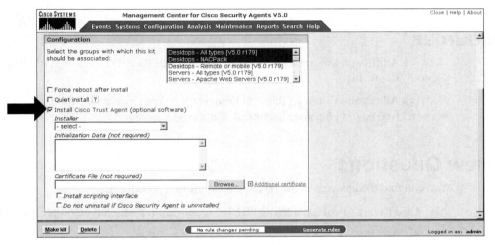

Bundling Cisco Trust Agent with CSA installation can represent a significant operational time savings, as well as decrease the interruption on the part of the user community.

Summary

Cisco Trust Agent is the NAC posture agent that is a fundamental component of NAC Framework providing the following two major functions:

- Acts as a broker, communicating with the NAC-enabled host applications and gathering credentials
- Communicates with NADs by way of EAPoUDP or EAPoL (802.1X)

Cisco Trust Agent communicates with various NAC-enabled host applications by way of their posture plug-ins. NAC third-party vendors must build their own posture plug-ins to communicate their credentials to the policy decision points. Each vendor is identified by a unique vendor ID that includes identifying its application type (for example, antivirus) and attributes (for example, version). ACS must be able to understand the NAC vendor's credentials. You might need to import partner attribute definition files (ADFs) into the ACS ADF dictionary.

Cisco Trust Agent also acts as a vital communication tool to users by informing them by way of message notifications in the form of pop-ups. It also guides users into remediation by the use of their web browser and URL redirections.

The presence of NAC-enabled applications and posture agents, in conjunction with the network access devices and the policy validation servers, allows the network to intelligently evaluate and enforce a security compliance policy anywhere in the network.

Resources

Network Admission Control EBC Presentation, Russell Rice, Director of Marketing, STG, Cisco Systems, Inc.

Network Admission Control Technical Frequently Asked Questions, http://wwwin.cisco.com/stg/nac/nac_technical_faq.shtml#anchor4.

Review Questions

You can find the answers to the review questions in Appendix A.

1 Cisco Trust Agent includes an 802.1X supplicant for which type of interfaces?

 a Any type of access interface

 b Only wired interfaces

 c Wired and wireless interfaces

 d All Layer 2 and Layer 3 interfaces

2 How is the protected EAP tunnel established between ACS and Cisco Trust Agent?

 a Both use a shared secret password only.

 b Choice of using either a shared secret password or certificate.

 c Cisco Trust Agent presents a certificate to ACS.

 d ACS presents a certificate to Cisco Trust Agent.

3 When evaluating identity and posture credentials, which EAP type must be used with 802.1X?

   a EAP-FAST

   b Protected EAP

   c EAP-TLS

   d EAP-GTC

4 Cisco Trust Agent communicates directly with which two NAC components?

   a NAD

   b ACS

   c NAC-enabled applications posture plug-in

   d Posture agents

5 Which type(s) of NAC vendor file is located in the host directory C:\Program Files\Common Files\PostureAgent\Plugins?

   a .dll

   b .log

   c .exe

   d .inf

6 Which common filenames are assigned to the two posture agent plug-ins?

   a ctapp.inf

   b CiscoHostPP.inf

   c CiscoHostPP.dll

   d ctaapi.dll

   e ctapp.dll

7 Which of the following statements is false?

   a A benefit of using CSA with NAC is that it can protect Cisco Trust Agent from being altered.

   b CSA MC allows the ability to install Cisco Trust Agent and required certificates along with the CSA quiet install.

   c CSA can discover and mark application traffic with DSCP values.

   d CSA is a posture agent and does not require the use of Cisco Trust Agent.

This chapter covers the following topics:

- Posture Validation Servers:
  - Cisco Secure Access Control Server
  - NAC Framework solution with external policy servers
  - Audit servers
- Posture policy planning
- Posture policy rules
- NAC agentless hosts and whitelisting techniques
- Authorization
- Enforcement actions

CHAPTER 4

Posture Validation Servers

A posture validation server acts as the central policy evaluation point in the *Network Admission Control (NAC)* Framework solution. A posture validation server inspects the attributes contained in the credentials it receives from a host and compares them against the network's access policy. The policy consists of specific rules that represent the requirements for the privilege of network access. If the host does not meet those requirements, that host can be denied network access or receive some minimal amount of access that can permit it to complete a remediation process and return to a healthy state. This chapter describes the process in which a posture validation server determines and enforces a policy. It also explains how rules are created and how actions are assigned.

This chapter describes the following items:

- How a NAC solution uses hosts with NAC-enabled antivirus (AV) applications
- A NAC solution that also uses an AV partner's external posture validation server
- A common patch and AV enforcement policy
- How a posture token is chosen
- Whitelisting techniques for NAC Framework, including identifying the technique that can be used for each of the three NAC implementation methods

A NAC solution consists of several elements in a data network. The network access devices (NADs) sense the presence of a new host attempting access and begin the authentication and/or posture validation process. An agent on the client undergoing the posture validation process responds to the NAD with one or more credentials containing type-length value (TLV) elements that represent the state of the client or the state of files or software residing on that client. These credentials and TLVs are evaluated by a posture validation server (PVS) and compared to a policy that determines whether the client is compliant with the policy for admission to the network.

Posture Validation Servers

Upon the attempt of a new client connection, the NAC Framework solution begins a new RADIUS session between the NAD and the posture validation server for each new host discovered. The condition of the host is requested as a set of credentials with attributes that represent various conditions on that host. These conditions can be the creation date of antivirus signature files, version numbers of software, and other identifying characteristics of applications running on a host. After the host has transmitted those credentials to the NAC solution, that host's condition must be evaluated for compliance with the network's access policy. The action of this evaluation is the function of the posture validation server, also referred to as a policy evaluation point. The posture validation server in the NAC Framework solution can be just a single server, namely the Cisco Secure Access Control Server (ACS), or it can be a variety of specific application vendor servers along with the Cisco Secure ACS. Currently, ACS is a requirement for the framework solution; ACS handles the communication between itself and the NAD by way of a tunnel, with the host undergoing admission control. No other authentication, authorization, and accounting (AAA) servers support this needed functionality. ACS also provides a policy engine that can logically evaluate the received client's TLV information and assign a relative health condition to the client.

Cisco Secure Access Control Server

Cisco Secure ACS can act as the entire policy evaluation point for a NAC Framework solution. In this case, all the policies and rules that you want to check are created in your ACS using a graphical user interface (GUI), as shown in Figure 4-1. On the left side of the initial screen is a column of buttons that lead you to the individual configuration areas in Cisco Secure ACS.

Figure 4-1   *Cisco Secure Access Control Server*

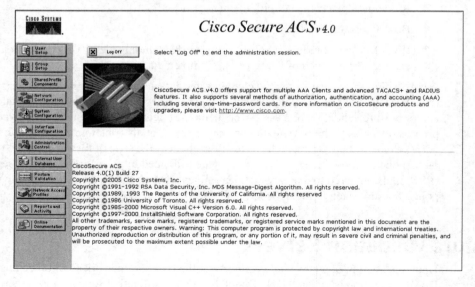

From the standpoint of the ACS, the NAC session begins with ACS receiving a RADIUS request from a NAD. This RADIUS authentication request is examined to determine the characteristics of the request by the ACS. The ACS can check a variety of characteristics about the RADIUS request to determine how to handle that request. The RADIUS request might have originated from a specific NAD's IP address or from within group of IP addresses that belong to a specific class of NADs. The request can have certain RADIUS attributes or RADIUS service types associated with it, and ACS can also perform further evaluation based on vendor-specific attributes (VSAs) contained in the RADIUS request.

A network access profile (NAP) allows a differentiation of authentication methods that can be performed on that RADIUS request. For example, if ACS receives a request for an administrative telnet login to a router, it would not require posture validation credentials to be part of the authentication request. After ACS has properly categorized the authentication request, it begins the authentication phase. Because a RADIUS request can contain multiple credential types, more than one authentication can take place for each particular RADIUS request. Figure 4-2 shows the initial configuration screen for NAP. From this screen, you can access the various configuration sections of multiple different profiles. Each profile can have configuration definitions for the authentication request itself, how the request is to be handled, the types of NAC profiles used on the request, and the authorization that the host is entitled to after the authentication request has been processed.

Figure 4-2   *Network Access Profiles*

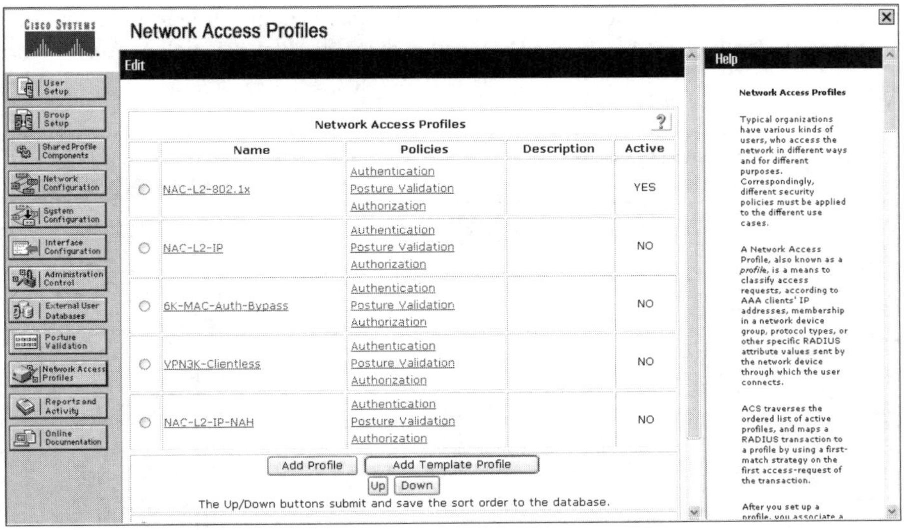

Figure 4-3 shows the configuration screen for a single profile. This screen is where you configure the individual characteristics of the incoming authentication request, including the protocol of authentication packet and any associated attributes.

Figure 4-3 *Profile Setup Window*

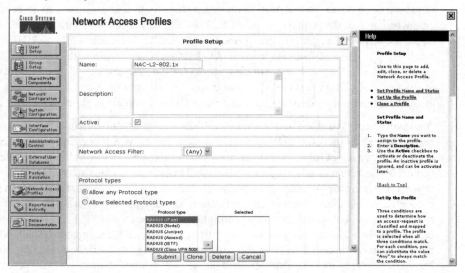

Figure 4-4 shows a NAP authentication configuration example where the network access policy requires a client to be checked for the identification of the user as well as verification of an active antivirus solution on the host the user is connecting to the network from. The user credentials can be checked against an external database such as Active Directory.

Figure 4-4 *NAP Authentication Configuration Window*

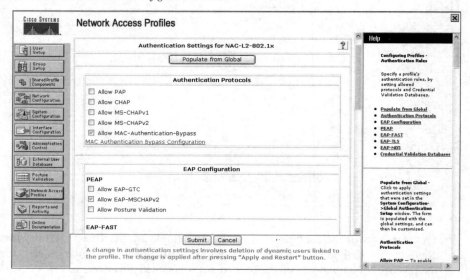

ACS can check the user credentials against its internal user database or against any configured external user databases, such as Microsoft's Active Directory. The next step in the posture validation process is the evaluation of the posture TLVs. The selection of the particular policy that is to be applied to the authentication request is determined by the set of NAC credentials received in the authentication request. The set of credentials is compared against the configured required credential types in the posture validation window. As shown in Figure 4-5, the first match that occurs in the posture validation rule list causes that specific posture validation rule to be chosen for that host.

Figure 4-5   *NAP Posture Validation*

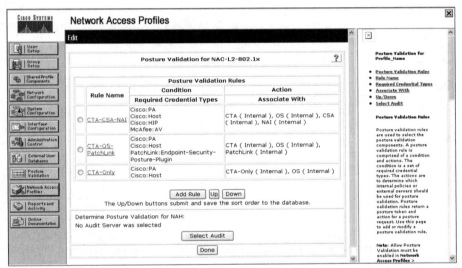

These posture validation rules take the form of a series of policies with multiple individual rules per policy and a final default rule at the end. Each rule contains one or more condition sets where the comparison against the received TLV is done. The rules are evaluated sequentially so that they appear in the ACS policy interface. The decision is made on a first-match basis; if a set of TLVs matches the requirements for all the condition sets that are required for a particular rule, rule evaluation processing terminates at that point for that specific policy. For this reason, the rules should be written in such an order that the most common posture token is first—usually this is the healthy posture token. If no rule matches, the policy rule checking falls through to the default rule, and the associated posture token for the default rule is assigned.

Figure 4-6 shows a closer look at policy posture validation rules. The name of the policy is shown along with a set of conditions for each rule that would result in a match of that rule. The resulting application posture token is also displayed along with any assigned actions for the matched rule. In this example, matched rules result in the hosts machine's default browser opening to the specific URL shown. The action is specific to the individual posture plugin.

Figure 4-6 *NAP Posture Validation Rules*

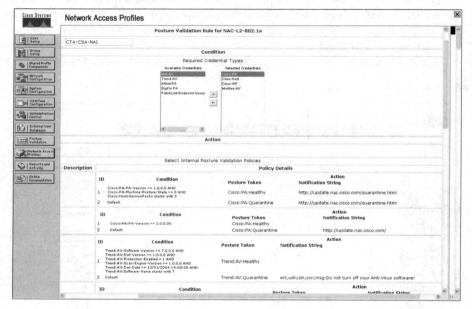

Optionally, ACS can also relay specific credentials to external posture validation servers implemented by third-party NAC program members who participate in the NAC Framework solution.

NAC Framework Solution with External Policy Servers

Alternatively, the evaluation of the TLV data can be performed by a third-party posture validation server. Many reasons for this exist. A third-party server can have a predetermined set of policies that can make a decision when a client is healthy or infected much more accurately than a manually configured policy, avoiding the need to configure a custom set of policy rules in ACS. The external server can also update itself automatically from the Internet; this eliminates the need to constantly change or update policy rules and relieves the administrator of this burden.

Figure 4-7 shows the ACS window for configuring external posture validation servers with which that ACS will interoperate.

Figure 4-7   *External Posture Validation Servers*

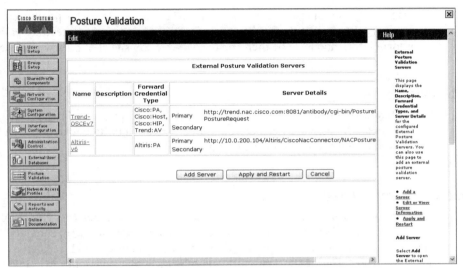

When an external posture validation server is set up here, ACS knows to send the configured credential or credentials to the third-party server for evaluation. The external server then responds with a result token for the policies that it has control over. These application posture tokens are merged with any other application posture tokens by ACS, and a system posture token is chosen and assigned to the client. This also determines the network access entitlements, restrictions, or any other actions that are to be enforced on that client. This information is shown in the Passed Authentications report in the Reports and Activity section.

The Cisco NAC Framework program includes participation from vendors that are external to Cisco Systems. The following sections include information available at the time of this writing. Some of these details might have changed, so check with the individual program vendor for the most current information.

Trend Micro OfficeScan

The Trend Micro OfficeScan solution (in version 7.3 as of this writing) integrates with the Cisco NAC Framework solution as an external policy validation server for an antivirus solution. OfficeScan can automatically update itself with antivirus pattern files across the Internet and provides relief from daily updating chores for the NAC administrator. More information is available from the Trend Micro website at http://www.trendmicro.com.

McAfee Policy Enforcer

The McAfee Policy Enforcer is in beta testing as of this writing. This product can scan managed or guest systems and verify compliance with your network security policies. Additional information can be found on the McAfee website at http://www.mcafee.com.

Audit Servers

While they are not strictly posture validation servers, we mention audit servers here briefly because, in many cases, they can be configured to return a posture token that can be used in the overall network admission control process.

The QualysGuard Appliance

The QualysGuard appliance is one auditing solution that integrates with NAC Framework. Beginning with ACS version 4.0, after determining that the host cannot communicate with the NAC solution, ACS can notify the QualysGuard appliance, which can begin a network audit of the host. During the audit, the QualysGuard appliance notifies ACS that the audit is in progress and should be placed in a transition state. Part of the transition state includes instructions to the NAD to open a communication path between the agentless client and the QualysGuard appliance. After completing an audit of a host, the QualysGuard appliance can return a posture token to ACS that can assist in the decision-making process for network access. Later versions of ACS will be able to take the information provided by the QualysGuard appliance, such as device type, and use that in the decision-making process.

McAfee Policy Enforcer

The McAfee Policy Enforcer also includes an audit server that communicates with the NAC solution through the Generic Authorization Message Exchange (GAME). This enables the scanning of nonresponsive hosts and a more accurate assessment of the host's security posture when dealing with those hosts. Additional information on the McAfee solution can be found on their website at http://www.mcafee.com.

Altiris

The Altiris solution manages the patch level and software update process for managed clients. The Altiris solution integrates through the Generic Authorization Message Exchange protocol to perform an audit on a client with a back-end server. The Altiris solution ensures that a host is compliant with currently authorized patches.

Current information regarding the Altiris products can be found on the Altiris website at http://www.altiris.com.

Posture Policy Planning and Policy Rules

The planning of a network access policy should begin with the enterprise security policy. This policy can state in broad terms the requirements for end stations, the acceptable use of the network, and other items that can help a network administrator make a decision about the type of rules that make up that enterprise's network access policy. It is the NAC administrator's job to translate the enterprise network security policy into a set of NAC policies and rules that resemble what is acceptable to the enterprise. The security policy can be translated into actionable rules with the knowledge of specific security software packages that the corporate information technology group has mandated should be installed. After specific packages have been identified, rules can be written to specify version numbers and other requirements that must be met prior to network access.

Posture Policy Rules

Posture rules are basically just checks against received values contained in attributes. The checks performed on the attributes depend on the data type of the attribute. These attributes can take the form of software version numbers, dates and times that files were created or became available, the names of files, hot fixes or other patches, and a variety of other information. Each of these attributes has a specific data type, and each data type has a variety of operators associated with it. Table 4-1 shows attribute data types.

Table 4-1   *Attribute Data Types*

OctetArray	Integer32	Unsigned32	String (UTF-8)	IPv4Addr	IPv6Addr	Time (4 octets)	Version (4 x 2-octet sets)
=, !=	=, <, >, !=, >=, <=	=, <, >, !=, >=, <=	=, !=, contains, starts with, regex	wildcards & mask	wildcards & mask	=, <, >, !=, >=, <=	=, <, >, !=, >=, <=

For example, the name of an antivirus package can be specified with a string. The string data type could be checked with a regular expression that searches for a word or phrase. Similarly, dates can be checked for an absolute value or a relative value, such as being no older than a certain amount of time.

Policy Evaluation and Choosing a Posture Token

Each client's credentials and attributes are evaluated separately. The policies and rules are evaluated sequentially, in the order configured in the ACS GUI in the Posture Validation Policy window. Figure 4-8 shows a sample policy.

Figure 4-8 *Posture Validation Policies*

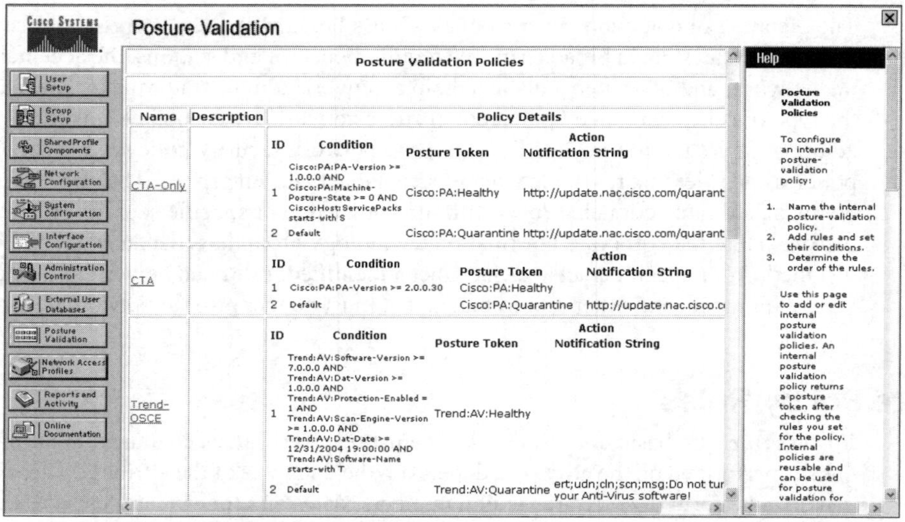

Clients can be assigned groups by both the posture validation process and by the user validation process. These two policies are combined by entries in a policy table that can define a unique set of access privileges for each combination.

NAC Agentless Hosts and Whitelisting

The NAC solution allows a variety of ways to handle hosts that do not or cannot participate in NAC. These can be IP-enabled appliances, such as printers, IP phones, or hosts, that run operating systems for which Cisco Trust Agent is not yet available. These hosts can be audited by an external audit server, or they can be exempted from the NAC process by using MAC Authentication Bypass (MAB), also known as *whitelisting*. As shown in Table 4-2, the whitelist technique chosen is determined by the NAC implementation method: NAC-L2-802.1X, NAC-L2-IP, or NAC-L3-IP.

Table 4-2 *Whitelisting Techniques for NAC Framework*

Component	NAC-L2-802.1X	NAC-L2-IP	NAC-L3-IP
ACS whitelist (centralized)	MAC-Auth-Bypass	MAC\IP wildcards (posture only)	MAC\IP wildcards (posture only)

Whitelisting is simply a list of MAC addresses or IP addresses that are centrally administered and cannot participate in the NAC process. MAB uses the MAC address information from a NAC-L2-802.1X session with a special RADIUS packet with a service type of 10 to access a list of MAC addresses in the ACS database. Figure 4-9 shows the window used to assign MAC addresses to user groups that allows MAB.

Figure 4-9   *MAC Authentication Bypass Setup*

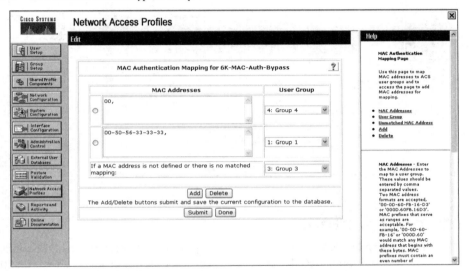

Look for future versions of ACS to allow Lightweight Directory Access Protocol (LDAP) access to external databases for MAC addresses.

Authorization

The next step in the NAC Framework process is the authorization of the client onto the network. If the client has been placed into a group as the result of user authentication, this group membership can also be taken into account as part of the network authorization. Figure 4-10 shows an example of a network authorization policy.

Figure 4-10 *Authorization Configuration*

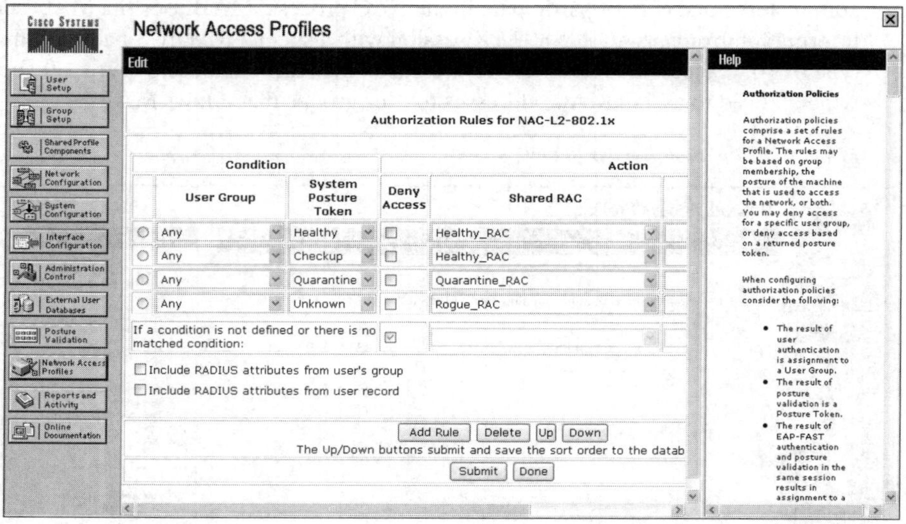

Enforcement Actions

The final step in a NAC Framework solution process is the selection and the configuration of the access entitlements that the client receives or the enforcement actions that the network places on that client. Currently, the two IP modes that NAC operates in share a common set of access entitlements and enforcement actions, whereas the 802.1X method uses a separate method. Table 4-3 identifies the enforcement action that can be used by the three NAC implementation methods.

Table 4-3 *Enforcement Actions*

Feature	NAC-L2-802.1X	NAC-L2-IP	NAC-L3-IP
VLAN assignment	✓		
URL redirection		✓	✓
Downloadable ACLs	6500 only (PBACLs*)	✓	✓
Posture status queries		✓	✓
802.1X posture change	✓		

*Policy-based access control lists

As of this writing, these enforcement actions are planned to change in the future so that NAC-L2-IP can get VLAN assignment as an enforcement action and NAC-L2-802.1X can get access list assignment or URL redirection.

RADIUS Authorization Components

The enforcement actions that the solution takes on a client are configured as a set of RADIUS Authorization Components (RACs). A RAC is simply a set of RADIUS attributes that are sent to the NAD as a response to the posture validation process. These attributes can cause the NAD to perform VLAN assignment, change timer settings, or cause web requests to be redirected to remediation server pages. Figure 4-11 shows a sample RAC configuration window for a healthy condition.

Figure 4-11 *RADIUS Authorization Component Configuration*

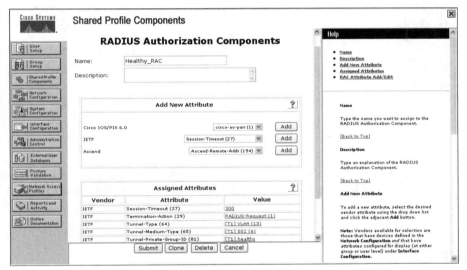

Downloadable access control lists can also be included as part of the enforcement actions when NAC is configured in one of the IP modes.

Posture Plug-in Actions

An additional method of enforcement or notification that NAC can use is the action field in the returned posture token. These actions are independent of any enforcement action that the network can place on a client. The action field is returned along with the result application posture token in the returned credential configured for the applicable policy. In the sample shown in Figure 4-12, the action for a Cisco:PA posture token can be a notification string formatted as a URL.

Figure 4-12 *Posture Agent Action Field*

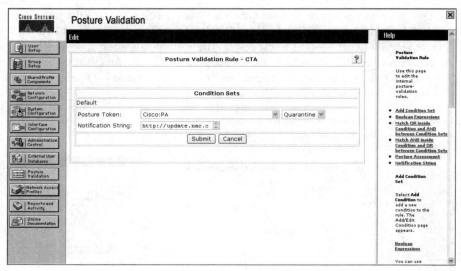

When a URL is configured in the action field for the Cisco:PA or Cisco Trust Agent, Cisco Trust Agent automatically opens the default web browser for the client to the configured web page.

Summary

The posture validation server(s) form the heart of the Network Admission Control Framework solution by acting as the policy evaluation point for your network. Administrators can translate network access policies into rules by using the graphical user interface in Cisco Secure ACS. ACS performs an automated evaluation of various client conditions before determining whether those clients are allowed access onto the network. ACS can also transmit client credentials to external posture validation servers that can make more detailed decisions about vendor-specific applications, such as the currency of various files being checked.

Refer to Volume 2 of this book for more information about how to configure policy validation servers for a NAC Framework solution.

Review Questions

You can find the answers to the review questions in Appendix A.

1 Which ACS version 4.0 NAP window is used to configure MAC Authentication Bypass to be allowed?

   a Posture Validation

   b EAP Configuration

   c Authentication Protocols

   d External Posture Validation Servers

2 Which of the following can be used as external policy server(s) for NAC Framework? Choose all that apply.

   a Trend Micro OfficeScan

   b McAfee Policy Manager

   c QualysGuard

   d Altiris

3 Which of the following can be used as external audit server(s) for NAC Framework?

   a Trend Micro OfficeScan

   b QualysGuard

   c McAfee Policy Manager

   d Altiris

4 Which of the following policy server(s) can logically evaluate the received client's TLV information?

   a Cisco Secure ACS

   b Trend Micro OfficeScan

   c McAfee Policy Manager

   d QualysGuard

5 Refer to Figure 4-7. For the Trend-OSCE policy rules for ID 1, if only one condition matches the policy rules, which posture token is assigned?

   a Trend:AV:Healthy for that rule because one match is all that's needed

   b Cisco:PA:Healthy for that rule because one match is all that's needed

   c Trend:AV:Quarantine because the healthy state requires all rules to be matched 100 percent

   d Cisco:PA:Quarantine because the healthy state requires all rules to be matched 100 percent

6 Which whitelist technique can be used for NAC-L2-802.1X implementations?

   a MAC wildcard for posturing hosts

   b IP wildcard for posturing hosts

   c MAB only

   d Any of the above

7 Which enforcement actions are *not* available for NAC-L2-IP when using NAC Framework Phase 2 (at the time of this writing)?

   a VLAN assignment

   b URL redirection

   c Downloadable ACLs

   d Posture status queries

This chapter covers the following topics:

- IEEE 802.1X technology overview
- 802.1X framework
- IEEE 802.1X operational overview
- RADIUS
- Authorization and enforcement
- Integration issues when using 802.1X
- NAC-L2-802.1X identity with posture validation and enforcement
- Leveraging an authenticated identity

CHAPTER 5

NAC Layer 2 Operations

The first Network Admission Control (NAC) Framework deployment rule of thumb is to use the NAC-enabled network access device (NAD) closest to the endpoints to check compliance; this helps enforce a least-privilege principle. In many cases, NAC is implemented at the switch port working at Layer 2.

This chapter describes how NAC works when implemented using NAC-L2-802.1X. The chapter begins by describing the 802.1X technology and how, when combined with NAC, it provides additional identity checking along with posturing.

This chapter describes the following items:

- Additional NAC benefits when combining 802.1X into the admission policy

- The functions of an 802.1X supplicant and authenticator

- Common RADIUS attributes used for 802.1X implementations

- The Extensible Authentication Protocol (EAP) authorization process and the most common EAP methods used

- Three attribute value pairs (AVPs) that are used for VLAN assignment by NADs providing the NAC-L2-802.1X method

- Some integration issues for hosts that are not 802.1X capable

- The posture validation process used in a NAC-L2-802.1X environment

- How VLANs are assigned to a host in a NAC-L2-802.1X environment

- Additional business benefits that can be leveraged from using an authenticated identity

IEEE 802.1X Technology Overview

The use of IEEE 802.1X offers an efficient framework to a protected network for authenticating and administering user traffic. Together with technology extensions and supplemental authentication techniques, NAC builds on 802.1X to establish a technology solution that can improve the security of physical and logical access to LANs. NAC incorporates all the capabilities defined in the IEEE 802.1X authentication standard and provides enhancements and extensions for improving identity-based access control and for making 802.1X technology easier to deploy in real-world network environments. For some enterprises, the basic authentication of users is not enough. Organizations require more visibility, traceability, and enhanced audit capabilities for authenticated users. By leveraging 802.1X, NAC can provide functionality to address these common issues currently faced by enterprise networks, in addition to ensuring software compliance.

802.1X Framework

Through the increased use of 802 LANs in public and semipublic places, a desire existed to provide a mechanism to associate identities with the port of access to the LAN to establish authorized access. Other potential motivations were the personalization of the network access environment and billing/accounting mechanisms, all while wanting to leverage existing authentication, authorization, and accounting (AAA) infrastructures with other forms of network access. The 802.1X technology ties the Extensible Authentication Protocol (EAP) to both the wired and wireless LAN media and supports multiple authentication methods. The technology defines a generic framework that can use different authentication mechanisms without implementing these mechanisms outside the back-end authentication infrastructure and client devices. The 802.1X technology specifies a protocol framework between devices desiring access to a LAN (supplicants) and devices providing access to a LAN (authenticators). For flexibility, differing credentials (such as token cards), Kerberos, one-time passwords, certificates, and public key authentication can be used with 802.1X. Primarily, 802.1X is an encapsulation definition for EAP over IEEE 802 media—EAP over LAN (EAPoL). This Layer 2 protocol transports authentication messages (EAP) between supplicant (user/PC) and authenticator (switch or access point). The 802.1X technology always assumes a secure connection, and the enforcement is done through MAC-based filtering and port-state monitoring.

Supplicant

The 802.1X authentication architecture consists of a client entity that requests service to a network system. In 802.1X terms, this client is referred to as a *supplicant*. A supplicant represents a user or host requesting a network connection.

As shown in Figure 5-1, the supplicant is on the left side, representing networked devices that need to attain network services through 802.1X authentication. Supplicant functionality is the software solution that provides 802.1X capability for wired and wireless networks. The 802.1X supplicants can support various EAP methods, including EAP–Message Digest 5 (EAP-MD5), EAP–Transport Layer Security (EAP-TLS), EAP–Tunneled Transport Layer Security (EAP-TTLS), Cisco Light Extensible Authentication Protocol (LEAP), EAP–Protected EAP (EAP-PEAP), EAP–Flexible Authentication via Secure Tunneling (EAP-FAST), and so on. NAC only works with EAP-FAST. Also, supplicant capability can be supported over various platforms, including but not limited to Windows XP, 2000, NT, 98, and Me; Pocket PC 2002; CE.net 4.1; CE.net 4.2; Mac OS X;

Palm Tungsten C; Solaris 8; Red Hat Linux; and so on. If an 802.1X supplicant is available on a specific platform, a network administrator can take advantage of security advances like NAC. The supplicant software communicates with an 802.1X AAA/RADIUS server to confirm a user's identity.

Figure 5-1   *802.1X Supplicant*

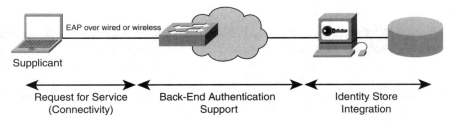

The type of identified credential used by an 802.1X supplicant depends on the EAP method. For EAP-TLS, it is a public-key infrastructure (PKI) certificate. For EAP-MD5, it is a username/password. NAC has the potential to use a combined identified credential through its use of EAP-FAST.

Authenticator

The 802.1X authentication architecture also consists of a network device or entity that facilitates the authentication of the supplicant. This device is generally known as the *authenticator*. The authenticator's primary role is to transpose an EAP conversation from supplicant to authentication server. From an EAP perspective, an authenticator is a pass-through device. The EAP conversation is transported by way of 802.1X from supplicant to authenticator. The 802.1X technology stops at the authenticator. The 802.1X authenticators include switches, routers, or wireless LAN (WLAN) access points, as indicated in Figure 5-2.

Figure 5-2   *802.1X Authenticator*

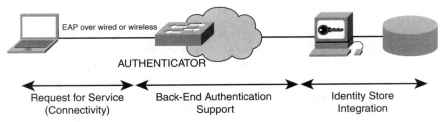

It is the authenticator's ultimate responsibility to provide or restrict network access. Providing network access can come in various levels of authorization as well, so it is also the authenticator's responsibility to enforce policy as a result of authenticating the identified credential from a supplicant.

Default Security of 802.1X

An 802.1X authenticator is responsible for providing network access for any supplicants. As a result, increased security is provided to the networked system. Regardless of media, 802.1X typically enforces a "guilty until proven innocent" data plane through its use of the EAPoL control plane. Specifically, access control is achieved through the use of controlled and uncontrolled ports. From the result of the authentication process, the authenticator can determine whether the supplicant is authorized to access any services. If the supplicant is not authorized for access, the authenticator sets access to its controlled port as a state of unauthorized. In the unauthorized state, the use of the controlled port is restricted. This operation is shown in Figure 5-3.

Figure 5-3   *802.1X Controlled/Uncontrolled Ports*

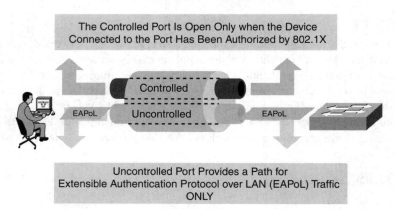

For Each 802.1X Switch Port, the Switch Creates
Two Virtual Access Points at Each Port

The Controlled Port Is Open Only when the Device
Connected to the Port Has Been Authorized by 802.1X

Controlled

EAPoL   Uncontrolled   EAPoL

Uncontrolled Port Provides a Path for
Extensible Authentication Protocol over LAN (EAPoL) Traffic
ONLY

As shown in Figure 5-3, one point of access, the uncontrolled port, allows the uncontrolled exchange of protocol data units between the supplicant and authenticator regardless of the authorization state. The other point of access allows the exchange of protocol data units only if the current state of the port is authorized. This is the controlled port. So from a network security standpoint, the only traffic that should be processed by an authenticator on the uncontrolled port is EAPoL. From a literal standpoint, it's just like an administrator having access to all ports in an enterprise and configuring a "permit EAPoL, deny any" access control list (ACL) on all ports until authorized by 802.1X.

Through the use of the IEEE 802.1X technology, you can improve your network security model and achieve stable premises for NAC. These include keeping the outsiders out and reducing potential network attacks. This way, only authorized users can gain network access, and unauthorized or unrecognized users can be denied access or granted guest access. Later in the chapter, the "Accounting" section examines how you can track usage for accountability and forensic information. The "NAC-L2-802.1X Identity with Posture Validation and Enforcement" section examines how NAC uses 802.1X to keep insiders honest, by also ensuring software compliance as part of an identified credential exchange.

Authentication Server

Although 802.1X does not mandate the use of a specific AAA protocol, an authentication server is a key component in port-based access control for 802.1X. Generally an authentication server is the entity that provides an authentication service to an authenticator. When used with 802.1X, this server typically executes EAP methods for the authenticator, and is typically located as an AAA facility. The authentication server is responsible for validating supplicant credentials and determining whether to authorize the authenticator to grant access for the host to any requested network services. Typically, the RADIUS protocol is used as the transport for EAP between the authenticator and authentication server, as shown in Figure 5-4.

Figure 5-4   *Authentication Server*

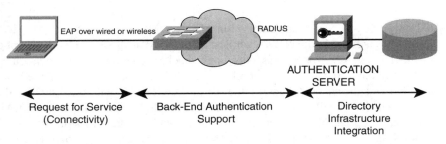

The architecture of EAP also allows EAP to extend beyond the AAA protocol or authentication server, as indicated in Figure 5-4. This allows the possibility of integrating with an existing directory infrastructure (like Windows Active Directory) to verify identity information.

IEEE 802.1X Operational Overview

Now that you understand at a high level how 802.1X identifies who someone is and/or restricts unauthorized devices from connecting to a LAN, we now review the underlying protocol messages. Until authentication has successfully completed, a supplicant only has access to the authenticator to perform authentication exchanges. After authentication is complete, a supplicant can be granted full access by an authenticator, or to specific services offered by the authenticator. The following sections describe how EAPoL makes this occur.

A supplicant typically announces its presence on the wire by way of an EAPoL-Start frame. This is an indication to an authenticator that a supplicant is present on one of its ports and would like to be authenticated. An authenticator should oblige this EAPoL-Start frame with an EAPoL-Identity-Request frame to ask the supplicant for its initial identity credentials defined in RFC 3748. A supplicant will respond to this frame by way of an EAPoL-Identity-Response frame. This process is shown in Figure 5-5.

Figure 5-5 *Initial EAP Exchange*

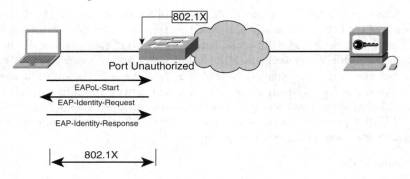

As shown in Figure 5-5, a supplicant-initiated authentication exchange occurs. All three of these frames are sent in the clear, regardless of the EAP method used by the supplicant or authentication server. Note that as a result, an attacker could use this information for exploit. The threat vector here is not related to 802.1X, however. The EAP method itself should provide the adequate security the session needs end to end. IEEE 802.1X does not mandate which side initiates authentication. As a result, the transmission of an EAPoL-Start frame is optional by a supplicant, and an authenticator can transmit EAPoL-Identity-Request frames on the wire periodically. These frames can be thought of as 802.1X hellos, and all Cisco products enabled for 802.1X transmit them. By default, an authenticator is also responsible for retransmitting any frame, unmodified, that it does not get a response for when it expects one. EAPoL-Identity-Requests frames are in this category. So, an authenticator will retransmit an EAPoL-Identity-Request frame periodically in an attempt to find a supplicant. This process continues until a supplicant is found, and 30 seconds is the default rate at which any retransmission of frames occurs from an authenticator. This process is shown in Figure 5-6. It represents EAPoL from an authenticator, even though no supplicant is yet present. If a supplicant never appears on the wire, an authenticator will never allow network access in this condition, nor should it.

Figure 5-6 *EAPoL from Authenticator in the Absence of Supplicant*

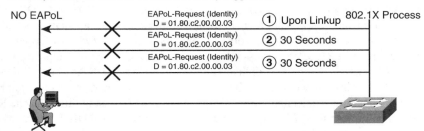

Multicast MAC Addressing

You should also understand the addressing components of EAPoL in an 802.1X exchange. As 802.1X assumes a secure connection that is point to point, it leverages the use of a multicast MAC address. This MAC address, 01-80-c2-00-00-03, is a special group of MAC addresses reserved by IEEE 802.1D in the Bridge Protocol Data Unit (BPDU) block. This is an important point to remember. From a protocol standpoint, this ensures that an authenticator must typically be the first Layer 2 hop. This ensures that EAPoL is not transparently forwarded by a MAC bridge. Furthermore, if other switches or network devices that also comply with 802.1D are inserted between an authenticator and supplicant, those devices will discard EAPoL frames by design. Authenticators could communicate directly with a supplicant using a unicast destination MAC address, but most supplicants use 01-80-c2-00-00-03 in the absence of an established pairwise association (like 802.11). This indicates another default security benefit for 802.1X. Until an authenticator finds a supplicant, the networked system is not aware of a device's MAC address. As a result, spanning-tree state in a LAN environment is not in a forwarding state until 802.1X has authorized a port.

EAP Data Frames

The rest of an authentication exchange is driven entirely by the supplicant and authentication server. At this point, an authenticator typically operates in pass-through mode, transposing the EAP conversation from 802.1X on the client side to RADIUS on the authentication server side (and vice versa). Technically, an authenticator receives EAP data packets in the form of EAPoL, then strips off the 802.1X headers, and then reencapsulates an EAP message unmodified inside a RADIUS packet. The same is true in the other direction as well. Other specifics depend on the nature of the EAP-Type itself.

RADIUS

The preceding sections examine the ability of an EAP conversation to be transported by way of 802.1X. The following section focuses on its transport using RADIUS. After an

EAP message is encapsulated, a RADIUS packet is initiated from an authenticator toward a RADIUS server, typically over User Datagram Protocol (UDP) ports 1645 or 1812. Also, a response from a supplicant to an authentication server is encapsulated as a RADIUS-Access-Request packet. Any response by an authentication server to a supplicant is usually in the form of a RADIUS-Access-Challenge. A RADIUS-Access-Request packet contains the EAP message from the supplicant unmodified in RADIUS Attribute [79] defined by RFC 3579. This attribute allows the authenticator to authenticate a supplicant by EAP without having to understand the EAP method it is also passing through. The RADIUS server can return EAP-Message attributes in most types of RADIUS packets, including Access-Challenge, Access-Accept, and Access-Reject packets. To prevent attackers from subverting EAP by attacking RADIUS, RADIUS also provides per-packet authentication and integrity protection. This is the Message-Authenticator attribute, or RADIUS attribute [80], also defined by RFC 3579. Other tertiary RADIUS attributes are in use as well, defined by RFCs 2865, 2868, 2869, or 3580. For illustration purposes, an example is shown in Table 5-1 for a Cisco Catalyst switch enabled for 802.1X/RADIUS, running Cisco IOS Release 12.2(25)SE.

Table 5-1   *RADIUS Attributes for 802.1X*

No.	Attribute Name	Request	Challenge	Accept	Reject	Description
1	User-Name	1	0	0	0	Copied from EAP Identity Response in Access-Request.
4	NAS-IP-Address	1	0	0	0	IP address of device acting as authenticator.
5	NAS-Port	1	0	0	0	Physical port of device on authenticator such as "50102", meaning "interface fastethernet1/0/2. "5" is for all Ethernet interfaces.

Table 5-1   *RADIUS Attributes for 802.1X (Continued)*

No.	Attribute Name	Request	Challenge	Accept	Reject	Description
6	Service-Type	1	0	0	0	Indicates framing to be used for framed access. This attribute indicates the type of service a user has requested or the type of service to be provided. It can be used in both RADIUS-Access-Request and RADIUS-Access-Accept packets. It has been used on switches in the past to enable RADIUS exec authorization and to launch a user into enable mode. Regarding 802.1X, it can have other uses, such as how to enable restriction based on a MAC address and/or username. Currently sent by Set as Framed "2" in Access-Requests and tracked by ACS in RADIUS Accounting logs.
8	Framed-IP-Address	0	0	1	0	Indicates the address to be used, set to all 1s by ACS.
12	Framed-MTU	1	0	0	0	Indicates the maximum transmission unit (MTU) to be used by the user. Set to "1500".
18	Reply-Message	0	0	0	1	Failure message used by ACS in an Access-Reject. "Rejected\012\015" is an example.
24	State	0-1	1	0	0	Sent by the server to the client; sent back in a new Access-Request reply to a challenge. Hence, not sent in first Access-Request.
25	Class	0	0	1	0	ACS currently includes this opaque value back to a client in Access-Accept.

Table 5-1   *RADIUS Attributes for 802.1X (Continued)*

No.	Attribute Name	Request	Challenge	Accept	Reject	Description
26	Vendor-Specific	0	0	0-1	0	Set for Microsoft Point-to-Point Encryption (MPPE) Send/Rcv keys. Windows XP was used for this test.
30	Called-Station-Id	1	0	0	0	MAC address of device acting as authenticator.
31	Calling-Station-Id	1	0	0	0	MAC address of device acting as supplicant.
61	NAS-Port-Type	1	0	0	0	Indicates the type of physical port on the authenticator. Set to "15" for Ethernet.
79	EAP-Message	1	1	1	1	EAP Response in Access-Request. EAP Request in Access-Challenge. EAP Success in Access-Accept. EAP Failure in Access-Reject.
80	Message-Authent-icator	1	1	1	1	Hash-based Message Authentication Code–MD5 (HMAC-MD5) to ensure integrity of packet.

Table 5-1 is for illustration purposes only. Consult specific product documentation to determine specific RADIUS attributes in use by differing products. As you can also begin to realize from Table 5-1, a networked system can begin to leverage the notion of an authenticated identity, not only as a security practice but also to enhance forensic or accounting capabilities.

EAP Negotiation

From our prior examples, RADIUS is initiated when a supplicant replies to an authenticator with an initial identity, all of which is in the clear. This initiation is in the form of a RADIUS-Access-Request packet. An authentication server then asks a supplicant to authenticate using a certain EAP-Type it is enabled for. This technically happens in a RADIUS-Access-Challenge packet, followed subsequently by an EAPoL-Request packet from the authenticator to the supplicant. The EAP message itself is a request to initiate the given EAP method. At this point, the supplicant can initiate the authentication request and proceed with the given EAP method, or choose another. If the supplicant is not enabled to, or does not want to, authenticate using the authenticator's recommended EAP type, the supplicant transmits an EAPoL–negative acknowledgment (EAPoL-NAK) to the authenticator, which in turn informs the authentication server of this event by way of another RADIUS-Access-Request packet. This is the supplicant's indication to the authentication server which EAP method it would like to authenticate with. This is typically known as *EAP negotiation,* all of which is legitimate for 802.1X and RADIUS.

End-to-End EAP

After the EAP method has been agreed upon by both the supplicant and the authenticator, specifics of each method can now commence. This is illustrated in Figure 5-7.

Figure 5-7   *End-to-End EAP*

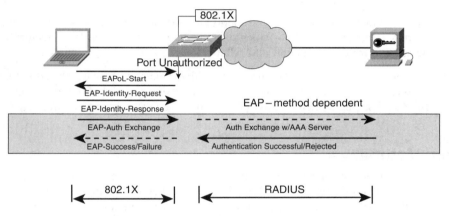

The specifics of each EAP method are not within the scope of this book, although EAP-FAST is described in later sections of this chapter.

Potentially the most crucial decisions you have to make regarding the deployment of 802.1X is which EAP authentication mechanism you will use. It boils down to which type of identified credential you need, coupled with any facets of the chosen protocol. EAP supports a plethora of authentication methods. EAP methods commonly used are as follows:

- The following challenge-response–based methods:
    - **EAP-MD5:** Uses MD5-based challenge-response for authentication.
    - **LEAP:** Uses username/password authentication.
    - **EAP–Microsoft Challenge Handshake Authentication Protocol (MS-CHAP) v2:** Uses username/password MSCHAPv2 challenge-response authentication.

- The following cryptographic-based method:
  - **EAP-TLS:** Uses x.509 v3 PKI certificates and the TLS mechanism for authentication.
- The following tunneled methods:
  - **PEAP:** Protected EAP tunnel mode that serves as an EAP encapsulator; tunnels other EAP types in an encrypted tunnel—much like web-based Secure Sockets Layer (SSL).
  - **EAP-TTLS:** Other EAP methods over an extended EAP-TLS encrypted tunnel.
  - **EAP-FAST:** Recent tunneling method designed to not require certificates for deployment.

Be aware that supplicants do not support all EAP methods. Likewise, all authentication servers do not support all EAP methods. In addition, many back-end directory infrastructures do not support all EAP methods.

Authenticators, however, should support all EAP methods, because they don't necessarily need to know the inner workings of each EAP protocol. Most of the time, your choice of EAP authentication method drives everything else used in your network.

Tunneled Method

Organizations that need the security of TLS, but do not want the complexity thereof, typically choose a tunneled EAP method. The authentication in EAP-TLS is typically mutual. Both parties authenticate each other. Tunneled methods typically use a server-side certificate to derive a mutually agreed upon encryption key. This initial process only authenticates the server, and an authentication can now occur within this encrypted channel that is established. This is the same basis for most secure web transactions and is the basis for tunneled EAP methods. This allows an identified credential to be sent back to the server in an encrypted manner, based on the SSL-like establishment of the one-way server trust, which constitutes the tunnel. However, in most tunneled methods, certificate trust is a necessity. In other words, the server's certificate authority has to be trusted by the supplicant so that the supplicant can verify the server's certificate by using the public key to decrypt the signature and ensure that it matches the data the server provided in its certificate. In comparison to the EAP messages described earlier, a tunneled method also services the notion of an outer and inner identity. An outer identity can be configurable by a supplicant and need not be the true user identity, because the true user identity is sent only after the tunnel is established. The network manager can also use a combination of EAP methods inside the tunneled authentication protocol, such as EAP-MSCHAPv2, EAP–Generic Token Card (EAP-GTC), EAP-TLS, and so on.

Authorization and Enforcement

Authorization is the embodiment of the ability to enforce policies on identities. Authorization can come in many forms. The most basic authorization notion is the ability to allow or disallow access to the network at the link layer. The notion of enabling a port configured for 802.1X after authentication occurs, while implicit, is a form of authorization, because the action grants network access. Typically, policies are also enforced using a group methodology, which allows easier manageability. In the simplest case, the authorized users group can have its ports enabled. The ultimate goal is to take this notion of group management and policies into the network infrastructure. Other forms of authorization include VLAN assignment, ACL assignment, quality of service (QoS) policy assignment, 802.1X with Address Resolution Protocol (ARP) inspection, and so on. In concert with 802.1X, authorization is reasonably straightforward. A RADIUS-Access-Reject packet typically contains a failure for EAP, a failure of authentication itself, and implicit instructions to the authenticator to deny supplicant access to the controlled port, or any other network resources. In contrast, a RADIUS-Access-Accept packet typically indicates an EAP success, or a positive authentication result. At this point, further policy or authorization instructions can be relayed from an authentication server to be carried out by the authenticator. The authenticator is also responsible for continually enforcing this network policy. This is shown in Figure 5-8.

Figure 5-8   *Authorization Process*

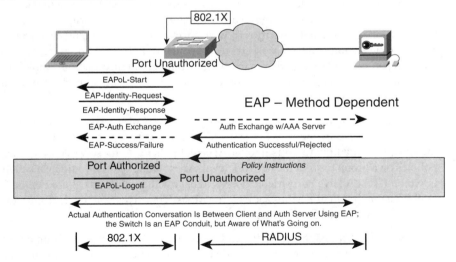

VLAN Assignment

VLAN assignment is an example of additional policy enforcement instructions that can be relayed to an authenticator. It is also the primary form of policy enforcement for NAC when 802.1X is used. VLAN assignment is accomplished primarily by way of RADIUS and RFC 2868. Three attribute value pairs (AVPs) are used for VLAN assignment, and are all Internet Engineering Task Force (IETF) standards. They are as follows:

- **[64] Tunnel-type–"VLAN" (13)**—Indicates the tunneling type parameter to be set by this RADIUS attribute. In this case, the value is "VLAN" (13).

- **[65] Tunnel-medium-type–"802" (6)**—Indicates the link layer topology to which the Tunnel-Type is being applied. For LAN technologies (Ethernet, Token Ring, wireless 802.11b, and so on), the value should be "802".

- **[81] Tunnel-private-group-ID–<VLAN>**—The string that indicates the specific tunnel (in this case, VLAN) that the authenticated client will be part of. This field is a free-form text string that can be matched against the names or numbers of configured VLANs on an authenticator.

By using this method, you can enable the flexibility of enforcing policies or access profiles to the network based on a network client's authenticated identity. By dynamically assigning VLAN values to client-connecting ports based on the client's authenticated identity, the network maintains the ability to group users per administrative policy. This allows the notion of groups and group applicable policy profiles to be carried down to the networking level. For example, different groups can be assigned different security access permissions based on duties, roles, and security risk level. An example of this would be if users in Group A were allowed unrestricted access, while users in Group B were limited to accessing only public resources and servers that maintain nonconfidential information. Applying the ability to limit access by risk criteria or levels allows a network administrator to minimize overall security exposure and risk.

By extending the notion of groups to the network by way of VLANs, you can control access by identity and group policies. The same holds true for group-specific QoS. By applying the grouping paradigm to users into VLANs and policies to those VLANs, you can apply policies on a group basis at the network level. An example of this would be an environment in which Users A have unrestricted access to bandwidth, but Users B are rate limited by QoS for a maximum of 8 Mbps for FTP functions. This gives you the flexibility to perform resource allocation and control on a group basis.

Ultimately, VLAN assignment is the end result of an authorization decision based on a successful authentication, based on an identified credential. This is also the basis of policy enforcement with NAC. As you see in later sections in this chapter, NAC adds the flexibility to make a more advanced authorization decision based on an identified credential plus numerous other data points.

Figure 5-9 shows the attribute value pairs (AVPs) that identify a VLAN assignment for the NAD to use for authorization enforcement.

Figure 5-9   *VLAN Assignment*

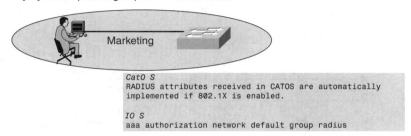

AV Pairs Used—All Are IETF Standard:
- [64] Tunnel-type—"VLAN" (13)
- [65] Tunnel-medium-type—"802"(6)
- [81] Tunnel-private-group-ID— <VLAN name>

```
CatO S
RADIUS attributes received in CATOS are automatically
implemented if 802.1X is enabled.

IO S
aaa authorization network default group radius
```

Integration Issues When Using 802.1X

Integration issues are common when implementing any type of security system, especially a network-based security system. As you consider 802.1X for a method of port-based access control, it is important to realize the benefit and potential drawbacks this has in an environment by carefully evaluating the systemic impact to a LAN. Integration is key to making 802.1X more deployable, especially in wired environments. The following is a list of integration issue examples you might face:

- How do you deal with devices that cannot speak 802.1X?
- How does VoIP interoperate with port-based access control?
- How do you support PC applications like remote wakeup/wake-on-LAN?
- How do you provide network visibility for authenticated identities?

The following sections explain each of these challenges and, in some cases, provides suggestions on how to overcome the challenge.

Default Operation

The 802.1X technology involves three primary components; supplicant, authenticator, and authentication server. Together they are used by a networked system to successfully provide authenticated access through port-based access control. One of the key components examined previously was an 802.1X supplicant, which is the entity seeking to attain services from a network. Without an 802.1X supplicant, network access should not typically be given. The protocol specification for 802.1X always assumes the key components are always there. In many network infrastructures, it might not be safe to assume that an entire LAN is composed entirely of 802.1X supplicants. This is especially true in wired deployments, where network devices range in age, multitude, and platform type. This includes legacy devices, such as printers or other application-specific devices that are incapable of supporting 802.1X supplicant functionality. To address this concern for wired topologies, Cisco has provided the Guest-VLAN. Before examining the Guest-VLAN, it is first helpful to understand the 802.1X default behavior for when a supplicant does not exist. This is shown in Figure 5-10.

Figure 5-10 *802.1X Default Operation*

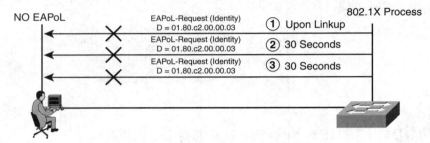

As shown in Figure 5-10, any 802.1X-enabled switch ports can send EAPoL-Identity-Request frames on the wire. The process occurs regardless of whether a supplicant exists. The beginning of this process represents an authenticator looking for a supplicant to authenticate while continuing to disallow port access. If a supplicant is not present on the wire, an authenticator defaults to providing no access because there is no EAPoL response to its requests. This process continues indefinitely by default, network access is never granted, and the port status remains unauthorized. The only thing that can transition out of this process is if an EAPoL-Start frame is received from a supplicant or if the periodic EAPoL-Identity-Request frames from the authenticator begin to be answered by a supplicant that appears on the wire. These answers would be in the form of EAPoL-Identity-Response frames from a supplicant.

The Guest-VLAN

Optionally, a Guest-VLAN can be configured on a port, primarily as a migration vehicle for 802.1X to allow you to easily migrate hosts to support 802.1X, while still providing some form of network connectivity. You might also want to attempt to use the Guest-VLAN for unauthenticated, third-party access. The deployment of the Guest-VLAN follows the same basic process as that described in the preceding section, with the exception of defaulting the port to allowing access when EAPoL-Identity-Request frames from an authenticator go unanswered. This is shown in Figure 5-11.

Figure 5-11 *The Guest-VLAN*

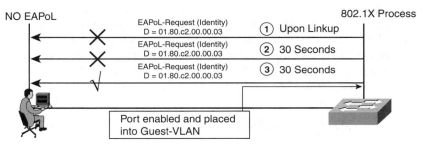

As shown in Figure 5-11, an authenticator's port can be moved to Guest-VLAN after the third EAPoL-Request. So, the port immediately transitions to an authorized state. Note that the deployment of a Guest-VLAN on an authenticator's port uses a default timeout of 30 seconds with three retries. This means that the total timeout period is 90 seconds by default for a port to be enabled in the Guest-VLAN if configured. The Guest-VLAN is a per-port feature and needs to be applied on all ports that might ever have devices that plug into them that lack 802.1X supplicant capability, but that also need to have network access in the absence of a supplicant. A device is also deployed to Guest-VLAN based only on the lack of response to an authenticator's EAPoL-Identity-Request frames. No further security or authentication is directly applied on a port with Guest-VLAN. It works just like having a network administrator deconfigure 802.1X and hard-set the port into a predetermined VLAN (by default, 90 seconds after the link comes up). This VLAN can be any VLAN, other than a voice or Remote Switch-Port Analyzer (RSPAN) VLAN. It can even be the same one already configured on the port, or it can be different, if you want to differentiate Guest-VLAN port access from 802.1 X-authorized port accesses from a VLAN standpoint. Finally, no machines that speak 802.1X, or that can respond to authenticator requests for identity through EAPoL, should ever go into the Guest-VLAN. Hence, no passed or failed 802.1X authentication attempt should have anything to do with the Guest-VLAN.

IP Telephony

Before examining the impact of port-based access control on IP telephony environments, it is first beneficial to understand how a telephony-enabled switch port provides network access to IP telephony devices. This process is shown in Figure 5-12.

Figure 5-12 *IP Telephony Port*

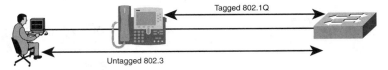

An IP telephony port is assumed to be a Multi-VLAN Access Port (MVAP). This is an access port that can handle two VLANs: a Native or Port VLAN Identifier (PVID) and an Auxiliary or Voice VLAN Identifier (VVID). The hardware on this port is set to an 802.1Q trunk. So, with MVAPs, a port can belong to two VLANs, allowing the separation of voice and data traffic. One of the benefits to a port of this type is that it can also enable 802.1X. To examine the impact of IP telephony on an 802.1X-enabled environment, it is first beneficial to understand how the authenticator assigns the default access to a port. This is shown in Figure 5-13.

Figure 5-13 *802.1X Controlled/Uncontrolled Ports*

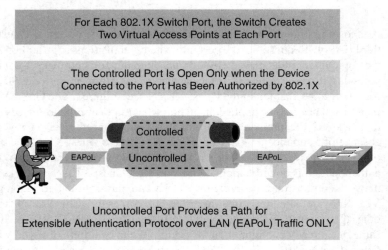

As you can see in Figure 5-13, no network access to a port is typically granted until 802.1X has authorized a port, and the only type of traffic that can be processed completely is EAPoL, because it is processed on the uncontrolled port. By default, this process becomes mutually exclusive with IP telephony environments if IP telephony handsets lack supplicant capability. At the time of this writing, a stopgap measure was needed, so Cisco provided a way to enable port-based access control and IP telephony. Figure 5-14 shows 802.1X with VVID.

Figure 5-14 *802.1X with VVID*

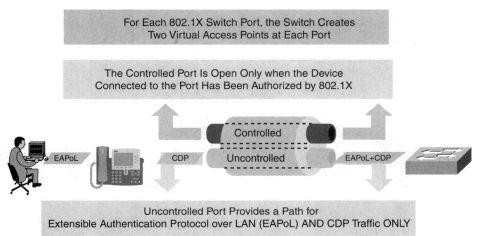

So, for ports that have been enabled for IP telephony and 802.1X, a data supplicant must still authenticate before getting access to a data VLAN. An IP phone handset lacking 802.1X supplicant capability can then get access to the voice VLAN after sending proper Cisco Discovery Protocol (CDP) packets, regardless of the 802.1X state of the port. This operation provides unauthenticated voice VLAN (VVID) access, while continuing to provide authenticated data VLAN (PVID) access for 802.1X data devices. This measure allows 802.1X and IP telephony to coexist so that the two advanced technologies are not in direct conflict with one another.

Management Utilities

Another integration concern is the ability for various types of device management applications to continue to work across wired topologies using 802.1X. Examples of management applications include remote control applications, alerting applications, and remote or peer-to-peer applications like Wake-on-LAN (WoL). WoL is an industry standard that is the result of the Intel-IBM Advanced Manageability Alliance. WoL creates a power management wake-up event. This is an advanced power management capability on many modern network interface cards (NICs) in the industry. NICs that support WoL have an extra connector and cable to connect to the motherboard. After a machine goes into low-energy suspend mode, it can be automatically reactivated when data from the network is received by the NIC. This capability can be used to wake up a mail server machine to deliver mail, for software management pushes, to deploy patches overnight, and so on. To examine the impact of 802.1X on these types of applications, refer once more to the notion of the 802.1X controlled ports shown in Figure 5-15.

Figure 5-15 *802.1X Controlled/Uncontrolled Ports*

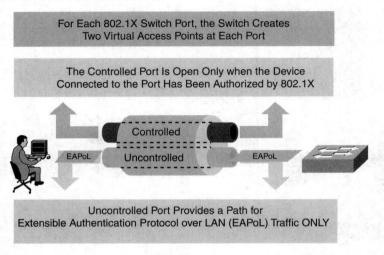

A bidirectional controlled port is shown in Figure 5-15. The authenticator exerts control restrictions on the controlled port in both directions. In other words, incoming and outgoing traffic through the authenticator's controlled port is strictly enforced. This causes applications like the ones mentioned earlier to break. Optionally, you can configure an authenticator's port to only exert control in one direction, for example, inbound to allow the applications to coexist with 802.1X. This indicates that control is not exerted on traffic exiting a networked system, but is still exerted for traffic attempting to enter a networked system. The operation described here is shown in Figure 5-16.

Figure 5-16 *802.1X with WoL*

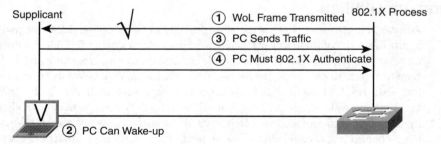

As shown in Figure 5-16, the use of a unidirectional controlled port allows management frames like those for use through WoL to be relayed through an authenticator, and allows the application to continue to operate as it did before 802.1X was present for port-based access control. This causes the notion of port-based access control to inevitably be reduced, because this allows any frames to exit an authenticator, not just the expected EAPoL control frames. In most cases, this is a reasonable vulnerability to undertake to allow these types of applications to continue to work in an integrated fashion. Furthermore, in this operation, you have allowed only the outgoing traffic to a port, while still dropping all the incoming traffic on a port that has not yet authenticated. Also, if a remote control application is integrating with 802.1X in this type of topology, a supplicant that has been restored by that application must then 802.1X-authenticate before network access can be granted through the port.

Supplemental Authentication Techniques

Another integration concern for 802.1X is to also provide a supplemental authentication technique in the absence of 802.1X supplicant capability, in addition to defaulting to some form of access like the Guest-VLAN does. Although 802.1X is a port-based authentication method increasingly used at the access layer, 802.1X supplicant capability cannot be ubiquitously assumed. You need to be aware of the following scenarios:

- The 802.1X supplicant capability comes as default in some operating systems (for example, Windows XP). But not all the hosts can have the supplicant functionality embedded into their system software. While 802.1X can be enabled by default in some operating systems (like Windows XP), the operating system can also lack native support of NAC through 802.1X.
- Scenarios where you want to give a guest type of access, but some of the devices (other than hosts, for example, printers and IP phones) need to be allowed into the network even without authenticating themselves using 802.1X.

To overcome these 802.1X supplicant challenges, an approach such as MAC Authentication Bypass (MAB) can be helpful as a supplemental authentication technique.

The primary goal of MAB is to provide network access control on a per-port basis that is based on a device's MAC address. Another goal of MAB is to dynamically apply policies to a client session that is based on its MAC address, very similar to how 802.1X can.

MAB is configured on a per-port basis. The switch makes a RADIUS request to a RADIUS server on behalf of the device needing network access with the MAC address of the host as the credential to be verified. If the MAC address is found in an identity repository, and the device is permitted onto the network, it gets assigned an authorized policy as a result. This feature is useful for allowing NAC agentless hosts (NAHs) access to the network as well. Because MAB is dynamic, you can configure it on all ports in the network, and you do not have to explicitly configure it on ports where nonsupplicant devices are connected.

There will always be devices that do not support 802.1X, for many reasons. MAB also provides a migration path from port-security, the Cisco User-Registration Tool (URT), and the Cisco VLAN Management Policy Server (VMPS) deployments, where applicable. More importantly, MAB allows NAC to deal with agentless devices. In contrast to the Guest-VLAN, a port is not given network access blindly when 802.1X times out on an authenticator's port. Alternatively, the MAC address is learned on a port, and RADIUS is initiated by way of EAP or RADIUS to authorize the MAC address the switch has just learned. At this point, network access can be granted based on this identified credential: the MAC address. Also, virtually all the same policy-enforcement techniques from RADIUS, such as VLAN assignment, can be automatically leveraged.

In summary, MAB provides a fallback mechanism to 802.1X. It should also stand alone as the only type of authentication configured on a port. Note that MAB does not serve as a way to deal with failed 802.1X authentication attempts. MAB can provide organizations that will not/cannot do 802.1X, but have bought into port security with configured MAC addresses, with more options. MAB also enables the processing of NAC agentless devices.

NAC-L2-802.1X Identity with Posture Validation and Enforcement

The primary goal of NAC-L2-802.1X is to integrate NAC functionality into Layer 2 switches and combine NAC with 802.1X to provide a unified authentication and posture validation mechanism at the Layer 2 network edge. This mechanism can help to protect your network from attack by machines with insufficient software compliance. Performing posture validation at the edge maximizes the portion of the network to be protected by port-based access control as well, and allows posture validation to be performed on switches directly that might not be providing Layer 3 routing services.

Posture validation in NAC-L2-802.1X is triggered by the standard 802.1X mechanisms. Either a supplicant sends an EAPoL-Start message to an authenticator or the authenticator probes the supplicant with an EAPoL-Identity-Request message. Posture information is then chained with user identity credentials for validation by back-end identity and/or policy servers using EAP-FAST. As with standard 802.1X, the authentication exchange between the supplicant and the authenticator is over EAPoL. Policy enforcement for NAC is done by assigning the authenticated port a specified VLAN, thus providing a form of segmentation and quarantine at Layer 2 for machines that are not compliant with policy. NAC-L2-802.1X can also restrict non-IPv4 traffic from nonpostured hosts, so it is preferred for deployments where such a restriction is a requirement.

In the future, look for more advanced auditing capabilities to leverage the techniques mentioned previously to handle agentless hosts by temporarily placing them into a VLAN where they are audited by a special audit server and, after being identified, are moved into another VLAN that provides an appropriate level of network access.

NAC-L2-802.1X provides posture validation triggered as part of the regular EAP exchange. This is where EAP-FAST comes in. More details on EAP-FAST are provided in a later section of this chapter.

Periodic Posture Reassessment

NAC-L2-802.1X also provides periodic reassessment of responsive postured hosts. This is done by way of a RADIUS-supplied session timeout. A host's posture can change, due either to changes on the host itself or from back-end policy rules. This means that hosts might need to be periodically reassessed to ensure that they are still postured appropriately. Ideally, reassessment should be triggered by events when possible to minimize the amount of time a host spends with its posture assessment out of sync with the new admission policy. This is the case for certain posture plug-ins for Cisco Trust Agent. With the right posture plug-in, an application can inform Cisco Trust Agent of a posture change directly. Then Cisco Trust Agent can inform the network that its posture has changed by initiating a reauthentication event by way of an EAPoL-Start packet. Alternatively, Cisco Trust Agent can also ask its suite of plug-ins for a status check periodically. If reauthentication is required from the network, 802.1X provides a mechanism for periodic reauthentication based on a configurable timer. When this timer triggers a reauthentication, the host is also repostured. When posture standards change on the authentication server, the switch is not currently told to trigger a reauthentication of all postured ports directly, so this can be a case for reauthentication. Another case for reauthentication is quarantined devices, and the network's ability to help a device get out of quarantine and back onto an active network.

A session timeout can come in the form of a fixed authenticator configuration, or can be supplied by RADIUS to the NAD. Supplying it by RADIUS means compliance with RFC 3580 and RADIUS Attributes [27] and [29]. So, on wired switches, it is either a local timer or the Session-Timeout value. This provides a way to enable reauthentication while avoiding the issue of configuring the authenticator to choose between two timers (a locally configured one or Session-Timeout). The operation of these attributes in combination with an authenticator is as follows:

- [027] Session-Timeout by itself acts as if [029] Termination-Action = "Default". These settings terminate the session, and the 802.1X state machine transitions to DISCONNECTED upon the end of the timer.

- [027] Session-Timeout + [029] Termination-Action = "Default" is the same as the previous bullet.

- [027] Session-Timeout + [029] Termination-Action = "RADIUS-Request". With this configuration, the host is reauthenticated passively, so the 802.1X state machine transitions to a CONNECTING state.

Any of these RADIUS attributes can be configured in Cisco Secure ACS.

NAC Supplicants for 802.1X

NAC-enabled 802.1X supplicants include Cisco Trust Agent and retailed versions of 802.1X available from Meetinghouse Communications at the time of this writing. Cisco Trust Agent is a free, wired-only supplicant. It is capable of EAP-FAST only with EAP-

MSCHAPv2, EAP-TLS, and EAP-GTC. It initiates an EAPoL-Start when a posture change is realized by the host. Cisco Lite can also renew its IP address when VLAN changes occur. For details on Meetinghouse's supplicant, see the Meetinghouse website (http://www.mtghouse.com) for specific product documentation.

EAP-FAST

EAP-FAST is the crux of NAC-L2-802.1X capability in providing user authentication and posture information in a single control plane. EAP-FAST uses symmetric key algorithms to achieve a tunneled authentication process. The tunnel establishment relies on a Protected Access Credential (PAC). An EAP-FAST authentication can be considered in the following phases:

- **Phase 1**—Uses PAC to mutually authenticate the supplicant and authentication server and establish a secure tunnel.
- **Phase 2**—Performs host authentication in the established tunnel.
- **Optional Phase 0**—Enables the client to be dynamically provisioned with a PAC.

This PAC can be dynamically or manually provisioned on the host. The PAC is a unique shared credential that mutually authenticates host and server. The PAC is associated with a specific user ID and an authority ID. PACs remove the need for PKI (digital certificates). The TLS Protocol typically establishes the secure tunnel between the supplicant and the authentication server. User authentication credentials can then be passed securely within the encrypted tunnel to the authentication server.

NOTE   At the time of this writing, Phase 0 is used extensively with Cisco Trust Agent to provision PACs through an in-band method only.

Various enhancements were added to EAP-FAST, one of which is support for NAC. EAP-FAST is the only current EAP method that supports inner method chaining and the exchange of arbitrary data. This way, EAP-FAST can supply identity verification (common to all EAP methods) and can perform posture validation in a single EAP session.

The NAC posture type-length value (TLV) exchange is not fixated on EAP-FAST. It could be used for other secure exchange methods in the future. Other forms of NAC, such as NAC-L2-IP and its use of PEAPv1 and TLVs can perform posture checking, but EAP-FAST is the only shipping EAP method that can support 802.1X and posture checks simultaneously.

Further details of EAP-FAST are not within the scope of this book.

Leveraging an Authenticated Identity

NAC and 802.1X are a technology solution that can improve the security of physical and logical access to local-area networks. For some businesses, the basic authentication of users is not enough, however. Some require more visibility, traceability, and enhanced audit capabilities for authenticated users. Some of these concepts can be achieved by leveraging the notion of an authenticated identity. The following sections examine one of these ways by using RADIUS Accounting in conjunction with 802.1X. Techniques such as this can provide functionality to address these common issues currently faced by enterprise networks.

Accounting

The 802.1X technology has the potential to leverage RADIUS Accounting features much the same as dialup, PPP over Ethernet (PPPoE), and virtual private networks (VPNs) already do. As one of the general AAA services, RADIUS Accounting provides the means to track user actions and general usage. The RADIUS Accounting services on an authenticator provide the network connection and usage information to an accounting server, such as Cisco Secure ACS or another similar accounting server. It saves the information in the form of records. You can then use the accounting information for the purposes of security, billing and resource allocation, and so on. RADIUS Accounting and 802.1X are similar to other accounting and tracking mechanisms that already exist using RADIUS, with the additional capability of operating through 802.1X as a Layer 2 transport. Accounting and tracking information can include basic billing, usage, and various events related to any 802.1X ports.

The combination of 802.1X and RADIUS Accounting enhances the overall value of NAC by providing the additional capabilities for network session awareness and the notion of an authenticated identity into an enterprise management infrastructure. One benefit of this solution includes increased network visibility. This gives businesses better control by explicitly allowing who and what gets on your network, and tracks when and where anyone gets onto your network. From an identity management perspective, you can also leverage who authenticates into your network and when authentication events take place.

Another benefit of RADIUS Accounting in a LAN is to increase auditing capabilities. This can allow you to trace network access and provide audit capabilities by recording the network access server (NAS) port for the physical port through which a session authenticates. This can also provide rapid traceback to problems on the network that supplements visibility.

Other possible uses of this as a solution include the following:

- Tracking utilization
- Billing for resource consumption
- Incident management/forensic analysis

You can also add other techniques, such as Netflow, to track usage on your network. RADIUS Accounting can supplement these techniques. For example, universities might be interested in tracking utilization per users/students. The integrated use of NAC can now provide easier user identification while also providing accounting in a single system. If you provide Internet access, you might want to control user access with 802.1X plus maximum session and/or MAC address control using ACS. This alone can be a strong reason for you to adopt 802.1X as well.

If you are exploring alternatives to providing your own billing mechanisms for your own resources, as well as resources shared or loaned to third parties, RADIUS Accounting tracks and documents all access to the network.

You might be interested in providing notification to a management platform for network anomalies. For example, when a virus breaks out, you might have no way to easily determine what users any reactive measure installed by network administrators can impact. RADIUS Accounting can give you this ability and allow you to know who else you would be impacting as a result of taking intrusive network action as a result of these events. RADIUS Accounting gives you assistance in debugging virtually any type of real-time or reactive network event. For example, if unauthorized access to intellectual property in your network has occurred, RADIUS Accounting can provide a means of rapid traceback and additional information for identifying the source of the unauthorized access.

Cisco Security Monitoring, Analysis and Response System (CS-MARS) can also help parse and correlate accounting logs in addition to other network-related events. This also helps organizations troubleshoot 802.1X and the chain of connections among the authenticator, the authentication server, and the back-end directory infrastructure. Specifically, CS-MARS can listen to the accounting logs to understand user behavior. In addition, CS-MARS can normalize, correlate, and report on authentication events from authenticators directly for a complete view of the topology. With a single interface, CS-MARS can report the IP address, username, connection start and stop times, interface, and MAC address of each 802.1X session on a networked system with a mitigation path displayed.

In summary, leveraging the notion of an authenticated identity can provide more solutions to specific problems in the broader sense of NAC. One way is through RADIUS Accounting, which includes Accounting-Request packets containing one or more AVPs to report various events and related information to an accounting server. You can also track user-level events by using the same mechanism. Similar to other accounting and tracking mechanisms that already exist using RADIUS, this can now be done through 802.1X as well. You can increase network session awareness. You can also provide information for a management infrastructure about who logs in, session duration, support basic billing usage reporting, and so on. Finally, this also provides a one-stop shop for a union of network information. You can use this information to map the information of an authenticated identity to a specific IP address and location on your network.

Summary

The combination of 802.1X technology and NAC (NAC-L2-802.1X) provides a unified authentication and posture validation mechanism at the Layer 2 network edge.

The 802.1X framework components consists of a supplicant, authenticator, and an authentication server. The supplicant is located on a host and works as a client to request service to a network system. The authenticator is a network device that transposes an EAP conversation from supplicant to authentication server. It also acts to enforce the policy received from the authentication server. The authentication server is the policy server that determines whether a valid host can access the network.

Many RADIUS attributes exist that allow the authenticator to authenticate a supplicant by EAP without having to understand the EAP method it is also passing through. The RADIUS server can return EAP-Message attributes in most types of RADIUS packets. Examples include Access-Challenge, Access-Accept, and Access-Reject packets.

An authentication server can ask a supplicant to authenticate using a certain EAP type for which it is enabled. The 802.1X supplicants can support various EAP methods, including EAP-MD5, EAP-TLS, EAP-TTLS, Cisco LEAP, EAP-PEAP, EAP-FAST, and so on. Not all supplicants support all EAP methods. EAP-FAST is the only currently supported EAP method for using 802.1X and NAC together. Cisco Trust Agent and Meetinghouse supplicants support this functionality.

NAC-L2-802.1X policy enforcement is accomplished by way of a VLAN assignment. Three RADIUS attribute value pairs (AVPs) assign VLANs by the NADs. The three AVPs are Tunnel-type–"VLAN", Tunnel-medium-type–"802", and Tunnel-private-group-ID–<VLAN>.

Some challenges exist when using some 802.1X supplicants. MAC Authentication Bypass (MAB) can be a helpful technique to overcome the challenges by providing network access control on a per-port basis that is based on a device's MAC address.

Forms of authorization include VLAN assignment, ACL assignment, QoS policy assignment, and 802.1X with ARP inspection.

Basic authentication of users is not enough for some businesses. Some also require visibility, traceability, and enhanced audit capabilities for authenticated users. These concepts can be achieved by leveraging the authenticated identity with the RADIUS Accounting feature.

Resources

"Designing and Deploying Secure Wireless LANs" from Networkers 2005, http://wwwin.cisco.com/Mkt/events/nw/2005/post/presos/docs/AGG-2011.ppt.

"Understanding Identity-Based Networking Services, Authentication and Policy Enforcement" from Networkers 2005, http://wwwin.cisco.com/Mkt/events/nw/2005/post/presos/docs/SEC-2005.ppt.

Review Questions

You can find the answers to the review questions in Appendix A.

1 Choose additional benefit(s) that can be observed when combining 802.1X into the admission policy.

   a   Identity-based access control

   b   Traceability of users for auditing purposes

   c   Visibility of users

   d   All of the above

2 Match the type with its function.

   ___ Requests service

   ___ Validates credentials

   ___ Enforces authorization policy

   a   Authentication server

   b   Authenticator

   c   Supplicant

3 Which of the following is a response from a supplicant to an authentication server?

   a   RADIUS-Challenge-Request packet

   b   RADIUS-Access-Request packet

   c   EAPoL-Start packet

   d   EAP-Identity-Request packet

4 Which three EAP tunneling modes can be used with 802.1X?

  a PEAP, EAP-TLS, EAP-FAST

  b EAP-TLS, EAP-TTLS, EAP-FAST

  c PEAP, EAP-TTLS, EAP-FAST

  d EAP-FAST, LEAP, PEAP

5 The main advantages of using 802.1X VLAN assignments are the ability to limit access by risk criteria and to assign access by a group, such as "guest" or "sales". True or false?

6 Which RADIUS attribute value pair (AVP) parameter specifies the link layer topology type to which a VLAN is applied for use with 802.1X?

  a Tunnel-type

  b Tunnel-medium-type

  c Tunnel-private-group-ID

  d Identity-type

7 What triggers a Guest-VLAN to be assigned to hosts that do not have an 802.1X supplicant?

  a By default after 30 seconds of no response from an authenticator's EAPoL-Identity-Request.

  b By default after the host has failed authentication from the authenticator.

  c By default after three retries of no response from an authenticator's EAPoL-Identity-Request.

  d By default, after 90 seconds of no response from an authenticators EAPoL-Identity-Request, the authenticator's port goes to a TRANSITION state.

8 When using a Cisco switch port that has been enabled for both IP telephony and 802.1X, the data port can never authenticate if the telephony device lacks an 802.1X supplicant. True or false?

9 Which switch-based Layer 2 technique provides network access to known devices that lack an 802.1X supplicant?

a MAB

b Guest-VLAN

c By using Cisco Trust Agent

d Exception table

10 Which RADIUS attribute(s) allow a host to reauthenticate passively, where the 802.1X state machine transitions to a CONNECTING state versus DISCONNECTED?

a Session-Timeout + Termination-Action = "Default"

b Session-Timeout = "RADIUS-Request" + Termination-Action = "NONE"

c Session-Timeout + Termination-Action = "RADIUS-Request"

d Session-Timeout = "Default"

This chapter covers the following topics:

- EAPoUDP framework
- EAPoUDP operational overview
- Voice integration issues
- Exceptions to NAC posture

CHAPTER 6

NAC Layer 3 Operations

Extensible Authentication Protocol over User Datagram Protocol (EAPoUDP) offers a flexible method to transport EAP information. EAPoUDP runs over IP, using UDP as a transport to allow the transmission and verification of posture credentials and host posture over any link-layer technology. The authenticator in this regard can be any network device capable of the protocol and need not be on the same link as the device seeking to attain authorized network service. Any network device capable of supporting EAPoUDP can be used for enforcement up to three hops away from a host.

Cisco Network Admission Control (NAC) assesses the state, or posture, of a host to prevent unauthorized or vulnerable endpoints from accessing the network. The main objective is to ensure software compliance and reduce exposure to a network virus by providing network access based on the requesting device's antivirus or otherwise device-specific software credentials. The act of detecting the credentials of a device requesting network access is referred to as *posture validation*. Ultimately, compliant devices are generally provided network access, while noncompliant devices are given a quarantine status and have limited or no network access.

This chapter describes the following topics:

- EAPoUDP Framework
    - Posture trigger mechanisms for NAC-L3-IP and NAC-L2-IP
    - Session initiation process
    - Credential Validation
- EAPoUDP Operational Overview
    - RADIUS
    - Authorization
    - Cisco Trust Agent
    - Policy Enforcement
    - Status Query Techniques
    - Agentless Hosts
    - Voice Integration
    - Exceptions to NAC posture

EAPoUDP Framework

The control protocol to transport EAP messages between an authenticator and client is EAPoUDP, which operates over a Layer 3 medium.

The authenticator is similar to an authenticator's role in IEEE 802.1X:

- The authenticator relays credential requests and responses between clients and authentication, authorization, and accounting (AAA) servers.

- The authenticator enforces network policy on a particular port or interface as an authorized result.

Authenticators for EAPoUDP offer similar base functionality compared to 802.1X. By default, authenticators operate in pass-through mode, which requires a AAA server. By default, the primary responsibility of an authenticator is to transport the EAP conversation through UDP on the client to the authenticator, and RADIUS on the authenticator to the AAA server. The only time AAA servers are not required is for status query requests, which are examined in the "Status Query Techniques" section, later in this chapter.

As mentioned, authenticators also enforce policy. The enforcement point is generally where (on a network device) EAPoUDP is configured. For NAC-L3-IP, this is a Layer 3 router interface. For NAC-L2-IP, this is the Layer 2 Ethernet switch port. Currently, NAC-L2-IP is to be used only at access ports, not trunk ports. ACLs persist in their use as an enforcement method for NAC-L2-IP. This allows VLANs to be statically or dynamically assigned through mechanisms such as 802.1X or other Layer 2 admission technology, without affecting NAC-L2-IP. The use of ACLs as a means to enforce policy also implies that they are applied for any VLANs of which a port is a member (for both voice and data VLANs).

An authenticator for NAC-L2-IP always initiates requests to the client for authorization. No facility currently exists to enable a client to initiate a session using the control path. The authenticator initiates an EAPoUDP session based on specific activity on the data path. This is known as a *posture validation trigger* method, discussed in more detail in the section that follows.

Posture Trigger Mechanisms for NAC-L3-IP and NAC-L2-IP

A posture validation trigger is the mechanism that initiates posture validation toward a client. Intercept ACLs serve as posture triggers for NAC-L3-IP on routers. DHCP-Snooping and Address Resolution Protocol (ARP) inspection are valid posture triggers for NAC-L2-IP on switches. They serve as match criteria to initiate a posture exchange of information. A posture trigger differs from IEEE 802.1X, because 802.1X functionality requires each locally connected host to posture-validate before access to any part of the network is allowed.

Intercept ACLs act on the reception of any type of network traffic and are completely configurable. An intercept ACL decides what can trigger posture validation for a host. A network administrator must configure an intercept ACL to trigger posture based on specific types of network traffic that is so desired. Upon reception of a data packet that matches an access control entry (ACE) in an intercept ACL, the authenticator first interrogates the source address of the packet. If no previous record of this source IP address exists, the authenticator then initiates credential validation for the client. If a session already exists for the client, an idle timer is reset and the packet is forwarded according to the current interface ACL. Intercept ACLs are generally used on Cisco routers performing posture validation for NAC-L3-IP methods. With NAC Phase 2, this functionality extends to Cisco switches as well through NAC-L2-IP.

NAC-L2-IP has two distinct methods of triggering posture—DHCP-Snooping and ARP inspection. In this regard, any host sending traffic must undergo posture validation. This differs from an intercept ACL, which must match an ACL to a trigger posture. Interface ACLs are needed for both methods and effectively define what traffic is to be allowed irrespective of posture, or while a posture check is being performed. For NAC-L2-IP, a default interface ACL must be in place, and it must permit DHCP or ARP to work effectively. Limits to the amount of traffic allowed before posture validation takes place are configurable.

An equivalent intercept ACL to match DHCP-Snooping would be one that permits DHCP client traffic on the correct UDP ports. An intercept ACL equivalent for ARP inspection would be an ACL to permit all ARP traffic. DHCP-Snooping and ARP inspection have applications outside of NAC, however, and are recommended security features already available on switches. NAC uses these mechanisms as a means to adequately detect the presence of all hosts. NAC can use either DHCP-Snooping or ARP inspection as a posture trigger. For DHCP-Snooping, when a host using DHCP acquires an IP address, a binding table entry is created on the switch. The creation of this entry is an immediate association between an IP and a MAC address for the client and is used as a means to trigger posture on a switch. To support clients that might have the network stacks statically defined, ARP inspection can also trigger posture. After an ARP frame of a host is recognized, this can immediately trigger EAPoUDP to initiate an authorization session for NAC.

Session Initiation Process

After posture has been triggered, EAPoUDP initiates for a given host on a port configured for NAC-L2-IP. This corresponds to the credential transaction that is needed between a client running Cisco Trust Agent and a AAA server like Cisco Secure Access Control Server (ACS). After posture is triggered, EAPoUDP begins at the authenticator. This initial effort is to find Cisco Trust Agent. This occurs through an EAPoUDP hello message over UDP port 21862. If a retransmission is necessary, this occurs as well, with the message identity not being incremented. Assuming that an agent is on the wire, an initial handshake occurs. Figure 6-1 depicts a high-level representation of posture trigger and session initiation.

Figure 6-1 *EAPoUDP Session Initiation*

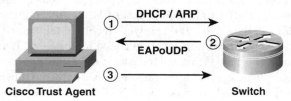

From Figure 6-1, DHCP or ARP happens and is realized by the authenticator, and should be permitted through a preconfigured interface ACL. Second, this DHCP or ARP instance initiates a posture session on the authenticator. Akin to 802.1X, the responsibility of retransmission lies solely with the authenticator. A client can retransmit a response only upon seeing a retransmitted request. This initial handshake must be completed for the EAPoUDP session to continue; otherwise, the authenticator would retransmit until it either receives a valid response or decides after a configurable number of attempts that the EAPoUDP association has failed. A switch can also rate-limit the transmission of requests to avoid dropping responses under load. After the initial handshake is complete, an EAPoUDP session should enter the credential validation phase, as described in the next section.

Credential Validation

After an initial EAPoUDP handshake is complete, an authenticator has initially communicated with a client (Cisco Trust Agent) and is ready to authorize the session. At this point, EAP is used persistently end to end from client to authentication server. The authenticator now encapsulates and relays EAP request and response messages and uses EAPoUDP and RADIUS as primary transport mechanisms. Specifically, the authenticator relays responses from the client to a AAA server by dynamically changing the underlying transport between EAPoUDP and RADIUS without modifying the EAP payload itself. The session ends in the sending of an EAP-Success/Failure as well. The authenticator's primary role is similar to 802.1X in this regard. Figure 6-2 depicts an entire NAC-L2-IP session.

Figure 6-2   *End-to-End NAC-L2-IP Session*

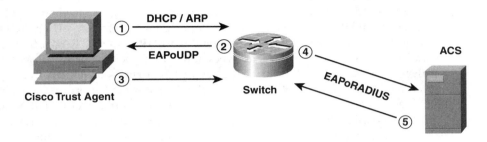

From Figure 6-2, DHCP or ARP happens and is realized by the authenticator, and should be permitted through a preconfigured interface ACL. Second, this DHCP or ARP instance initiates a posture session on the authenticator. After the posture session begins at Step 3, the session is then relayed by the authenticator to the AAA server to determine the client's posture for network access.

EAPoUDP Operational Overview

The NAC-L2-IP model is similar to the model created in NAC Phase 1 functionality. Operationally, traffic is always subject to the configured interface ACL. As a prerequisite, port-based ACLs must be configured on switch ports for EAPoUDP to operate appropriately. As soon as a port is in the forwarding state for Layer 2, the port binds the traffic path to the traffic allowed in the interface ACL. Because EAPoUDP is a Layer 3 mechanism and control plane, specific protocols need to be allowed to serve as a supporting control plane for the environment. At a minimum, DHCP should be allowed, along with UDP port 21862 (the UDP port for EAPoUDP itself). The addition of more services in this ACL might be required, depending on the conditions and needs in a pre-NAC type of traffic path. Windows Networking is an example of something that might need to be explicitly permitted before NAC takes place on a port. The EAPoUDP conversation from the client to authenticator is then transported by the authenticator to the authentication server in the form of RADIUS traffic.

RADIUS

The preceding sections examine the ability of an EAP conversation to be transported through EAPoUDP. This section focuses on RADIUS as the transport for a posture session.

After an EAP message is encapsulated, a RADIUS packet is initiated from an authenticator toward a RADIUS server, typically over UDP ports 1645 or 1812. Also, a response from a client to an authentication server is encapsulated as a RADIUS-Access-Request packet. Any response by an authentication server to a client is usually in the form of a RADIUS-

Access-Challenge. A RADIUS-Access-Request packet contains the EAP message from the Cisco Trust Agent (CTA) unmodified in RADIUS Attribute [79] defined by RFC 3579. This attribute allows the authenticator to authenticate a client through EAP without having to understand the EAP method it is also passing through, although for EAPoUDP, this method is always Protected Extensible Authentication Protocol (PEAP). The RADIUS server can return EAP-Message attributes in most types of RADIUS packets, including Access-Challenge, Access-Accept, and Access-Reject packets. To prevent attackers from subverting EAP by attacking RADIUS, RADIUS also provides per-packet authentication and integrity protection. This is the Message-Authenticator attribute, or RADIUS attribute [80], also defined by RFC 3579. Other tertiary RADIUS attributes are in use as well, defined by either RFCs 2865, 2868, 2869, or 3580. Table 6-1 provides a sample list of attributes contained in RADIUS packets for a Cisco Catalyst switch enabled for EAPoUDP/RADIUS, running Cisco IOS Software Release 12.2(25)SE.

Table 6-1 *RADIUS Attributes for 802.1X*

No.	Attribute Name	Request	Challenge	Accept	Reject	Description
1	User-Name	1	0	1	0	Copied from EAP Identity Response in Access Request.
4	NAS-IP-Address	1	0	0	0	IP address of network access device (NAD).
24	State	0-1	0-1	0-1	0	State attribute includes audit result information. Not interpreted by NAD.
26	Vendor-specific Cisco = 9,1 CiscoSecure-Defined-ACL (IOS)	0	0	0+	0	ACL name (see EDCS-120236).
26	Vendor-specific Cisco = 9,1 sec:pg	0	0	0+	0	Policy-based access control list (PBACL). sec:pg = <group-name>
26	Vendor-specific Cisco = 9,1 url-redirect url-redirect-acl	0	0	0-1	0	URL redirect (string) with support for concatenation of audit-session-id.
26	Vendor-specific Cisco = 9,1 posture-token	0	0	1	0	Posture token.

Table 6-1   *RADIUS Attributes for 802.1X (Continued)*

No.	Attribute Name	Request	Challenge	Accept	Reject	Description
26	Vendor-specific Cisco = 9,1 status-query-timeout	0	0	0-1	0	Sets status query timer.
26	Vendor-specific Cisco = 9,1 aaa:service	1	0	0	0	Indicates EAPoUDP (string). Value = "ip_admission" Note: Needed where unified policy not supported.
27	Session-Timeout	0	0-1	0-1	0	Sets revalidation timer (in seconds).
29	Termination-Action	0	0	0-1	0	Action on session timeout. Default: Terminate session Radius-Request: Re-auth
30	Called-Station-ID	1	0	0	0	IP address of authenticator or the interface IP address on which the client is seen or the MAC address.
31	Calling-Station-ID	1	0	0	0	MAC address of client.
61	NAS-Port-Type	1	0	0	0	15 = Ethernet 19 = Wireless
79	EAP Message	1+	1+	1	1	EAP Request/Response Packet in Access Request and Access Challenge. EAP Success in Access Accept. EAP Failure in Access Reject.
80	Message Authenticator	1	1	1	1	HMAC-MD5 to ensure integrity of packet.

Table 6-1 is for illustration purposes only. Consult the specific product documentation to determine specific RADIUS attributes in use by differing products.

Authorization

The EAP used in NAC-L2-IP to carry posture validation is Cisco-PEAP, or PEAP version 1. PEAPv1 carries the posture information between a client (Cisco Trust Agent) and the AAA server (ACS). The PEAPv1 details are outside of the scope of this book; however, one important characteristic enables NAC. This is the ability for the session to carry EAP type-length values (EAP-TLVs).

Phase 2 of PEAP for NAC consists of one or more EAP-TLV exchanges carried within the encrypted channel negotiated and established by Phase 1 of PEAP. User or device identity is not carried within the PEAP session. Phase 2 of a NAC PEAP session occurs only when a Transport Layer Security (TLS) session has been negotiated by Phase 1, and never occurs if the AAA server has returned an EAP-Failure to the client. This means that certificate trust issues must be resolved in advance of a deployment of an architecture supporting NAC. Hence, all the exchanges during Phase 2 of a NAC PEAP session are protected by the TLS cipher suite that was negotiated during Phase 1, except for the final success/failure issued by the AAA server. All tunneled information is encapsulated in a TLV format. PEAP also defines a vendor-specific TLV that carries vendor-specific data inside the tunnel. Cisco defines a vendor extension to carry posture information. The extension consists of the following two types of messages:

- **Posture TLV**—The AAA server uses this TLV to request posture information from one or more posture applications running on the end host. The response contains the queried posture information.

- **Posture notification TLV**—The AAA server uses this TLV to notify posture plug-ins of the result of the posture validation and any actions that need to be taken.

The client software informs the network of a device's posture in the form of these TLVs and is classified in the following section.

Cisco Trust Agent

The NAC-L2-IP authorization architecture consists of a client entity that responds to requests for posture information from a network system. This is analogous to a supplicant from the 802.1X context defined previously. Cisco Trust Agent is expected to be resident on an end station to broker posture information of the end station and to represent the device in its need to attain network services. Cisco Trust Agent communicates directly with an authenticator through EAPoUDP, and to a AAA server through PEAPv1. For a full view of this from the client perspective, see Figure 6-3.

Figure 6-3   *Cisco Trust Agent Communication*

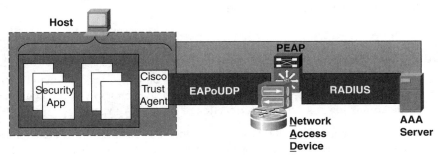

As you can see from Figure 6-3, the authenticator or Network Access Device (NAD) is the primary place in the system to enforce network policy as a result of authorization or interrogation of a client's posture. Policy enforcement is discussed in the following section.

Policy Enforcement

NAC-L2-IP uses access lists for NAC policy enforcement. ACLs are enforced as an authorized result for the determination of a client's posture. By default, the ACLs received as a matter of policy from the AAA server are assumed to be per-host ACLs. The specific information downloaded contains the information of the name of an ACL whose ACEs might already be configured on the switch, or might need to be updated dynamically from the AAA server. Also, all ACLs deployed to support NAC-L2-IP are assumed to be source-based ACLs and are assigned to a host session based on the NAC policy assigned. Specifically, each ACE of an ACL is dynamically modified to replace a source address **any** with the actual host's source IP address (which the switch also knows from the original posture trigger). This ACL applied at the end of a session also overrides the default interface ACL configured on a port. The interface ACL remains enforced on the port, although the per-host ACEs applied through NAC policy are inserted at the top of the ACL. Another expectation of ACLs of this type also implies that the ACEs never have implicit **deny any any** at the end of them like normal ACLs do. This allows the interface ACL to govern network access to the network for packets that do not match the host policy ACL. An example might be traffic from a new host that appears on the wire.

In addition to ACLs, URL redirect is a feature that can also be applied per host session. This policy specifies a URL to which any HTTP GET requests are redirected. URL redirect functionality is typically used when remediation of a host is needed and to enable a machine to become compliant with network policy. The redirect happens only for HTTP packets from the host destined to an address that matches the intercept ACL and does not match any of the ACEs in the posture policy ACL for the host. This functionality helps to avoid redirect loops. After a posture session has been concluded and policy has been enforced, a need exists to determine a periodic check of software compliance, or a keepalive mechanism of the client's attachment to the network.

Status Query Techniques

The preceding sections examine the capability of an EAP conversation to be transported through EAPoUDP and RADIUS. This section focuses on status-query techniques to aid in the determination and periodic verification of a device's posture.

EAP-Status-Query (EAP-SQ) is an EAP method designed to be executed between a client and the authenticator based on a previously established session. This process does not need to involve a AAA server. This process also works in conjunction with the EAP-TLV-Posture resident inside a PEAP session for NAC-L2-IP. Fundamentally, EAP-SQ provides a keepalive mechanism to ensure that Cisco Trust Agent is still resident on a host, and that it is the same device. This process also allows the communication of attributes that might modify the validation method and might trigger events.

Based on a periodic timer, an authenticator sends an EAP-SQ request to Cisco Trust Agent, assuming that a session has been previously authorized on the wire. Cisco Trust Agent then sends an EAP-SQ response, indicating that the host posture has not changed since being first authorized onto the network. If the host posture has not changed, an authenticator sends back an EAP-Success response. If the host posture has changed for the device, Cisco Trust Agent either does not respond to an EAP-SQ request or responds directly indicating the posture has changed, to which an authenticator can send an EAP-Failure as a result. After Cisco Trust Agent acknowledges the failure, the authenticator initiates a full revalidation to ascertain what has changed on the host and could potentially quarantine the device to assist with the remediation of the device. If no response to an EAP-SQ request is received, this triggers a revalidation as well.

Full revalidation of a host's posture might also be desirable to assess whether the host posture has changed, or to indirectly enforce new policy definitions. So, the revalidation process is executed through a periodic timer, or as a result of EAP-SQ failure or timeout.

Agentless Hosts

Hosts are deemed *agentless* if they have been subjected to posture validation and have been nonresponsive to posture requests. A classic cause of this is when the hosts lack Cisco Trust Agent capability. Devices like this include IP phones, printers, UNIX stations, and so on. In these cases, an authenticator can perform a pseudo-authentication on behalf of the end station as a matter of network policy. This functionality is not enabled by default when enabling NAC-L2-IP and needs to be configured explicitly. A host can be deemed agentless if the host does not respond to the EAP identity requests after a maximum retry value has been exceeded. This means that Cisco Trust Agent could be resident but is unresponsive for some reason as well (such as interoperation with a personal firewall). In either case, if a host is deemed agentless, an authenticator proxies for the host by sending an EAP request to the AAA server with a specific username and password combination. At this time, the host's source IP address and MAC address are relayed to the AAA server, which increases network visibility. After the IP or MAC address information is supplied, AAA deploys either a default policy based on the information relayed to it or a policy based on an external audit server determination. Ultimately, an EAP-Success/Failure message is received by the authenticator from AAA, similar to Cisco Trust Agent being on the wire. This process facilitates various types of audit capabilities, including fingerprinting. When auditing is desired, remember to take this into account when planning for interface ACL policy; the default interface ACL must allow access to an audit server for the audit server to reach the host and determine how to treat it.

Voice Integration

If EAPoUDP is in use as a control plane for NAC-L2-IP, the solution should provide Voice VLAN Identifier (VVID) access and authorized Port VLAN Identifier (PVID) access based on posture. The solution also allows EAPoUDP and voice to coexist.

EAPoUDP provides a different type of architecture and access control environment than 802.1X, mainly because it is Layer 3 in nature. The specific differences in the control plane types, and best-practice guidance on when to deploy either control plane, are not within the scope of this book. Cisco switches also support EAPoUDP and voice in conjunction with any IP phone. Furthermore, because EAPoUDP is available only on access ports at the time of this writing, the functionality is provided using auxiliary VLAN ports. From a deployment perspective, it is not necessary to configure a VVID along with EAPoUDP (although a separate VVID is not typically recommended). A VVID need not be separate from a PVID either, which is typically a configuration restriction on an 802.1X-enabled port (although this is not typically recommended either). Cisco IP Phones should be able to be exempted from EAPoUDP rules based primarily on Cisco Discovery Protocol (CDP). An alternative to this approach includes a configured static exception. Overall, a typical expectation of the solution should typically define that IP phones should not be treated specifically as agentless devices. Rather, they should be exempt from NAC entirely, based on another form of supplemental identification (MAC address) or control plane (CDP). Authenticator operation is configurable based on network or security policy. So, an IP phone should be connected to a port that has EAPoUDP configured, and the phone should get access to the VVID by 802.1Q-tagging its packets by default, just like it does without EAPoUDP. This should leave the PC behind the phone to be postured before getting access other than what is defined for the default interface ACL on the port.

For switches that support EAPoUDP, the default configuration of EAPoUDP for NAC-L2-IP added onto a port could break IP telephony through the use of an interface ACL. After EAPoUDP is enabled on a port, all traffic is subject to the default interface ACL configured, unless exceptions exist. For voice to work, you would need to explicitly make exceptions for IP phones. This is in contrast to 802.1X, where you can allow IP phones by default. Additionally, you might not want voice traffic to be suspect to the same posture verification rules as data traffic. The following example demonstrates an IP phone plugged into a port with a "default" configuration for an ACL that allows only EAPoUDP and limited network services before EAPoUDP takes place on the port and would break voice operation:

```
Switch#show access-lists interface_acl
Extended IP access list interface_acl
    10 permit udp any any eq 21862
    20 permit udp any eq bootpc any eq bootps
    30 permit udp any any eq domain
    40 permit tcp any host 10.0.200.30 eq www
    50 permit icmp any any
    60 deny ip any any
```

At the time of this writing, no posture agents exist on IP phones. Because of the architecture of EAPoUDP mentioned previously in this chapter, you also have no way to stop a posture trigger on a switch. Also, any device that lacks a posture agent can revert to agentless if configured. So, a solution goal might be to exempt Cisco IP Phones from posture entirely. A configurable option for this is as follows:

```
identity profile eapoudp
  device authorize type cisco ip phone policy PHONE-ALLOW
identity policy PHONE-ALLOW
  access-group PHONE-ALLOW
ip access-list extended PHONE-ALLOW
  permit ip any any
```

The configuration must attach a policy to the **device authorize** statement. This allows the switch to look for the platform string in the CDP cache. The access list referenced by the policy also permits all traffic. Optionally, it could be tuned to only allow bearer and control traffic from an IP phone and/or from a specific voice subnet for further restriction.

This configuration should allow IP phones to be immediately exempt from the default ACL configured on the port (and NAC posture). This configuration works for all IOS-based switches. However, with CatOS, IP phones are allowed by default (similar to the 802.1X operation). This is because of the policy configuration. The primary configuration of policy on CatOS is a VLAN-ACL (VACL). Hence, the VVID can be exempt from this by nature. If the policy configuration were attempted as a port-based ACL (PACL), the configuration would be rejected because of the mandatory DHCP-Snooping ACE. DHCP-Snooping is required to trigger posture for NAC-L2-IP on CatOS. So, by default, IP phones on a configured VVID should work fine, regardless of an EAPoUDP deployment or configuration for CatOS. No other special considerations are required.

Impact of Trust Agent Disappearing

The EAPoUDP state does not go away on direct linkdown from a switch. So, it should not be expected to go down when a Cisco Trust Agent is unplugged from an IP phone either. Even if a client plugs directly into an authenticator that becomes unplugged, this linkdown event does not generate an EAPoUDP-session teardown or the removal of the MAC address in the session, as Figure 6-4 illustrates.

Figure 6-4 *Cisco Trust Agent Disappearing*

For a session that has been unplugged, when the link comes back up, a switch also does not use an immediate ARP for the stored MAC address to re-create a presumed session. An EAPoUDP session is persistent until EAP-SQ or an ARP probe triggers it again. It also matters whether the new session is from the same MAC address. If the new session is from the same MAC plugging back in, the session simply resumes. However, if the device plugging back in is from a different MAC, a switch can always try to posture the device automatically. So, if a session is moved within a switch, posture might not be performed, and the device might be suspect to whatever is in the default ACL. The primary issue different for phones and the examination of this topology is that link rarely goes down. So, this has little impact on EAPoUDP as described. As a reminder, information contained in the EAPoUDP state can be easily spoofed. If the device tracking table is enabled for posture initiation, this should time out a session if a client is disconnected indirectly from an IP phone environment by default in 30 seconds. Also, a switch should send an ARP probe to determine whether a session is still there. This mitigates some risk and removes stale entries, but antispoofing mechanisms are recommended for a best-practice defense mechanism.

Voice Integration Summary

Agentless behavior might not be desired for a phone (unless requirements dictate otherwise). Cisco IP Phones can be exempted from NAC based on CDP, or they must be configured with a static exemption.

You must take some considerations into account for the impact of EAPoUDP on voice. For NAC-L2-IP, an entry added to the Layer 2 device tracking table (or a DHCP-Snooping binding table entry) controls when a device should be posture-checked. This is hard-coded behavior in a switch and cannot be controlled. As a result, at the initiation of a posture check, a switch looks for Cisco Trust Agent. However, a switch does not look for Cisco Trust Agent if it knows not to through an exemption like the processes previously described. If an IP phone cannot be exempt from EAPoUDP, it will always time out if Cisco Trust Agent is not on the wire and revert to agentless (if configured). At this point, the MAC address of a presumed phone could be sent to the ACS so that it can be wildcarded. However, during this time, the device is subject to the rules on the default ACL and describes agentless behavior, which might not be an ideal deployment scenario for voice devices. The presence of CDP should allow Cisco IP Phones to be exempt from any posture. This, however, is not as a default condition for IOS-based switches, while it is for CatOS-based switches.

However, with the solution described in the previous paragraph in place, any enforced NAC policy does not necessarily need to take voice into account explicitly. From a security standpoint, the EAPoUDP state can also be easily spoofed. CDP for phones or IP/MAC info for hosts can all be mirrored. Attempting to mitigate these concerns with EAP-SQ or ARP probes does not address these potential concerns directly. If this is a concern, antispoofing techniques, such as Dynamic ARP Inspection or IP-Source-Guard, should be considered and are highly recommended.

Exceptions to NAC Posture

Exceptions to NAC posture might need to be dealt with as part of a NAC architecture that supports a heterogeneous environment. Otherwise, you need NAC agents (presumably Cisco Trust Agent) applied on everything conceivable, potentially including new closed products from other vendors. Most of the basis from this is because of the need to appropriately handle agentless requests. Some of these devices were briefly described earlier, and the preceding section demonstrated how to exempt IP phone devices from posture. An alternative to attempting to leverage a control plane for this technique is through a static configuration on a switch that supports NAC-L2-IP. This is typically called an *exception list* and would provide a switch with device information in advance to allow a switch to bypass posture on a certain device. However, per-device exception lists on separate switches are typically not a scalable technique for most enterprises.

Exception lists specifically come into play after the first packet that matches an intercept ACL is intercepted—also referred to as *interesting traffic*. Remember, though, that the default posture initiation process cannot be controlled on a switch. So, before the switch starts the posture process, it can check whether the host is present in the exception list. If the host is present, a specific configured policy is associated to the exception entry. This specific policy might, in turn, reference an ACL to blindly allow unrestricted network access based only on the criteria identified (MAC or IP). In this way, the switch does not start the posture process, when it would otherwise. Of course, even if exception lists are configured, if no matching entries exist in an exception list, the posture process starts normally. EAPoUDP session state is maintained, even for devices in an exception list. For scalability reasons, this could be a potential disadvantage.

Regardless of whether Cisco Trust Agent is resident on a device, a switch could be configured to check with AAA first before beginning a posture. In other words, you can optionally treat the device as agentless before posture begins (provide a posture exemption) or provide access based on this request alone if the device is indeed agentless (provide a posture exception). This is typically termed *EAPoUDP bypass*. Either way it is used, you can attempt to provide network access based on a switch-identified credential, such as a

MAC address. For example, using wildcard masking for hosts within ACS could be an acceptable way of dealing with many device types that have a low risk of propagating worms or viruses.

In summary, creating exception lists on separate switches that support NAC-L2-IP could be daunting. Partners could help in this regard, though. In addition to providing ways to provide manageable exemptions, or NAC exceptions for devices incapable of Cisco Trust Agent, ways are available to support the verification of auditing technologies. These auditing technologies, coupled with network policy, provide a ubiquitous way to handle devices incapable of speaking NAC.

Summary

Applying EAPoUDP on a switch (NAC-L2-IP) provides a posture validation mechanism at the Layer 2 network edge.

The EAPoUDP framework consists of a client, an authenticator, and an authentication server. The client (Cisco Trust Agent) is located on a host and works to broker posture information from an end station and provide it to the network. The authenticator is a network access device (NAD) that transposes an EAP conversation from Cisco Trust Agent to the authentication server. It also acts to enforce the policy received from the authentication server. The authentication server is the policy server that determines whether a valid host can access the network.

NAC-L2-IP policy enforcement is accomplished by way of an ACL assignment. The ACLs received as a matter of policy from the AAA server are assumed to be per-host ACLs. URL redirect can also be used by an authenticator to support the notion of device remediation, and device cleaning after being quarantined.

The implementation for EAPoUDP and IP telephony should allow a successful interoperation of voice and network device posture as well. This interoperation needs to be explicitly configured in IOS-based switches, however.

Agentless devices can be handled as exceptions to NAC posture. Some devices can be handled as exemptions to NAC posture, through static configurations or EAPoUDP bypass techniques.

NAC-L2-IP allows you to integrate into an existing network topology, while providing posture capability directly. It is an L3 control plane, so the network need not support a single-host-per-port topology.

Resources

"All about Network Admission Control" from Networkers 2005, http://wwwin.cisco.com/Mkt/events/nw/2005/post/abstracts.shtml#242.

"Understanding and Deploying Network Admission Control" from Networkers 2005, http://wwwin.cisco.com/Mkt/events/nw/2005/post/abstracts.shtml#206.

Review Questions

You can find the answers to the review questions in Appendix A.

1 Which protocols should be allowed so that the EAPoUDP Layer 3 mechanism and control plane can operate?

  a DHCP

  b EAP port 21862

  c UDP port 21862

  d TCP port 443

2 The RADIUS Message-Authenticator attribute prevents attackers from subverting EAP by providing per-packet authentication and integrity protection. Which Message-Authenticator attribute found in Table 6-1 is used for HMAC-MD5 for a Catalyst switch?

  a Attribute No. 1

  b Attribute No. 29

  c Attribute No. 79

  d Attribute No. 80

3 ACLs deployed to support NAC-L2-IP and NAC-L3-IP are assumed to be source-based ACLs that are used on a per-host basis and accomplished by what statement in an ACE?

4 Which method(s) allow IP phones to be exempted from NAC?

    a   Enabling Cisco Discovery Protocol

    b   Static exemption using phone IP address

    c   Static exemption using phone MAC address

    d   All of the above

5 Which Catalyst switch security features can prevent spoofing of EAPoUDP states?

    a   EAP-Status-Query

    b   IP-Source-Guard

    c   ARP probing

    d   Dynamic ARP Inspection

This chapter covers the following topics:

- NAC Framework lifecycle process
- Preparation phase
- Planning phase
- Design phase
- Implementation phase
- Operation and optimization phases

CHAPTER 7

Planning and Designing for Network Admission Control Framework

You must consider many things before deploying a Network Admission Control (NAC) Framework solution into your network. As with most security solutions, if it is not carefully planned and designed, when implemented, it could cause more disruption to your users than from the malicious activity you are intending to protect them from.

After NAC is implemented, the work is not done. You must be prepared to monitor its effectiveness and tweak the policies and rules to stay current with the latest updates that make up your admission policy.

This chapter identifies important tasks that help you prepare, plan, design, implement, operate, and optimize a NAC solution. You learn to do the following things:

- Identify the six phases of a NAC Framework lifecycle process
- Learn preparation tasks that identify security policies as well as staff role and responsibilities
- Learn NAC Framework solution objectives and implementation strategies that should occur in the planning phase
- Identify key areas to consider when designing for NAC and learn components that should be part of a NAC policy
- Identify major installation tasks for implementing the Cisco NAC Framework
- Identify tasks that are completed in the operation and optimization phases

NAC Framework Lifecycle Process

When deploying a NAC Framework solution, you have much to do on the front end before you even start designing your solution. Likewise, you have much to do on the back end after your NAC Framework infrastructure is in place. Because of the volatile nature of software patching and security updates, you must constantly monitor your NAC solution and make changes as needed. Most likely, you are aware and probably doing some of the steps suggested throughout this chapter when operating an ever-changing high-tech technology such as NAC.

Your NAC Framework lifecycle should have the following six phases:

- Prepare
- Plan
- Design
- Implement
- Operate
- Optimize

Sometimes these phases are referred to as *PPDIOO*. PPDIOO is a Cisco process that defines the continuous lifecycle stages and is shown in Figure 7-1.

Figure 7-1   *NAC Framework Lifecycle*

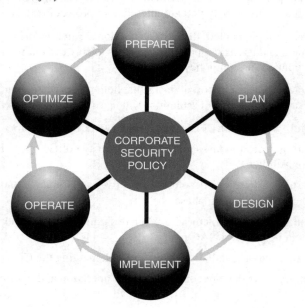

As shown in Figure 7-1, at the heart of the NAC Framework lifecycle is your corporate security policy. Your security policy should be the blueprint that defines the design and implementation of NAC. NAC is just one technology that protects your business's assets, and when implemented correctly, it can guarantee the proactive measures that you specify are in place prior to granting a user or device network access.

This chapter covers each of the six lifecycle phases, with more attention spent on the planning and design phases. It also provides some recommendations regarding what should be done in each phase through some lessons learned. Obviously, you will experience additional steps as you progress through your own NAC Framework implementation and operation, so this chapter is not all-encompassing. Also, this chapter does not provide configuration examples. For detailed configuration examples, refer to Volume II of this book, *NAC Framework Deployment and Troubleshooting*.

Preparation Phase

This should be the first phase of your NAC solution lifecycle. Before you even begin your planning phase, you should already have an established security policy that can assist you in defining the NAC policy. In addition, you need to identify the security management personnel that should work together to develop a business case for making a technology change such as NAC. Without these in place, it will be difficult to sell NAC to the business decision makers as well as to the various departments that will most likely have to implement your plan. This section identifies different tasks and events that should be agreed on, documented, and shared with all who will be affected by implementing and managing this new technology change.

Define Your Corporate Security Policy

All businesses should have a corporate security policy that serves as a model of what is an acceptable security level for the business and identifies employee responsibilities. It also serves to help build a business case for adding NAC to existing security practices. If it is not important for your business to have a security policy, selling NAC to the business decision makers can prove to be a difficult task.

A corporate security policy should have at least the following components or individual policies:

- Information security policy
- Acceptable use policy
- Network access control policy
- Security management policy
- Incident-handling policy

As shown in Figure 7-2, all the components together define the corporate security policy.

Figure 7-2 *Information Security Policy*

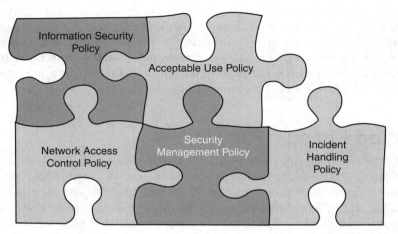

Each policy should explicitly state the policy, the user's responsibility, and the group responsible for monitoring, managing, and enforcing the policy.

Information Security Policy

At a minimum, explicitly state the following items in this policy:

- Identify what are considered corporate assets; not all are obvious to employees. For example, identify company-provided PCs, servers, telephones, cell phones, personal digital assistants (PDAs), lab equipment, external media, documentation, and intellectual capital.

- Describe business security practices that must be observed by employees around these corporate assets. For example, a laptop with secure financial information should not be left in a car.

- Describe the process used for patching desktop software. Is it an automated process, or does it require user intervention? Identify who is responsible for ensuring a desktop is patched.

- Describe acceptable risks. Examples include the following:

    — Contractors who have a certain clearance can access sensitive information or gain access to certain areas of the network.

    — A PC or server that is not patched with the latest noncritical update is allowed onto the network, whereas devices missing critical updates are placed in quarantine until they are properly patched.

- Identify the process for handling NAC agentless devices.
- Identify areas of protection and clarify who can be allowed to access this area.
- Identify which areas of the network that guests (visitors) are allowed to access.
- Identify other security-related organizations and define their responsibilities.

Acceptable Use Policy

This policy describes the business's acceptable use of information and should be written in an easy-to-understand language so that it cannot be misinterpreted. At a minimum, explicitly state the following in this policy:

- Outline users' roles and their responsibilities.
- Describe the consequences for when the policy is not followed.
- Identify how this acceptable use is communicated, as follows:
  — For employees, will this communication be a one-time or a periodic reminder, or when noncompliance is observed?
  — For guests, will a communication be displayed on their devices when network access is attempted? Will the message include an acceptable-use consent before access is granted?

Network Access Control Policy

This policy describes how data is categorized and clarifies who can access it. At a minimum, explicitly state the following:

- Define data categories and describe business sensitivity such as highly confidential, restricted, internal-only, and public use.
- Define who can access the data by category.
- Describe the network access control policy for all access methods in your network. For example, is the policy different for users who are wired or wireless, or who are using a virtual private network (VPN) or extranet?
- Will users be assigned to a group or role that can be used by the entire corporation for a consistent labeling that identifies network and/or data access (for example, staff, engineer, sales, human resources, contractor, and guest)?
- Define the policy for network access if a device is slightly out of compliancy and is not critical, several versions out of date but not critical, critical update required, and required security software not running or device infected.

Security Management Policy

You must understand your business's security management process and identify who is responsible for the various tasks. Include all the groups within your business that must work together throughout all the NAC lifecycle stages. This group should contribute to the design and ongoing management of the network admission policy, and will be called the *NAC team* going forward in this document. The following should help you identify who to seek out and determine what processes are in place or are not yet determined:

- Identify and document the organizations that are responsible for the following:
  - Information security, which typically entails defining who is responsible for corporate information and asset policy definition and enforcement
  - Network operations, including LAN, WAN, wireless, remote access, extranet, and network monitoring
  - Information technology operations that include desktop, server, and applications
  - Security operations that include firewalls, intrusion prevention, antivirus, identity, and security monitoring
  - Help desk staff who are the first contacts when employees need help
- Identify who is responsible for your business's security policy creation, communication, and enforcement? Is more than one group doing this? If so, document each group and its responsibility.
- Describe the process for making changes to the security policy, and identify who owns this responsibility.
- Describe the communication process for informing employees about security changes. Identify who is responsible for communicating these changes.
- Decide whether network access is or will be based on user identity, software compliance, or both. Identify locations where network access policy can differ. Also, identify whether exceptions are allowed for certain users or locations. For example, if the CEO is noncompliant, is that person still granted access?
- Describe the admission policy for nonstandard devices that connect to the network. Examples include IP phones, videoconference devices, labs, extranet, kiosks, video surveillance, badge readers, guests, and consultants.
- Describe the admission policy for unmanaged devices that connect to the network. Examples include printers, shared storage, and shared servers.
- Describe the policy for resolving errors in the system that can disable ports that are in an error condition. Prior to NAC, if the error-handling policy was to wait 24 hours before an errored port was reenabled, users could circumvent this restriction by

plugging into a different port to attempt access. In a NAC environment using the same error policy, the error will most likely follow the user from port to port, not allowing the user access from anywhere for 24 hours.

Incident-Handling Policy

This policy describes how a security incident is handled and should include the following:

- Describe the process for employees to report security problems, and identify a reasonable time in which the problem should be resolved.

- Identify who to contact when an incident occurs. Will this contact differ given the type of incident? Identify who is responsible for resolving the incident reported.

In summary, you must have these policies defined up-front before you begin your NAC planning. These polices will be used as inputs in defining your NAC policy in addition to identifying the group responsible for implementing and managing the NAC solution.

Use the list of questions in this section to describe, document, and communicate the various security policies that make up your corporate security policy. Also, define security administration and management roles and their responsibilities. This can help identify all parties that should be included in the rest of the PPDIOO phases for implementing your network admission policy enforcement.

Planning Phase

This section helps you gather necessary information to plan your NAC Framework solution. The planning phase includes the following major tasks:

- Describe your NAC solution objectives and prioritize them as to your business importance. This can help identify the mandatory requirements that should be part of the implementation strategy.

- Document your existing infrastructure. Understanding what you have is important to size what is needed to implement NAC.

- Identify infrastructure components that should be included for integration and interoperability with NAC. Describe the integration strategy.

- Describe the operational strategy for managing, monitoring, updating, and supporting the NAC Framework solution components.

- Describe the NAC Framework proof of concept implementation and how success is evaluated.

- Describe the migration strategy for rolling out the NAC Framework implementation. Identify whether the implementation will be accomplished in phases. If so, identify in which phase the various NAC objectives will be implemented.

- Estimate project costs for your NAC Framework implementation.

NAC Solution Objectives

NAC must provide certain objectives for your business. More requirements will add implementation complexity and also increase your cost. Identifying these objectives up-front with priorities can help you size your initial deployment and help you identify the other desirable features that can be phased in later.

Use the following list to identify your NAC solution objectives:

- List the problems that NAC must solve for your business.

- List the problems that are desirable for NAC to solve.

- Do certain government-regulation requirements need to be observed? If so, describe the requirements and identify users or network areas affected.

- Do you need to be able to monitor and provide reports of compliant and noncompliant devices? Do you need the same capabilities for users?

- Are historical logs of noncompliant users required? If so, how long should they be stored?

- Do you plan to manually or automatically remediate noncompliant devices? If so, do you currently have a remediation solution in place that you plan to integrate? If not, has a remediation solution been identified but not yet been put in place?

- How are agentless devices and guests going to be handled?

- Will integration and interoperability requirements be part of the NAC policy. Examples include interoperability with an external user store database such as Lightweight Directory Access Protocol (LDAP), the ability for IP telephony to coexist with NAC, and the ability to check and enforce VPN users.

Prioritize your solution objective list and determine which objectives are required at the initial implementation and which can be added at a later phase.

Table 7-1 is an example of solution objectives and how they can be prioritized.

Table 7-1   *NAC Framework Solution Objectives Example*

NAC Framework Solution Objective	Priority	Implementation Phase
System compliance enforcement of operating system (OS) and antivirus (AV) software for all hosts and servers at main campus before granting network access to LAN/WAN users.	Mandatory	1
System compliance enforcement of OS and AV software for all hosts and servers at remote sites and for VPN users before granting network access to users.	Mandatory	2
Only corporate employees (identities) who successfully authenticate with corporate LDAP database are allowed full access to the business intranet. Contractors are allowed access to areas of the network in which they work, and access is based on their physical location and job function.	Mandatory	1

Table 7-1   *NAC Framework Solution Objectives Example (Continued)*

NAC Framework Solution Objective	Priority	Implementation Phase
System capable of handling NAC agentless devices.	Mandatory	1
Guests (visitors) only have access to the Internet.	Mandatory	1
A centralized enterprise-class management system for administration and monitoring of NAC.	Mandatory	1
Historical reports required for one year for the following: Successfully authenticated devices and users Noncompliant devices and level of deficiency	Highly Desirable	1
Check and enforce the use of corporate-provided host personal firewall and host intrusion protection system. Quarantine the host if not enabled.	Highly Desirable	1
Detect and control the use of an external storage device on a system.	Desirable	2
Network location awareness to determine whether a device is in the office, lab, or hotspot, or is remote. Must be able to enforce different admission policy and log device and location.	Desirable	2

Documenting Your Existing Infrastructure

You must understand your current infrastructure to determine your gaps. This section helps you define the deployment scenarios, identify the network access devices (NADs) to be used as the policy enforcement point, and identify the policy servers. You should perform the tasks described in the following sections.

Surveying Your Network

Determine the devices that are physically connected to the network. Three major categories exist: NADs, hosts that are NAC capable, and NAC agentless hosts (NAHs).

Determine whether existing NADs are supported or require an upgrade. Perform the following review:

- Describe your current network topology and document it.
- Identify NADs acting as the policy enforcement points (PEPs) and document the following:
    - Do your NADs support NAC today, or is an upgrade or replacement required?

— Do the NADs' software release and image support NAC (that is, a router using a security image), or is an upgrade required?

— Do the NADs have enough memory to support NAC images, or is a memory upgrade required?

— Document the current NAD access control lists (ACLs) and VLANs (before NAC integration).

TIP   A tool, called Cisco Network Profile Collector (CNPC), is available to Cisco System Engineers (SE) to quickly identify IOS NAD hardware and software. The SE must connect to your network to use the tool to scan for IOS network devices that have Cisco Discovery Protocol (CDP) enabled. The tool gathers an inventory of hardware, such as model and memory installed, as well as software information, such as host name, IP address, IOS image, and version running. The Cisco SE can then upload the collected information to an internal Cisco web dashboard and produce a report with your network device details. This tool was developed to help SEs identify end-of-life hardware and software for their customers. You can use this tool to save time from performing a physical audit.

Another NAC tool is available using Cisco Works Interface Configuration Manager. It can perform a NAC profile, and this profile can be saved in a report format. Refer to the following URL for more information:

http://www.cisco.com/en/US/products/ps6903/
products_user_guide_chapter09186a0080636258.html

A sample topology is shown in Figure 7-3. It serves as a reference for the examples used throughout this chapter.

A sample NAD worksheet is shown in Table 7-2 for the sample network topology shown in Figure 7-3. Identify the NADs and determine whether they currently support NAC and whether upgrades are necessary.

Figure 7-3 *Sample Network Topology*

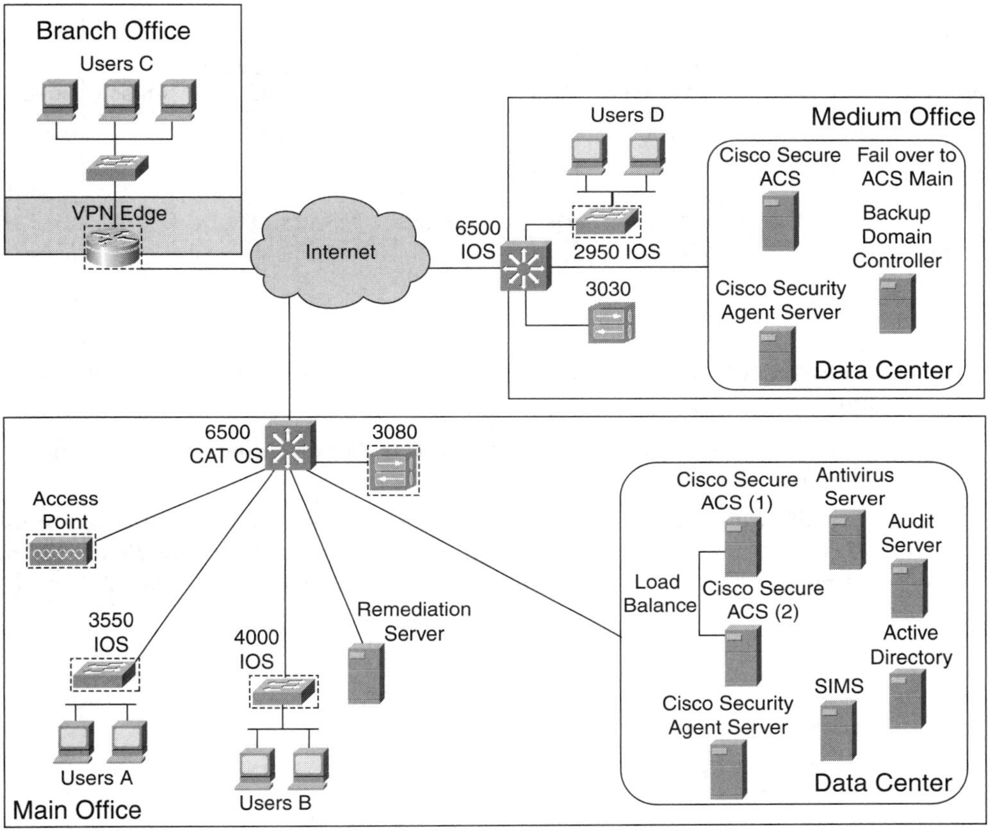

Table 7-2 *NAD Support for NAC Worksheet (Sample)*

Location	NAD Role	NAD Platform	IOS Software Release Version	Memory	Supported/ Upgrade	Authorization Method	Phrase	Notes
Main Campus	Desktop gateway A	Catalyst 3550	12.1(22)EA	OK	Upgrade	NAC-L2-802.1X	1	Upgrade to 12.2(25) SED
	Desktop gateway B	Catalyst 4000	11.2.(7)A	OK	Upgrade	NAC-L2-802.1X	1	Upgrade to 12.2(25)SG
	Wireless access point	Aironet 1200	12.2(13)JA2	OK	Upgrade	NAC-L2-802.1X	1	Upgrade to 12.3(7)JA
	VPN concentrator	VPN 3080	v4.0	OK	Upgrade	NAC-L3-IP	2	Upgrade to v4.7

continues

Table 7-2   *NAD Support for NAC Worksheet (Sample) (Continued)*

Location	NAD Role	NAD Platform	IOS Software Release Version	Memory	Supported/ Upgrade	Authorization Method	Phrase	Notes
Branch Offices	Small office Layer 3 gateway	2811 Router	12.3(8)T	OK	N/A	NAC-L3-IP	3	Use as is
	Medium office Layer 2 desktop gateway	Catalyst 2950	12.1(11)EA	OK	Upgrade	NAC-L2-802.1X	2	Upgrade to 12.1(22)EA6

Determine the NAC mode of operation that is to be used for each NAD identified on your worksheet as follows:

- Identify which implementation phase NAC will be enabled in to enforce policy at the NADs listed.
- Identify which of the NAC Layer 2 or Layer 3 authentication methods will be used. Refer to the NAC Phase 2 implementation decision tree in Figures 7-4 and 7-5 to determine the recommended implementation method based on your NAD capability.

Figure 7-4 *NAC Framework Phase 2 Implementation Decision Tree, Part 1*

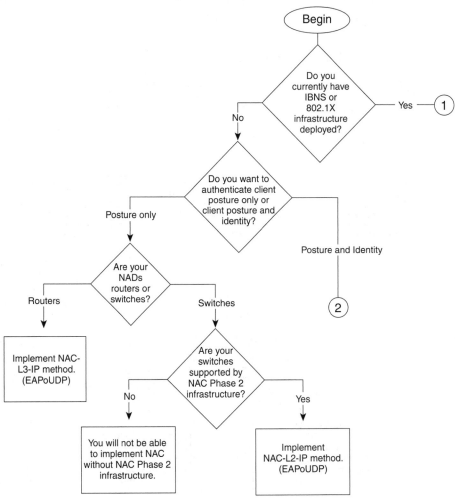

Figure 7-5 *NAC Framework Phase 2 Implementation Decision Tree, Part 2*

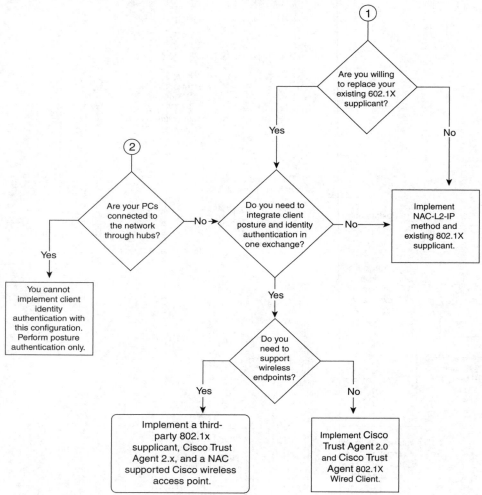

- Identify the NAC policy server(s) that are to be used (for example, Cisco Secure Access Control Server [ACS] and other partner servers), as follows:

   — Identify the model and software release.

   — Identify whether they exist or must be purchased.

   — Identify whether the existing policy server supports NAC or whether an upgrade or replacement is required.

- List all host and endpoint device operating systems and versions used by your business. A sample worksheet is shown in Table 7-3. Are all the OSs supported by Cisco Trust Agent? Which applications are NAC enabled and will be part of the admission policy?

Table 7-3 *Sample NAC-Supported Endpoint Worksheet*

Device Type	OS/Version	NAC-Supported?	NAC-Enabled App/Version
Employee laptops and desktops	Windows XP Professional Version 2 SP2	Yes	Cisco Security Agent v4.5 VirusScan Enterprise v8.0
Corporate server standard	Windows Advanced Server Version 2 SP2	Yes	Cisco Security Agent v4.5 VirusScan Enterprise v8.0
Development servers—Linux	Red Hat Linux v9.0 Enterprise v4	Yes	Cisco Trust Agent v2 Cisco Security Agent v4.5 VirusScan Enterprise v8.0
Graphics workstations	Silicon Graphics	No	No

- List all NAHs that must be exempted from the NAC enforcement policy. A sample worksheet is shown in Table 7-4.

Table 7-4 *NAC Exemption Worksheet (Sample)*

Device Type	OS	Location	Strategy	Notes
Graphics workstations	Silicon Graphics	All over	Audit server	—
Guest laptops	Various	All over	Audit server	—
Voice mail	Linux	Main and medium offices	Enter host in NAD exception list	IT managed, exclude 00-0D-70A4-27-C9
Print server	—	Two HQ Cat 3550 One Cat 4000	MAC Authentication Bypass (MAB)	At least three different Organizational Unique Identifier (OUI) codes
Printer—HP	—	Ten HQ Cat 3550 Six Cat 4000	MAB	At least eight different OUI codes
Surveillance camera	—	Lobby and outside doors, all locations	Enter host in NAD exception list	Gather MACs
Badge readers	—	Lobby and outside doors, all locations	Enter host in NAD exception list	Gather MACs
Polycom VC unit	—	All HQ and main office conf. rooms	Enter host in NAD exception list	Gather MACs
Cisco IP Phones	—	All locations	Voice VLANs	—

NOTE   An audit server that supports Generic Authorization Message Exchange GAME Protocol is needed to perform dynamic auditing of agentless devices, where static entries can be manually administered in Cisco Secure ACS and the NADs to exempt known agentless devices.

Integration Strategy

Identify infrastructure components that should be included for integration and interoperability with NAC. Identifying common infrastructure includes the following:

- Identifying Dynamic Host Configuration Protocol (DHCP) server(s) and DHCP pools that are to be used with NAC.
- Identifying directory services to be used, as follows:
  — Do you currently use an identity application for network authorization? If so, list the application(s) and software versions.
  — Identify directory services application(s). Examples include Microsoft Active Directory and LDAP. Identify their software versions.
- Identifying whether your current directory services application can support additional queries or whether an upgrade or additional server(s) are required.
  — Identifying your current public-key infrastructure (PKI). Examples include Microsoft Windows 200x server and a certification authority (CA) vendor. If you do not have a certificate authority vendor, self signed certificates can be generated from Cisco Secure ACS. In either case, Cisco Trust Agent must use a certificate to establish a secure protected EAP (PEAP) session with Cisco Secure ACS. Do you have plans to manage or purchase individual certificates from a CA vendor?
  — Do you understand the long-term support, migration, and scaling issues of self-signed certificates?
- Identifying whether the choice of NAC enforcement for a NAD requires changes to the existing network topology.

NOTE   Implementing NAC-L2-802.1X enforcement requires VLAN enforcement across all NADs at the time of this writing.

Operational Strategy

NAC team members and representatives from all affected groups (Network Operations [NetOps], Security Operations [SecOps], Desktop Services, and Support) need to meet and reach agreement on how the different groups will work together to manage, monitor, update, and support the NAC Framework solution components.

Your business's security management policy should serve as an input to your operational strategy. At a minimum, document the following:

- Policy compliance
- Project information sharing
- Monitoring and support strategy

Policy Compliance

Establish a policy that describes the process and organization(s) responsible for developing and maintaining the business's software conformity and standards. This policy should identify the following:

- Describe the software application deployment model, software maintenance procedures, and patch distribution process.
- Identify who is responsible for determining the latest patch updates. Identify who is responsible for determining compliance rules.
- Identify the process for implementing a new admission policy rule.
- Identify which policy management components exist and who is responsible for administering the updates. These could be different teams. For example, ACS can be managed by the NetOps or SecOps team and the antivirus application server can be managed by the Desktop Management team.
- Agree on a minimum time frame from update identification to administration of change. What is the priority of the change request to the group administering the NAC components?
- Describe the primary policy server where updates should be controlled (that is, credential attribute rules within ACS or antivirus application, or a mixture of other posture validation servers).
- Describe the process for how NAHs will be identified, registered, and approved.

Project Information Sharing

All organizations working on various NAC Framework components must proactively identify how information is shared and keep current. Identify the following items:

- Create a NAC solution contact list and escalation list.

- Propose and get agreement from all NAC project parties regarding the governance method to be used to make decisions and communicate with all involved parties.

- Identify where the NAC operational shared storage area exists so that all teams know where to find project-related information and contacts.

- Identify the person who is responsible for keeping this information current.

Monitoring and Support Strategy

Describe the process and organizations responsible for evaluating compliance to the admission policy. Also, describe the support strategy for problem resolution. Identify the following items:

- Identify who is responsible for supporting end-user workstations, desktop security applications, OS security support, and policy servers.

- Document the solution escalation process. Identify support responsibilities from the first level of contact through the escalation path to the subject-matter expert. Describe the procedures for escalating NAC-related issues and the process for problem closure.

- Describe the level of monitoring for compliance usage. What event triggers contacting the next level of support?

- Determine whether compliance reports are generated. What information should be captured and from what management tools? Who generates the reports and how often should the reports be generated? Who receives the reports? How long should the reports be stored and where are they kept?

Proof of Concept

Determine how you are planning to test your design. Are you planning to conduct a proof of concept (POC), or will you use one of the initial phase steps to prove your design?

The recommended way to test your design is to conduct a POC in the lab first, followed by a deployment in a monitor mode to evaluate the concept in production, followed by a cutover on a group-by-group basis until the implementation is complete.

If a separate POC will be carried out, document the following:

- What are the POC objectives?

- How much of the design is to be proven?

- What is the POC setup and test plan?
- Who is responsible for task responsibilities and time frames?
- Will external help, such as Cisco, a partner, or professional services, assist with the POC? If so, is a cost associated with the outside help?
- Are you planning to perform a demonstration of your POC that is shown to the decision makers?

Migration Strategy

A migration strategy should be developed to serve as a checklist of tasks for the implementation phase of your NAC Framework solution. You might even need to go through multiple, staged phases for implementation. The migration strategy is where you should describe how to accomplish the solution objectives, describe the steps and their requirements, and identify who is responsible for performing the tasks.

Use your NAC Framework solution objectives listed in Table 7-1 as inputs for the migration strategy. A sample migration strategy is provided in the "Implementation Phase" section, later in this chapter.

Cost Considerations

When you prepare your NAC Framework plan, be prepared for the question: "Sounds good, but what will it cost me?" At a minimum, you should determine the costs listed in this section.

Software Costs

Estimate the software costs for hosts and policy servers that will be used as part of your NAC Framework solution. Identify the following:

- Host costs:
  - What is the posture agent software cost (Cisco Trust Agent is no charge)?
  - Will host operating systems require an upgrade?
  - Will 802.1X be used? If so, does an 802.1X supplicant need to be purchased?

NOTE   Verify whether Cisco Trust Agent is bundled with a partner vendor's application software or an 802.1X supplicant.

- Policy management costs:
    - Do you need to purchase or upgrade ACS?
    - Do you plan to use the purchasable Server Load Balancing (SLB) for RADIUS IOS feature?
    - Do you have a NAC-enabled application in place that will be integrated? Does it need to be upgraded?
    - Do you need to purchase or upgrade your remediation system?
    - Do you plan to use an audit system? If so, do you plan to purchase or upgrade?
- If you plan to have a management or monitoring tool to support NAC, determine the cost if you need to purchase or upgrade.

Hardware Costs

Estimate the hardware costs for NADs and servers that will be used as part of your NAC Framework solution. Identify the following:

- Do the NADs acting as policy enforcement points (PEPs) need to be upgraded to a security image or need a hardware upgrade, or will you purchase new ones? Refer to Table 7-2.
- Are servers in place that can support the NAC policy management server(s) and/or management monitoring tools? If so, do they need a hardware and/or software upgrade?

Installation/Operation Costs

Estimate the costs for preparation, installation, and day-to-day operations for your NAC Framework solution. These costs are not as obvious as the hardware and software costs, but should be accounted for in the complete implementation cost for your business. Consider the following:

- Identify training costs for operations personnel to install, configure, and troubleshoot NADs, policy servers, remediation, and audit systems.
- Identify training costs for support personnel to manage and monitor day-to-day support tasks.
- Identify external services:
    - Determine whether professional services will be used for any phase of the NAC lifecycle. If so, identify the costs.
    - Identify additional maintenance or technical support costs incurred by implementing and operating NAC.

- Identify internal resource costs and time estimates for the following tasks:
  - Site survey and design
  - Installation/upgrade/configuration of NADs
  - Installation/upgrade/configuration of ACS
  - Installation/upgrade/configuration of NAC-enabled applications, remediation system, and audit system
  - Installation/upgrade/configuration of management monitoring tools
  - Installation/upgrade/configuration of host agents
  - Creation of websites for communications and registering NAHs (if applicable)
- Determine whether travel will be necessary for subject-matter experts to go on location to perform tasks. How often and how long are planned trips?
- Identify additional annual costs that should be expected for NAC solution administration. This cost could be spread across multiple organizations that manage the different components that make up the NAC Framework solution.
- Identify additional annual costs that should be expected for support and/or help desk personnel. Estimate more cost at the initial implementation, progressing to less cost as the solution matures.
- Identify costs for NAC integration with NAC partner products such as remediation, antivirus, patch management, and auditing:
  - Are professional services used to design, install, or integrate these products with NAC?
  - Are additional licenses or upgrades required for existing partner products to become NAC compatible?
  - Will subscription services or additional licenses be required to receive updates?

Design Phase

Most customers' primary reason for deploying NAC is to prevent problems associated with unauthorized and noncompliant network hosts. When designing the network admission policy, business and security objectives, acceptable uses, and acceptable risks must be known by the designer. These inputs should influence the overall architecture design and are just as important as the network topology and device configurations.

The following sections describe the many components of a NAC policy, including gathering and organizing requirements that can be used later in the implementation phase.

These sections also identify scaling and high-availability considerations that are critical to providing a resilient NAC solution that protects while not impeding user productivity.

Network Admission Policy Definition

At a minimum, designers should use their business's Acceptable Use Policy and Network Access Control Policy as inputs to their network admission policy.

For many, the admission decision encompasses more than just identity and can involve compliance of the host OS and multiple client-side agents, applications, and even hardware.

As previously mentioned, many organizations can manage all these applications and infrastructure, so representatives from each of the organizations should participate with the NAC team in defining the admission policy and rules that contain the following:

- Policy definition
- Credential definition
- Identity definition
- Network virtualization and isolation
- Quarantine and remediation services
- NAH definition

Policy Definition

Network admission policies are typically structured around several of the following authorization decision elements:

- **Who**—Differentiated network access that is based on the requestor by one of the following:
  - **User identity**—A username, a group, or by a guest privilege.
  - **Host identity**—A corporate asset versus a device that is not managed by corporate.
  - **Host posture**—Software compliance state such as healthy, quarantine, and so on.
  - **Machine identity**—Independent verification of machine identity or verification that a machine is bound to a specific user.

- **Where**—Differentiated policy based on the requestor location:
  - — **Geographic**—Building, city, country, or other region requiring unique enforcement of a specific set of rules or laws.
  - — **Local unique requirement**—Staff area versus lobby, conference room, lab, or high-security area.
- **When**—Differentiated access that is time based and can be tracked by the following:
  - — **Calendar**—Time of day and day of week.
  - — **Quotas**—Session limits based on account balance, time duration, or number of active instances.
  - — **Logs**—Track events for accounting and auditing purposes, such as resource usage and security forensics.
- **How**—Based on network access method and protocols used:
  - — **LAN**—Access using 802.1X or Layer 2 switch port.
  - — **Wireless**—Access within and around buildings.
  - — **WAN**—Access within a Layer 3 routed network.
  - — **VPN**—Access for remote users.
- **What**—Network privileges and features based on the capability of the access method:
  - — **Open**—No restrictions.
  - — **Group**—Logical network virtualization based on group or role.
  - — **Extranet**—Partner connectivity.
  - — **Utility**—Dedicated shared devices such as a print server.
  - — **Guest**—Nonemployees with Internet-only access.

The previous list can be part of your NAC decision policy. For your initial policy (such as Phase 1 of your implementation), it is best to start with some simple decisions to satisfy your mandatory NAC objectives such as the "who" decision. Then, as you gain confidence with your implementation, add more decisions to grow your policy.

A network access security policy does not have to be complicated to be effective. A simple policy could be as follows:

- Authenticate employees with compliant hosts.
- Force employees with noncompliant hosts to remediate with access only to the quarantine zone until compliant.
- Allow guests and unauthorized users Internet-only access.

A simple basic policy is shown in Table 7-5.

Table 7-5   *Basic NAC Policy*

Who	Where	When	How	What
User: Employee Posture: Healthy	Any	Any	Any	Any
User: Employee Posture: Not healthy	Any	Any	Any	Quarantine zone only
User: Guest	Any	8 a.m.–6 p.m.	Wireless only	Internet only

A customer who desires a more complex restrictive policy uses more decisions; an example is shown in Table 7-6.

Table 7-6   *More Complex NAC Policy*

Who	Where	When	How	What
User: Employee Host: CorpAsset Posture: Healthy	HQ Branch offices	Any	LAN, WAN, wireless	Any
User: Employee Posture: Healthy	Remote access	Any	VPN	Any
User: Contractor Host: CorpAsset Posture: Healthy	HQ Branch offices	7 a.m.–6 p.m.	LAN, wireless	Local intranet and Internet only
User: Employee User: Contractor Host: Not CorpAsset	HQ Branch offices	Any	LAN	Restricted to their group LAN
User: Employee User: Contractor Posture: Infected	Any	Any	Any	No network access
User: Employee User: Contractor Posture: Not healthy and not infected	Any	Any	Any	Quarantine zone only
User: Guest	Any	8 a.m.–6 p.m.	Wireless only	Internet only
Shared resources (printers, servers, voice mail, and so on) Host identity: MAC	Any	Any	LAN	Allow exceptions (see worksheet in Table 7-4)

The more complex example uses a combination of decisions to determine the type of authorization identified in the "what" column. Determine all the combinations of who, where, when, and how. Keep it simple, and try to minimize your "what" that determines network privileges.

A more simple and manageable approach is to start with a basic policy that is less restrictive, such the example shown in Table 7-5. As you gain confidence in your solution, start to increase the decisions incrementally to be more restrictive and monitor for results.

TIP   This NAC policy incremental implementation is a good approach and can be planned as part of your NAC lifecycle IOO phases, which are discussed later in this chapter.

Credential Definition

NAC Framework uses credentials provided by NAC-enabled security applications informing the policy server(s) about the health of those applications. Each credential has one or more attributes that has data associated with it. Refer to Chapter 3, "Posture Agents," to refresh your memory on credentials, attributes, and their syntax. This section focuses on defining the posture validation, which uses host credentials and policy rules. Together they determine the host posture compliance. Posture tokens identify the level of compliance. The possible tokens include healthy, checkup, transition, quarantine, infected, and unknown. Not all tokens are required to be used. The designer determines which are necessary to satisfy the solution.

In the section "Surveying Your Network," earlier in this chapter, a worksheet (Table 7-3) was used to gather information on the NAC applications; it is used as an input to define host use cases and identify the host credentials used. Also, identify the various states of each credential evaluated and the posture that is to be assigned. Determine the enforcement for each posture state, such as the access capability, redirection to a remediation or audit server, and enforcement actions, such as a message to the user or a string used by a NAC partners device (for example, a string that triggers an auto-remediation for a host).

Begin by identifying your business's different use cases and their actions. An example is shown in Table 7-7.

Table 7-7 *Host Use Case Worksheet (Sample)*

OS	NAC Application	State	Posture	Access	Redirect	Enforcement Actions
Windows XP / Windows Advanced Server / Red Hat Linux	Cisco Trust Agent installed Cisco Security Agent (CSA) installed VirusScan installed	Cisco Trust Agent enabled and current OS current CSA enabled and current VirusScan enabled and current	Healthy	Full	No	None; business as usual
	Cisco Trust Agent installed CSA installed VirusScan installed	Cisco Trust Agent not current, but enabled OS current CSA and VirusScan enabled and current	Checkup	Full	Yes	Pop up "checkup" message Redirect to remediation website
	Cisco Trust Agent installed CSA installed VirusScan installed	Cisco Trust Agent current and enabled Old versions of OS, CSA, or VirusScan CSA and VirusScan enabled	Quarantine	Restricted	Yes	Pop up "quarantine" message Restrict access to quarantine zone Redirect to remediation website
	Cisco Trust Agent installed CSA installed VirusScan installed	Cisco Trust Agent disabled OS current CSA and VirusScan enabled and current	NAH	Restricted	No	Need to enable Cisco Trust Agent automatically Actions transparent with no user notification
	Cisco Trust Agent not installed CSA installed VirusScan installed	OS, CSA, and VirusScan current and enabled or disabled/old version	NAH	Restricted	Yes	Need to remediate, but no pop-up available to user Redirect to remediation website

Table 7-7   *Host Use Case Worksheet (Sample) (Continued)*

OS	NAC Application	State	Posture	Access	Redirect	Enforcement Actions
	Cisco Trust Agent installed CSA installed VirusScan installed	Cisco Trust Agent current and enabled OS current or out of date CSA or VirusScan disabled	Infected	None	No	Pop up "infected" message User must call desktop support for help

NOTE   Redirection is an enforcement feature supported on NAC-L2-IP and/or NAC-L3-IP implementations. At the time of this writing, NAC-L2-802.1X does not support redirection, but is planned to be offered in the future.

The next steps are to take the host use cases, determine the NAC application attributes in which the decisions will be based on, and design the policy rules.

The designer can take this information and further detail the decision for each applications posture plug-in. The designer must know the application attribute values (AVs) available for each vendor that will be checked by ACS. The vendor that supplies the plug-in should describe its specific AVs and provide the attribute definition files (ADFs) needed to import into ACS. Use the worksheet in Table 7-8 to finish defining host credentials for the different posture states for your NAC policy.

TIP   This step might be completed closer to the actual implementation because attributes that contain versions and dates will likely have incremented.

NOTE   If an external posture validation server (PVS) or NAH audit server performs the compliance checking, some of these attributes do not need be defined here. In this case, the administrator for the PVS/audit server defines the compliance-checking conditions and posture token results in those servers.

Table 7-8 can serve as a worksheet for designing your policy and rules. The NAC applications identified in Table 7-7 should be an input into this worksheet. Later, in the implementation phase, this can be used to configure the ACS posture validation database.

Table 7-8 *Host Credential Worksheet (Sample)*

Policy Name	Rule	Condition	Posture	Action	Policy Location
Cisco Trust Agent	1	OS version >= 2.0.0.30 AND Machine-Posture-State >= 1 (See the following note.)	Healthy	None; business as usual	Internal
	2	Else	Checkup	Pop up "checkup" message url-redirect= http://update.nac.cisco.com/checkup status-query-timeout=3600	Internal
Windows	1	OS-Type contains Windows XP AND ServicePacks contains 2 AND HotFixes contains KB826939 AND HotFixes contains KB912919 OR OS-Type contains Windows 2000 Advanced AND ServicePacks contains 4 AND HotFixes contains KB911193 AND HotFixes contains KB910491	Healthy	None; business as usual	Internal
	2	Else	Quarantine	Pop up "quarantine" message Restrict access to 192.169.1.2 or VLAN "Quarantine" Redirect to http://update.nac.cisco.com/quarantine status-query-timeout=120	Internal

Table 7-8 *Host Credential Worksheet (Sample) (Continued)*

Policy Name	Rule	Condition	Posture	Action	Policy Location
Red Hat Linux	1	OS-Type: Red Hat Enterprise Linux ES AND OS-Kernel-Version >= 2.6.17.13	Healthy	None; business as usual	Internal
	2	Else	Checkup	Pop up "checkup" message url-redirect=http://update.nac.cisco.com/checkup status-query-timeout=3600	Internal
CSA	1	CSA Version >= 4.5.0.0 AND CSA Operational State=on	Healthy	None; business as usual	Internal
	2	CSA Version < 4.5.0.0 AND CSA Operational State=on	Quarantine	Pop up "quarantine" message Restrict access to 192.169.1.2 or VLAN "Quarantine" Redirect to http://update.nac.cisco.com/quarantine status-query-timeout=120	Internal
	3	Else	Infected	Pop up "infected" message No network access	Internal
VirusScan	1	McAfee AV Version >= 8.0.0.0 McAfee AV Scan-Engine-Version >= 4400.0.0.0 McAfee AV Patch-Version >= 11 AND McAfee AV protection enabled	Healthy	None; business as usual	Internal
	2	McAfee AV protection not enabled	Infected	Pop up "infected" message No network access	Internal
	3	Else	Quarantine	Pop up "quarantine" message Restrict access to 192.169.1.2 or VLAN "Quarantine" Redirect to http://update.nac.cisco.com/quarantine status-query-timeout=120	Internal

---

NOTE   The Machine-Posture-State attribute specifies the running state of the machine. The states
are as follows:

      1—Booting; not all Windows services are running yet.

      2—Running; Windows services are running but the user is not logged in to the
machine.

      3—Logged in; user successfully logged in.

A posture validation policy is defined for each of the different NAC applications that are to
be checked. Each policy has conditions that are checked that contain a set of required host
credential types and values.

An action can be specified, if desired, such as sending a notification string to Cisco Trust
Agent, instructing it to launch the default web browser on the host. For example, you can
automatically launch a browser for a quarantine assessment by entering **http://x.x.x.x/
quarantine** (or by using the fully qualified domain name in place of *x.x.x.x*) in the posture
assessment notification string of a rule. Again, these actions vary by application. The
designer should consult the vendor for the available actions and required syntax for entering
into ACS.

Identify where the policy is managed and evaluated. Is it managed internally within ACS or
externally with a vendor's policy validation server?

Also, identify the posture tokens to be used and identify what conditions exist for each. In
our example, the following posture tokens are used for the host use cases:

- **Healthy**—Compliant with policy.
- **Checkup**—Slightly out of compliance but not critical enough to reduce access
  privileges.
- **Quarantine**—Out of compliance; requires remediation.
- **Infected**—With host security deactivated, it is assumed to be infected. Therefore, the
  user must seek assistance from desktop support to remediate locally, with no access
  to the network for safe measures.
- **Transition**—The posture validation process has not yet completed. Two scenarios
  can cause this posture: The machine has not fully booted and the evaluation cannot
  yet occur, or the host is agentless and is in the audit process.

Identity Definition

Using identity and posture information together to determine network access is one of the
strengths NAC provides. However, not all NAC assessment methods can determine the
authorization level for both identity and posturing simultaneously. Designers need to ensure
that the NADs can support the security policy being implemented. For example, if machine

identity is a mandatory requirement, designers need to ensure that their NADs are capable of supporting 802.1X.

For those who want to use NAC in a monitor-mode deployment based on identity authorization, switches are the types of NADs needed. They need to be 802.1X capable and should be configured with the following features:

- **Guest-VLAN**—Allows non-802.1X hosts to access the network that uses 802.1X authentication on a port-by-port basis.

- **Failed authorization VLAN**—Allows supplicants that failed three authentication attempts to have access to the network. This can be done on a port-by-port basis.

<table>
<tr><td>**NOTE**</td><td>The same VLAN can be used for both Guest-VLAN and failed authorization VLAN if no network differential is needed for non-802.1X hosts and supplicants that failed to authenticate.</td></tr>
</table>

- **MAC Authentication Bypass (MAB)**—Allows NAHs to bypass the 802.1X default security policy by way of the hosts' MAC address. A wildcard MAC OUI can be configured to allow like devices versus single static entries. MAB is often used on network printers. MAB is not available on all switches; the Catalyst 6500 only supports MAB at the time of this writing. Refer to the Cisco Feature Navigator for the latest NADs that support MAB.

Table 7-9 shows the NAC deployment methods and their identity and posture capabilities at the time of this writing.

Table 7-9   *Assessment Method Posture and Identity Capability*

Feature	NAC-L2-802.1X	NAC-L2-IP	NAC-L3-IP
Machine identity	✓		
User identity	✓		
Posture	✓	✓	✓
Audit		✓	✓

The NAC authorization decision can use identity and group membership to provide differentiated levels of access depending on the identity and posture results. This allows designers to prioritize access based on either attribute.

Identity and group membership plays an important role in determining network admission; however, the host's posture should typically take precedence in the NAC decision. For example, if the host posture is not healthy, in most cases, the threat of a vulnerable or infected host does not warrant overriding the privilege of a group identity. In contrast, with healthy hosts, the group identity determines the authorization level and network access capability for the user.

Authorization priorities can be determined by creating a table of user groups that use the same network requirements, such as employees, contractors, and guests. You then assign each group with identity and posture combinations, using names to identify the combinations for a particular security policy.

TIP	Use a standard naming convention throughout your design to make it easy to understand how the NAC field and attributes are used. For example, use a standard name for posture token, user groups, and message notifications. A consistent standard makes it easy for those who must implement and troubleshoot NAC. In this book, the names used describe the posture (healthy, quarantine, infected, and so on).

An example of defining user groups for posture and identity is shown in Table 7-10.

Table 7-10 *User Groups Based on Posture and Identity*

User Group	Posture: Healthy	Posture: Checkup	Posture: Quarantine	Posture: Infected	Posture: Unknown
Employee	Employee	EmployeeCheckup	EmployeeQuarantine	Infected	EmployeeQuarantine
Contractor	Contractor	ContractorCheckup	ContractorQuarantine	Infected	ContractorQuarantine
Guest	Guest	Guest	Guest	Guest	Guest

NOTE	In this example, Guest access is for unmanaged devices used by nonemployees. Therefore, Cisco Trust Agent is not present, and no capability exists for determining different posture states.

An example of defining user groups for posture only is shown in Table 7-11. In this simple example, the user group chosen reflects the posture token name.

Table 7-11 *User Groups Based on Posture Only*

User Group	Posture
Healthy	Healthy
Quarantine	Quarantine
Infected	Infected
Unknown	Unknown

Network Virtualization and Isolation

Each user group is then associated with a specific set of network access rights that control what network behaviors are permitted.

After an authorization decision is made by the NAC policy server, it pushes the respective actions for that policy to the NAD for enforcement on the host and user. As described in Chapter 2, "Understanding NAC Framework," the most common enforcement mechanisms are VLAN assignments, ACLs, URL redirections, and QoS parameters.

These enforcement mechanisms are available to administrators to segment the network, permitting user access to authorized network resources only.

Network Virtualization

Before implementing NAC, you should understand what network resources you are trying to permit or deny access to and which mechanisms are possible given the capability of your NADs. Using IEEE 802.1X on LAN switches and wireless access points to dynamically assign hosts to VLANs is a common method of network virtualization. This ensures that users can only talk to other resources within the same VLAN and are subject to VLAN ACLs. VLANs are the recommended solution for virtualization at the time of this writing; no consistent way to use downloadable ACLs exists at this time.

For scalability, we recommend using named VLANs such as "Quarantine" or "Guest" versus numbering.

For VPNs, remote-access networks, and LANs, ACLs limit destinations by IP address and protocol. We recommend that you use named ACLs (for example, "Healthy" or "Quarantine") versus numbering here as well.

Refer to Table 7-8. The Action column identifies the segmentation to take when quarantining hosts for the sample topology.

Isolation

Segmenting a network based on requestors' identity and posture is the primary purpose for deploying NAC. However, where you choose to enable NAC to enforce these polices is just as important. NAC should be enabled at the very edge of your network to detect and isolate a virus-infected host from any other network host other than hosts used for antivirus and remediation. If the NAD at the edge is not NAC capable, enable NAC at the closest NAC-capable NAD to the hosts. Be sure that NAC is not enabled at multiple NADs throughout the network; a host should only be validated and enforced by one PEP.

Enabling NAC in the distribution or core of a network can seem like a simpler approach to managing less NADs, but it does little to contain a virulent host located at the access layer. Enabling NAC at all network access edges is the recommended and most effective defense.

Default Network Access

When creating a NAC policy, a designer must understand the default security policy, which is the network access given to users and hosts that fail authorization. Users and hosts that fail authorization are considered unauthorized, which in the past were typically thought of as nonemployees, visiting guests, or hackers. With NAC, unauthorized users could even be legitimate users that, for some reason, failed authentication. This failure might have been caused by a failure in the authentication, authorization, and accounting (AAA) services because of scalability or availability. Regardless of the reason, users are left with the default network access that is provided by the NAD, and they can vary.

At the time of this writing, the following are the network access defaults that are determined by NAC assessment methods:

- **NAC-L2-802.1X**—No access is allowed.
- **NAC-L2-IP**—Whatever the default port or VLAN ACL allows is permitted.
- **NAC-L3-IP**—Whatever the default interface ACL allows is permitted.

Depending on the NAD and assessment method, administrators can configure the default access that satisfies your security access policy. Options are no access, full access, Internet-only access, or some customized set of network services.

Quarantine and Remediation Services

The following sections describe two methods that can be used for remediating quarantine devices: integrating patch management and using content engines for software updates.

Patch Management

Organizations need to have a patching strategy in place to ensure that software is kept up to date (healthy). When a host is detected out of compliance, it should be quarantined and forced to remediate. Describing your businesses patching process was a recommended step in the "Information Security Policy" section, earlier in this chapter.

Patching solutions vary by businesses. Some use a manual process, where a support technician walks over with software CDs and updates a machine. This method does not scale for large organizations. Instead, these organizations typically use an automated process, where patching is done in the background and is transparent to users. Either way, the result is to keep devices compliant and healthy.

A web server that contains all required software updates provided by a patch vendor is a scalable patch management approach. A dedicated patch management solution that integrates with NAC to automatically trigger patching upon network quarantine is an even better approach and is highly recommended. A list of third-party partners can be found at http://www.cisco.com/go/nac.

The following actions can be configured when a noncompliant host is detected:

- User notification by way of a Cisco Trust Agent pop-up dialog message. As a common courtesy to users, this action should always be provided whenever they are redirected.
- Browser auto-launch by way of Cisco Trust Agent to a specific URL. This URL could be to the patching web server or directly to the patching vendor's website.
- Browser URL redirection to specific URLs that could also be the same as those noted previously.
- Patch client triggered by network authorization or quarantine enforcement action.
- Patch client triggered by patch server notification upon network authorization.

You must understand the capabilities supported by the patch vendor used; features vary by NAC participants. Some can only provide posture credentials to Cisco Trust Agent, while others offer complete integration between ACS and their own posture validation servers, providing customized client notifications. When choosing a vendor, ask what Cisco NAC integration options it provides for the easiest and most efficient patching solution.

In Table 7-8 in the Action column, the designer identified the following steps to take to quarantine hosts in the sample topology:

- Send a pop-up "quarantine" message.
- Restrict access to the quarantine zones that include 192.169.1.2 or VLAN "Quarantine".
- Redirect to remediation website for patching at http://update.nac.cisco.com/quarantine.

Content Caching

Organizations are under pressure to provide updates or patches quickly to hosts, regardless of their location. As a result, these updates can be frequent. Adding this additional requirement to typical network traffic can cause network performance problems, especially at remote sites with limited WAN bandwidth for distributing software as well as limited IT resources to oversee the process.

A content engine can improve network performance and work-force productivity by delivering software intelligently, prepositioning files closer to the hosts that need them. Cisco Application and Content Networking System (ACNS) is a content-caching solution that is available in dedicated appliances or integrated in Cisco routers by way of a network module.

In addition to pushing security software updates to their servers and host devices, quarantine users can also be redirected to a local content engine for software updates.

The enforcement is similar to the familiar remediation process, where the device is automatically redirected to a web or remediation server; here it can obtain the required software to make the device compliant. However, when a content engine is deployed, it can be preloaded with the web or remediation server pages and software. When the URL redirect matches the content engine preloaded URLs, it serves as the source for the remediation web page instructions as well as the software library from which the update is downloaded. In this case, the cache engine is physically closer to the hosts that need the software updates than the web or remediation server that ACS had originally assigned. Users are unaware that the cache engine is servicing them. The result is that the user experience is faster and network bandwidth is conserved.

Refer to http://www.cisco.com for more information on this topic. Search for the document "Application and Content Networking System Solution for Network Admission Control Integrated Within a Cisco Router." It provides a configuration example. The steps are the same when using the dedicated ACNS appliance.

NAC Agentless Host (NAH) Definition

What is your plan for managing NAHs? Earlier, the NAHs were identified in Table 7-4. The options for exempting agentless hosts vary by NAD and by their NAC methods, which are described in Table 7-12.

Table 7-12 *Options for Exempting NAHs*

Component	Method	Pros	Cons
NAD	CDP using NAC-L2-802.1X	Allows detection and exemption of Cisco IP Phones Can be placed into voice VLAN for NAC exemption	Not available for third-party IP phones
NAD	Static MAC address Use with: NAC-L2-IP NAC-L3-IP (support begins with IOS Release 12.4.6T)	Single MAC address MAC wildcard	First hop only for routers Maintains static list Does not scale well
NAD	Static IP address Use with NAC-L2-IP and NAC-L3-IP	Single IP address IP wildcard	Maintains static list Does not scale well
ACS	Network access profile filter	Centralized list of MAC/IP wildcards Scales better than static list at NAD	Maintains static list

Table 7-12   *Options for Exempting NAHs (Continued)*

Component	Method	Pros	Cons
ACS	MAB group mapping Use with NAC-L2-802.1X	Centralized list of MAC/IP wildcards Provides Guest-VLAN and failed authentication VLAN Scales better than static list at NAD	Maintains static list
Audit server	Automatically trigger audits with: NAC-L2-IP NAC-L3-IP (support begins with IOS Release 12.4.6T)	Scales best	Requires additional component

Use the worksheet in Table 7-4 to describe the host, its location, and the NAD servicing it as well as the method used to exempt the host. Preconfiguring NAHs can be accomplished with a static single entry or a wildcard entry for MACs sharing a common OUI from a specific vendor. The most scalable option is to use an external audit server that can automatically scan an NAH and determine compliance.

Solution Scalability and High-Availability Considerations

Most modern networks have some form of AAA implemented to control who can access the network and what these users can do. Traditional AAA challenges typically occur for ingress traffic at VPN or wireless access points. Most other user authentication occurs from a separate back-end directory services database.

With NAC, every host that attempts access can now require a successful authentication prior to network access. After they are on the network, hosts must continue to pass posture revalidation checks to stay on the network. Using NAC increases demands on an organization's AAA infrastructure. Designers must plan for the following:

- Are the AAA policy servers scaled for the increased demand?
- Does the design of the network provide a high-availability service, especially if the AAA policy is not reachable?

Failure to increase both scalability and availability of the AAA infrastructure can result in legitimate users and healthy hosts being unable to access the network, making them nonproductive. The following sections describe the capabilities that exist at the time of this writing that should be considered when designing for NAC.

Scalability Considerations

Many factors must be considered when deploying NAC. While individual factors might not cause significant impacts, the combination of any of these can seriously affect the performance of the ACS server as well as user productivity in a NAC deployment.

All requests for NAC must be authorized by ACS, which, at the time of this writing, is the only AAA server that currently supports NAC. For this reason, ACS is the most important component in the framework architecture to size and scale when designing a NAC solution. You need to be aware of the following factors when designing for NAC:

- Location and number of NADs and ACSs within the network
- Number of hosts and users
- NAC policy complexity and organization
- Protocol authorization rates
- NAC timers in ACSs and NADs
- Replication and synchronization of ACS databases
- Cisco Secure ACS redundancy

Location and Number of NADs and ACSs Within the Network

In a large network, NADs can be dispersed geographically with a variety of speeds and feeds. When NAC is implemented, the NADs must communicate with the NAC policy server (ACS). In the past, organizations might have had ACS in centralized locations because AAA might have been used for only network access for some users and devices, and local store directories for the majority of user authorization. With NAC, all authorizations must go through the AAA policy server. Now, more AAA policy server(s) might need to be installed as well as spread out geographically to accommodate this wider use.

Also, the ACS database is not unlimited. Maximum configuration entries exist; increasing memory in the ACS servers can expand some entries. For example, ACS 4.0 has a maximum of 50,000 addressable entries for NADs. This might seem like a large number, but large enterprises can exceed this. Remember that NADs can be switches, routers, wireless access points, and VPN concentrators. Some integrated network devices, such as Integrated Services Routers, have a combination of these NAD functionalities in one device (router, switch, and access point) that can use different policies that depend on their access function. To allow scaling large numbers of NADs, rather than using the NAD individual IP addresses, instead use ranges of IP addresses. Even better practice is to use a single wildcard entry (*.*.*.*) to avoid having to continually update the list of NADs in the ACS database.

Number of Hosts and Users

A designer needs to determine the total number of users and hosts that connect to your network. This provides an initial count for the minimum number of authorizations per day that you can expect on your AAA servers. When counting, keep in mind which authorizations your security policy dictates:

- **Identity only**—Add one authorization check per user.

- **Posture only**—Add one authorization check.

- **Posture and identity**—This can be done in one authorization check (NAC-L2-802.1X) or two authorization checks (NAC-L2-IP or NAC-L3-IP).

Also, consider user behavior throughout the day because some users connect multiple times through different access modes. For example, in a single day, a user might begin from home connecting using a VPN, come into the office and connect to the LAN, go to meetings and roam wirelessly, return to his desk, possibly restart his computer, and then end the day by checking e-mail at home using the VPN. Sound familiar? Many of these events trigger a new authorization process.

Users who reboot or roam should average out to a normal load on the AAA services because these events are done randomly through the day. Problems can occur when too many users attempt to connect simultaneously or within a short period of time. An example is when everyone turns on his computer at the start of the work day or when everyone is coming back online at the same time following a power outage. In the planning process, identify the local work schedule. Maybe the solution is to use multiple AAA servers to service different areas of the network or incorporate load balancing at strategic network points. The power outage scenario is much harder to control and can occur infrequently, where the cost of implementing for this worst-case scenario might be an acceptable risk identified in your organization's security policy.

Designers should be mindful of the NAD's capacity and the amount of hosts it can service as well. For example, when using NAC-L3-IP with routers with NAC enabled, additional memory requirements must be considered; 6 KB of memory is used for each successfully authenticated host (healthy, quarantine, infected, and so on) in the form of a dynamic ACL. In addition, each downloadable ACL from ACS uses an additional 0.8 KB of memory. This consideration is especially important for legacy routers with a fixed amount of memory. Use the **show memory statistics** IOS command to view IOS NAD memory usage prior to NAC implementation to get a good baseline of normal network use.

When sizing a AAA infrastructure, the number of users, average daily authorizations per user, and NAD capacity need to be taken into consideration.

NAC Policy Complexity and Organization

The NAC policy within ACS is organized by rules and conditions (attribute and values). Larger policies take more time to evaluate versus smaller policies. Over time, some rules with old conditions that are now included into new software should be removed. This should be part of your Operate and Optimize lifecycle phases. An example is where older software patches can now be included with new software patches or software versions. Because the new software version or patch is now a healthy requirement, why also have ACS look independently for the old patch? As more rules and conditions are added to the NAC policy, the time in which ACS must evaluate also increases. Then multiply that for every host being checked.

The order in which rules are checked can also have an impact on the performance. For example, if ACS checks first for noncompliant hosts and most hosts are compliant, ACS must process many more rules than if the rules are ordered to check for a healthy state first. This order example might have been relevant for the initial deployment, but over time, your policy and rules might need to be adjusted and reordered to grow with your organization's NAC use.

Protocol Authorization Rates

You have many network authentication protocols to choose from, ranging from lower security and/or less features to higher security and/or more features. Higher security and/or features can affect the rate of authentication. An example is the use of an encrypted tunnel that requires many round-trip communications and negotiations, lengthening the time it takes for the overall authentication process. With mixed NADs, different protocols are most likely used, so mileage can vary in the authorization rates. Part of the transactions per second (TPS) calculation covered later includes using the protocol authorization rate to determine the number of ACS servers required for your business's deployment.

NAC Timers in ACS and NADs

Timers exist within the NADs as well as within ACS for various NAC processes. As it works today, each timer has a global default value in the Cisco IOS of each NAD. These global IOS values can be edited using an IOS configuration command. The NAC timers can also be configured in ACS on a per-session basis; when used, the ACS timer overrides the NAD's timer. This means that ACS timers take precedence over NAD timers.

When setting timers, short times are not always good, so pay attention to each timer. Setting them incorrectly could impact the NAD's performance by requiring too much control plane overhead from NAC. An example is setting all host postures to be revalidated every few minutes, when normally this is not needed. The good news is that most NAC timer default values work well and can serve as good initial guides. Then over time, you can adjust them as needed and monitor the results.

The following describes key NAC timers that are configured in ACS under the RADIUS Authorization Components (RACs) screen. RADIUS attributes and timers can be specified and then applied to NADs during the network authorization process as follows:

- **Session timeouts/revalidations**

  In ACS, the session timeout (RADIUS attribute 27) triggers a complete NAC revalidation of user and/or host credentials. This is the most critical timer affecting AAA scalability because it controls the revalidation period for every host in the network.

  However, the similar-function timer in NADs affects only those hosts it services. An example of a NAD revalidation timer in IOS is **eou timeout revalidation**, which defaults to 36000 seconds (10 hours).

- **Extensible Authentication Protocol over User Datagram Protocol (EoU) status queries**

  The EoU protocol challenges hosts for their posture over Layer 3 connections. In between revalidations from the RADIUS session timeout, the NAD initiates a status query to periodically poll the authorized host and verify that it is still the same host. In addition, the NAD requests Cisco Trust Agent to verify the host posture is still the same since the last revalidation. If anything has changed, revalidation is initiated for that host. Fortunately, status queries are lightweight operations and have little impact on NAD performance. A status query by the NAD reduces frequent revalidations by ACS, which in turn improves overall solution performance. An example of a NAD status query timer is **eou timeout status-query**, which defaults to 300 seconds.

- **Hold period**

  NAHs that fail authentication with EoU are left with the default interface network access. They are not challenged again until this hold timer expires. In the meantime, the hosts are in a holding pattern, being ignored even if they repeatedly try to reinitiate authorization. An example of a NAD hold timer is **eou timeout hold-period**, which defaults to 180 seconds.

Replication and Synchronization of ACS Databases

Replication of the NAC policy is crucial for scaling policy changes. Initial policy creation can be a lengthy process. As a result, we recommend that you use the ACS replication features, providing a centralized policy change that is replicated throughout the business in a timely, consistent matter. This is especially important when the policy is updated to combat an impending known viral outbreak. Refer to the Cisco Secure ACS Configuration Guide for instructions on setting up database replication and synchronization.

Cisco Secure ACS Redundancy

To improve the performance of ACS in a NAC environment, ACS servers can be load-balanced with an external device such as a Cisco Content Services Switch (CSS) or Cisco Content Switch Module (CSM). A secondary but equally important benefit is to provide a AAA failover in the event that the primary AAA server is not reachable by the NADs. Both of these topics are described in detail in the "High-Availability Considerations" section, later in this chapter.

Calculations

When it comes to NAC scalability, most organizations are most interested in the number of authorizations that can be completed within a period of time and how this can impact user productivity.

The measurement of authorizations is typically rated in transactions per second (TPS). Many factors exist when determining the TPS. Factors include host and user factors, ACS factors, and back-end authentication server latency, such as Active Directory database lookups.

The following calculations can be used as guidelines for how to scale the Cisco Secure ACS for a Cisco NAC deployment at the time of this writing. The number of ACSs required to support a specific size of user database depends on many factors. In our calculations, we assume a minimum of one transaction per day per user as an average, but your transactions per day can vary.

NOTE   The material in the remainder of this section relies heavily on the content in "Network Admission Control Framework Deployment Guide," located at http://www.cisco.com/application/pdf/en/us/guest/netsol/ns617/c649/cdccont_0900aecd80417226.pdf.

For your calculations, you also need to increase the average number of transactions to account for variables including the number of session/revalidation timers per day as well as daily user behaviors. These considerations include the following:

- Number of revalidations that can be calculated by the RADIUS session timeout value.
- Number of daily VPN remote-access logins.
- Number of multihomed accesses on wired and wireless network interfaces.
- Number of daily users roaming wirelessly.
- Number of daily user restarts because of patches and updates, or general occasional problems with operating systems and applications.

- Average number of users working with multiple devices, such as desktops, laptops, PDAs, and so on.

- Average daily number of host posture changes. This can be relative to the number of updates and software policy changes.

Counting the previously listed timers and behaviors, you can now approximate the number of transactions per day with the following formula:

$$\text{Transactions\_per\_Day} = \text{Transactions\_per\_User\_per\_Day} * \text{Number\_of\_Users}$$

Now convert this to TPS by dividing by the number of seconds in a day using the following formula:

$$\text{Transactions\_per\_Second} = \text{Transactions\_per\_Day} / (24 * 60 * 60)$$

From this average transaction rate and the ACS authentication protocol performance numbers, you can estimate the minimum number of ACS servers needed to support the amount of users with the given TPS. Use the following formula:

$$\text{No. of ACS} = \text{Transactions\_per\_Second} / \text{ACS\_Protocol\_Authorization\_Rate}$$

The number of ACSs is an absolute minimum because it is an average for all times of the day. This assumes a continual 100 percent load, which is not realistic. This number does not take into account server downtime, which could be for policy replication, maintenance, and an occasional link going down. You should divide the final ACS count by 0.4 to account for some of this unknown until actual rates and loads can be verified by testing.

High-Availability Considerations

When a AAA request fails to receive a response from any of the AAA servers in a NAD's method list, the AAA client typically is designed to fall back to a local policy. With NAC, the NAD's local database cannot act as a policy server for posture decisions at the time of this writing. If the ACS policy server(s) are not reachable, authentication fails. The AAA survivability actions taken by NADs vary as follows:

- Failed authentication results vary. For NAC-L2-IP and NAC-L3-IP, failed authentication uses the default interface ACL to dictate network access. In 802.1X, failed authentication by default denies network access.

- Some NADs have a AAA fail open or fail closed option. This allows an administrator to choose the AAA failed condition: access to everything or no access.

Check the AAA capability for your NADs and be sure to look at recent software release notes on http://www.cisco.com. A number of feature enhancements have been added to AAA survivability, and the list keeps growing.

At the time of this writing, you can use three other methods to increase AAA availability, which include implementing the following:

- IOS RADIUS server failover
- External posture validation server failover
- Load balancing among the ACS servers

IOS RADIUS Server Failover

IOS NADs can be configured for AAA server failover to multiple RADIUS authentication servers. In the IOS NAD, configure a group or list of AAA servers in the search order in the event that a AAA server is not reachable. If a RADIUS server fails, the NAD automatically, after a timeout period, contacts the next RADIUS server to authenticate the clients. As a last resort, the local database can also be configured to allow users and devices to authenticate, but it cannot act as a posture validation server.

Timeout periods can be configured using the following commands:

- **timeout**—Number of seconds a NAD waits for a reply to a RADIUS request before retransmitting the request. Default is five seconds.
- **retransmit**—Number of times a RADIUS request is resent to a server. Default is three times.
- **deadtime**—Number of minutes a RADIUS server is not responding to authentication requests before it is passed over for authentication requests. Default is ten minutes.

To minimize the time required to fail over from one ACS server to another, values should be short enough to initiate failover but not so short that it causes the NAD to time out unnecessarily and mark a server as nonresponsive. Testing has shown that the default values perform well for NAC during ACS failover.

To further reduce the time in an ACS failover, tests using the following timeout values also worked well:

- Timeout to three seconds
- Retransmit to two times
- Deadtime to two minutes

These settings allow a NAD six seconds before deciding that an ACS server is nonresponsive, moving to the next server in the list for AAA service. The deadtime timer provides two minutes for a nonresponsive ACS server to recover or restart before tagged as being dead.

For more information on AAA RADIUS failover configuration options, refer to http://www.cisco.com/en/US/partner/products/ps6350/products_configuration_guide_chapter09186a00804ec61e.html#wp1001206.

External Posture Validation Server Failover

When an external posture validation server (PVS) is configured in the NAC policy, ACS communicates and sends the vendor's posture credentials to the PVS for evaluation. If ACS cannot communicate with the PVS or any of the backup PVS servers, authentication fails for all hosts that send that vendor's credentials. This results in the default interface ACL dictating the access policy, which is typically no network access for most traffic.

To increase availability when using external PVSs, use a primary and secondary PVS to allow failover options. The external PVS is configured in ACS at the External Policies screen; it allows configuration of multiple servers. The primary server is the first PVS that ACS sends the posture credentials to. If ACS cannot communicate with the primary server, it looks to the secondary server listed in the external policy.

Load Balancing Cisco Secure ACS

Configuring for ACS server load balancing improves the performance of ACS, as well as provides failover. Load balancing can be configured in one of two ways:

- IOS server load balancing (SLB)
- Load balancing and failover through the use of a CSS or a CSM

Load Balancing Using IOS

IOS RADIUS SLB is an IOS feature available on the 7200 router and the 6500 series switch platforms at the time of this writing. The ACS servers are placed in a AAA RADIUS server group the same way as described in the previous section. This feature can provide performance optimization for the AAA server group by using a load-balancing algorithm.

Another significant advantage of the IOS SLB for RADIUS load balancing is that the load can be directed based on the calling station ID. This can be beneficial in two ways. First, a more even hash result spreads the load better than a source IP method. Second, all the RADIUS accounting records for a particular session always go to the specified RADIUS server; hence, you don't have to reconcile start/stop records on an accounting reporting server.

When using SLB with NAC, we recommend that you use the Weighted Least Connections option versus the Weighted Round Robin default. Making this selection load-balances both the RADIUS authentication and RADIUS accounting traffic.

For more information, refer to http://www.cisco.com/application/pdf/en/us/guest/netsol/ns377/c649/cdccont_0900aecd800eb95f.pdf.

Load Balancing Using a Content Services Switch

A network load-balancing device, such as the Cisco Content Services Switch (CSS) or Cisco Content Switch Module (CSM), can also be used to balance authentication requests between the NAC authentication devices and the ACS servers.

As shown in Figure 7-6, the NAD points to a virtual IP address. In this example, 192.168.2.10 is configured on the CSS or CSM to represent a virtual ACS server. Each of the AAA servers is placed in a AAA farm and referenced in the virtual server.

Figure 7-6 *RADIUS Load Balancing Using Content Services Switch*

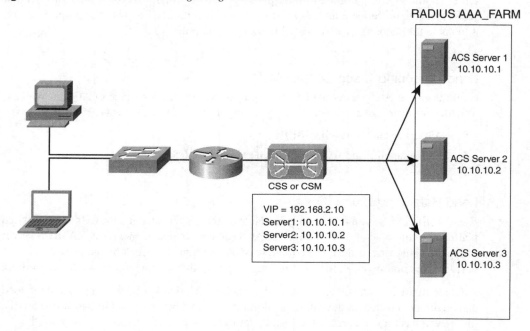

<table>
<tr><td>NOTE</td><td>While you can configure failover between sites, the best option is to use a local ACS server to fail over to on the same LAN. This provides the fastest and most reliable authentication for the local network.

For more information, refer to http://www.cisco.com/application/pdf/en/us/guest/netsol/ns377/c649/cdccont_0900aecd800eb95e.pdf.</td></tr>
</table>

Implementation Phase

Thorough information on the implementation phase requires a book within itself, and *Cisco Network Admission Control, Volume II: NAC Framework Deployment and Troubleshooting* provides detailed information and examples.

The following sections look at the implementation phase from a planning perspective, so when the implementation phase begins, plans and steps are already in place.

Completing the implementation phase requires following a migration strategy. The following is a quick summary of the high-level installation tasks and the suggested sequence that might make up a migration strategy:

1 Upgrade or install and configure the NAC policy server (ACS).

2 Upgrade or install and configure the external posture validation server(s).

3 Upgrade or install client(s) on hosts.

4 Upgrade or install and configure Cisco IOS NADs for NAC. Enabling NAC on the NADs should be the last step, because when enabled, NAC is then operational for those devices it services. If the other tasks were not completed, users will most likely have no network access.

5 (Optional) Upgrade or install and configure the NAC management console.

6 Verify operation with no unexpected outages.

NOTE   This installation task summary assumes a working network is in place and NAC functionality will be added.

Before going through the implementation phase, review the integration strategy and migration strategy created during the planning phase. Then tweak as necessary. It should have described the steps and requirements carried out in the implementation phase.

Staging Implementation

The migration strategy should identify whether multiple, staged phases are needed for implementation. Consider whether NAC is to be implemented in a monitor mode first, to gain confidence while not impacting users, and then follow up by increasing live implementation. Or, a section of the network could pilot the real policy for a determined amount of time.

The following section describes an example of a migration strategy for implementing phase one of our sample network shown in Figure 7-3.

Phase 1 Migration Strategy Sample

NAC will initially be deployed in a monitor mode to a small section of the HQ network (User A subnet) in the phase one implementation. NAC implementation will be done in a monitor mode only so that we can validate our Phase 1 design, and it serves as a proof of concept to help the NAC team gain an understanding of NAC compliance as well as to identify and record NAHs. The support team will also gain experience with NAC and the monitoring tools.

The NAC team will use five business weeks to evaluate implementation for a small segment of the HQ network. After success is determined and acceptance received by NetOps and the Support group, monitor mode will be enabled for all other HQ local user access for five additional weeks of evaluation.

If monitor mode is determined to be successful and acceptance is received by NetOps and the Support group, all other NAC implementation phase one components will be enabled and evaluated for three more weeks.

After monitoring is fully in use and information is gathered, such as agentless host and current policy conformance, a decision will be made on when to move forward with the enforcement mode.The NAC team, NetOps, and the Support group will collectively make a decision on whether to proceed with enabling enforcement at the HQ.

This is our migration plan.

Phase 1—Step 1

The following requirements *must be completed* in Step 1:

- NAC team sends e-mail to all HQ users notifying them of the upcoming deployment of NAC and describing how to get ready. Fliers will be posted on all internal bulletin boards to provided secondary notification.

- Desktop Services group uses CSA with Cisco Trust Agent bundled and will deploy to all corporate-provided hosts and servers by way of the corporate current patch management system. These updates are also made available by Desktop Services to the internal software download center.

- HQ's Catalyst 3550 access switch servicing the User A subnet has been upgraded by NetOps and is running the currently recommended standard IOS version.

- Cisco Secure ACS servers are in service running software version 4.1 by SecOps.

- Host antivirus policy server is in service running software version 8.0 (NAC-enabled) by Desktop Services.

- SecOps has the Cisco Works Security Information Management Solution (CW-SIMS) management system in service running the software version (NAC-enabled) for administration and monitoring.

- NAC support plan is delivered and accepted by Support Operations team(s).
- Support training is complete for Support Operations teams that will support and troubleshoot network access problems where NAC is to be enabled.

Phase 1—Step 2

After Step 1 conditions are met, monitor mode can begin to the User A subnet. Configuration begins in ACS and the NAD by the NAC team. In this mode, all endpoints are granted network access regardless of host posture or NAH status. Cisco Trust Agent message notifications are disabled in ACS, so even if the host is identified as quarantined, this will be transparent to users.

The monitor mode should satisfy the following objectives:

- NAC team is to gain an understanding of the current local compliance levels before policy enforcement begins. Monitor "healthy" state is assigned to devices with current OS and antivirus updates, and with host firewall enabled. Devices not compliant will be assigned "quarantine" state (which is only used at this time for tracking noncompliance).
- The operations and support teams should gain confidence with NAC in the monitoring mode and become familiar with the new management tools before enforcement mode begins.
- NAC team is to verify that known NAHs bypass posture validation and identify unknown/unmanaged NAHs that should also be exempted prior to the enforcement phase. The NAC team will use this information to inform NetOps and SecOps of unmanaged devices. After approval is granted for each device, the NAC team will update the NAH Exemption Worksheet and edit exception tables, adding only permitable MAC addresses for devices that are to be exempted statically.

NOTE   Tools are available from NAC partners to create MAC exceptions automatically and also be stored in an NAH database. Vendors that provide this capability are Great Bay Software and Altiris.

The following tasks *must be completed* in Step 2:

- NAC team is to notify NetOps, SecOps, Desktop Services, and Support teams that monitor mode is being enabled. No support burden is expected from monitor mode, but all groups must be aware the NAC implementation has begun.

- NAC team is to enable monitor mode for the User A subnet. Allow five working weeks to expose potential problems with monitor mode. NAC team will check with the NetOps, SecOps, Desktop Services, and Support teams every four hours during the business day on weeks one and two to verify no outages or user complaints. Weeks three through five will use daily follow ups.

NOTE This example uses five weeks to evaluate the monitor mode. Choose a time frame that is suitable for your deployment.

- NAC team reviews the rate of help desk calls, identifies NAC-specific activity, and compares to pre-NAC call levels. A NAC-related report is generated and identifies and refines the NAC deployment process. Improvements will be implemented and evaluated at the next deployment and should help reduce the amount of issues and calls.
- NAC team compares NAD and ACS logs with CW-SIMS reports to gain confidence that the authentication and compliance/noncompliance reports are capturing information as expected.
- NAC team uses NAD and ACS logs to identify NAHs that should be added to the NAC Exemption Worksheet shown in Table 7-4.

NOTE Some people prefer to use an automatic NAH tool to create MAC exceptions versus the manual, time-consuming approach of identifying and configuring each host as previously mentioned.

If the NAC, NetOps, SecOps, Desktop Services, and Support teams are confident with Step 2 implementation, proceed to Step 3 and implement monitor mode to all HQ user access subnets.

Phase 1—Step 3
The following tasks *must be completed* in Step 3:

- NAC team must notify the support teams that monitor mode is being enabled for all HQ local user access subnets.
- NAC team implements monitor mode for User B and wireless access point subnets.

NOTE   Some people can choose to move directly to the policy enforcement phase or might want to mix enforcement for previously monitored areas and monitor for new NAC areas. At the time of this writing, when Cisco Trust Agent message notifications are enabled in ACS, all users whose devices are NAC enabled and whose posture requires a pop-up message will receive the same message, regardless of whether they are in monitor or enforcement mode. For example, if noncompliant devices are deemed to have a posture of "quarantine" and a pop-up message is assigned to the quarantine group, all quarantine postures will receive the pop-ups regardless of whether they are configured for monitor mode. This could present both a communications and a support challenge because NAC suddenly becomes visible to new users in monitor mode. That is why, in this example, we stayed with monitor mode until we felt confident with the deployment before going to enforcement mode with the message notifications.

- Allow five working weeks to expose potential problems with monitor mode for all users. NAC team checks with the NetOps, SecOps, Desktop Services, and Support teams and verifies no unexpected outages or increased user complaints.

NOTE   This example uses five weeks for evaluating the monitor mode. Choose a time frame that is suitable for your deployment.

- NAC team reviews the rate of help desk calls, identifies NAC-specific activity, and compares the activity to pre-NAC call levels. A NAC-related report is generated and identifies and refines the NAC deployment process. Improvements will be implemented and evaluated at the next deployment and should help reduce the amount of issues and calls.
- NAC team compares the ACS logs with CW-SIMS reports to gain confidence that the authentication and compliance/noncompliance reports are capturing information as expected and to identify NAHs that should be exempted from the posturing process.
- If the NAC, NetOps, SecOps, Desktop Services, and Support teams are confident with Step 3, implementation gets approval to proceed to Step 4 to enable the remaining NAC components.

Phase 1—Step 4

In our example, this is the last monitor-mode step, adding the following mandatory functionality and gaining confidence with all Phase 1 components before the enforcement mode:

- Trending and historical reporting are in service by SecOps.
- Remediation server and redirection instructions for users are in place by Desktop Services.
- NAC agentless host auditing server is in place by the NAC team. This is to be used for dynamically detecting agentless hosts.

NOTE   Before enforcement is enabled, you should have a solution in place to deal with NAHs. Some customers prefer to use the auditing server in the first step rather than waiting until Step 4 as in this example.

TIP   Adding more NAC components as the migration progresses eases troubleshooting when the solution is not working as expected. This slower process also allows for support personnel to get familiar with new equipment and tools gradually versus many at one time.

- Desktop Services sends an e-mail communication to users reminding them of the NAC implementation, describing how this affects them and indicating what to expect.
- NAC team has turned on Cisco Trust Agent pop-up message notification in ACS. It is displayed to all hosts that are not compliant to provide them with instructions on how to become compliant. In the pop-up, also include the date when compliance is required and issue a reminder that after this date, network access is denied until compliance is observed.
- This last monitoring will occur for three working weeks using all NAC components.
- NAC teams gathers and analyzes policy compliance reports for the HQ site. Consult with the NetOps, SecOps, Desktop Services, and Support teams to get approval to move forward with enforcement mode. Make sure that they are comfortable with NAC and management tools before enforcement is turned on.
- All teams make a joint decision on the time frame to migrate from monitor to enforcement mode at all HQ local user access subnets.

Phase 1—Step 5
The following tasks are completed in Step 5:

- NAC team notifies NetOps, SecOps, Desktop Services, and Support teams that enforcement mode is being enabled for all HQ local user access subnets at least 48 business hours in advance.

- Desktop Services sends a final e-mail communication to users reminding them of the NAC implementation and describing how the enforcement phase affects them.
- NAC team alters the NAC policy from monitor mode to enforcement mode.
- For five business weeks following the transition to enforcement, the NAC team will continue monitoring NAC posture data closely through the monitoring and reporting interfaces. The NAC team is to work closely with the operations and support teams to understand the volume and type of support-level issues experienced.

Migration Strategy Summary

Use the preceding example as a guide when creating your migration strategy. The strategy should be written for the impending implementation phase versus trying to describe all steps in all phases.

At the end of first implementation phase, have all the teams that worked together meet and document lessons learned; these lessons can be included in the next implementation phase's migration strategy.

Regardless of how many phases your implementation will have, you should initially deploy with a loose policy, editing and tightening over time. If you instead begin with a restrictive policy, when implemented, it could cause a large disruption to the users and workplace and be considered a negative return on investment.

The less restrictive approach was used in this migration strategy example, starting with monitor mode. Even though users might receive numerous messages for preparation, many will ignore the messages. A tight initial policy could result in a massive loss of user productivity, and the help desk and support groups could get overwhelmed at cutover. To prepare users in advance, provide communication to educate them on what is about to change, including what is in it for them if they do or don't comply.

Communication to Users

Most organizations communicate by way of e-mail at least a few weeks prior to enforcement. The following message can serve as a model for your user communication:

ATTENTION ALL USERS,

Subject: Changes to your network access are coming soon with the implementation of Network Admission Control (NAC)

On <Date>, your location will begin enforcing a stronger corporate network access security policy (NAC) on all devices. This change will help us combat worms and viruses.

NAC verifies that your computer software is compliant with our security policy before giving you access to our network. Computers that fail to meet the defined security policies are considered to be noncompliant and will *not* be able to access the network. Noncompliant computers will be quarantined with no network access until they are remediated and found compliant.

What do I need to do?

To ensure that you comply with the new security policies, please determine your computer type and click the appropriate link that follows for actions *you* have to take by <Date> to continue gaining to access the network:

- I am a Windows or Red Hat Linux user. My device is a corporate asset and is managed by corporate-receiving updates.
- I am a Windows or Red Hat Linux user. My device is a corporate asset but is not managed by corporate and is not receiving updates.
- I am a Windows or Red Hat Linux user, but my device is not a corporate asset.
- All other users.

What does this mean to you?

When any device connects to the network, the device security state will be evaluated and considered either Healthy or Quarantine. All corporate-owned and -managed Windows and Red Hat Linux devices that get regular updates are considered healthy and will have normal access to the network. No visible indicators of a healthy status will exist; it is business as usual, requiring no action from healthy devices.

After implementation at your site, noncompliant Windows and Red Hat Linux devices will display a pop-up message stating that these users have been quarantined. If your device is noncompliant, you can launch a browser and be automatically redirected to an internal quarantine zone. The quarantine zone is the *only* area that you can access, and it is where you can obtain the latest software versions. After downloading the latest software, you will regain full network access.

All other devices that connect to the network must be registered using the <state your method here> to continue to access the network. Registration must occur before <Date>.

Please contact <state here> if you require assistance or have questions.

To learn more about this new security implementation, please visit the Desktop Services website at <URL>.

Please ensure that you have updated or installed the necessary software on your device by going to the appropriate link by <Date> to continue your network service.

Thank you for your immediate attention.

This may appear to be a lengthy message, but it covers what the user needs to know, how the user can make the correct determination, and how the user can comply prior to implementation.

Operation and Optimization Phases

As discussed in the section "Policy Definition," earlier in this chapter, we highly recommend an incremental policy implementation.

The operation and optimization phases are where operations personnel monitor the levels of compliance while also determining the impact on user productivity. Different tools are available for this.

This is where tightening the policy, maybe reordering the policy, and fine-tuning NAC timers can be done to increase security while improving performance.

If your NAC implementation is phased in, use the lessons learned and the tweaking of the solution as inputs into the next design cycle of your NAC deployment.

Refer to Volume II of this book for more details about the operation and optimization phases.

Summary

You have many things to consider when deploying a NAC solution into your network. If the solution is not carefully planned and designed, when implemented, it could cause more disruption to your users than from the malicious activity you are intending to protect them from. After the solution is implemented, the work is not done. You must be prepared to monitor its effectiveness and tweak the policies and rules to stay current with the latest updates that comprise your admission policy.

Six NAC lifecycle phases exist: prepare, plan, design, implement, operate, and optimize. These are summarized as follows:

- Preparation tasks include identifying security policies and staff roles and responsibilities. You then use them as inputs when creating NAC objectives and policies.

- Planning tasks include describing your organization's NAC objectives and prioritizing them. You then take inventory of your network infrastructure, identifying the policy servers and the NADs that act as policy enforcement points. Next, develop and document the following NAC plans: how to test your proof of concept, implementation strategy, and migration strategy. You should also determine the NAC implementation costs.

- Design tasks include creating definitions for NAC admission policy, credentials, and identity. You then define how the network will be segmented for isolation and how noncompliant hosts can remediate. Also define how NAHs get handled. Size your network so that it can scale and be highly available for the additional requirements that NAC introduces.

- Implementation is where the network infrastructure is installed, upgraded, and then configured for NAC. Additional devices, such as policy servers, external posture validation servers, audit servers, remediation servers, and patch management services, can be added to the network infrastructure, providing additional NAC capabilities.

- Operation and optimization comprise daily tasks, such as managing the various components and updating the policy to stay current with new software updates and patches. You also monitor the levels of compliance and tweak NAC timers and policies to reduce the impact on user productivity while strengthening policy rules and enforcement capabilities.

Each NAC lifecycle phase has unique tasks that, when completed, are prerequisites to tasks identified in subsequent phases. If one lifecycle phase is skipped to save time, the result is often more time spent fixing something that was overlooked. Each phase plays an important role in rolling out a successful NAC implementation. The best advice from lessons learned is to spend the time up-front preparing and planning before designing and implementing. If this is not done correctly, the result could cause a disruption to user productivity in the operation phase.

Resources

"Network Admission Control Framework Deployment Guide," http://www.cisco.com/ application/pdf/en/us/guest/netsol/ns617/c649/cdccont_0900aecd80417226.pdf.

"Network Admission Control Release Notes Phase 2," http://wwwin.cisco.com/stg/nac/ #techdocs.

"Technology Application Support External Security Posture Assessment" data sheet, http://www.cisco.com/application/pdf/en/us/guest/products/ps5619/c1262/ cdccont_0900aecd800ce539.pdf.

Review Questions

You can find the answers to the review questions in Appendix A.

1 Which lifecycle phase should security administration and management roles and their responsibilities be defined?

   a Operate

   b Plan

   c Prepare

   d Design

2 You want to implement posture and identity to hosts connected to hubs. What are your options? Hint: Refer to the NAC Framework Phase 2 Implementation Decision Tree in Figures 7-4 and 7-5.

   a You cannot use hubs for any type of NAC detection; replace hubs with Cisco switches.

   b Only posture can be accomplished through the use of hubs.

   c Use an 802.1X supplicant for this NAC method.

   d Hubs work fine with NAC.

3 Match the following NADs to the NAC method.

a NAC-L2-802.1X

b NAC-L2-IP

c NAC-L3-IP

d Can't be done

__ Router with posture and identity

__ Router with posture only

__ Switch with posture and identity

__ Switch with posture only

4 Match the definition with its NAC policy type.

a MAC exception

b Group membership

c Who, what, when, how

d Software update not current

__ Identity definition

__ Policy definition

__ Credential definition

__ NAH definition

5 Three decision elements can determine who has network access. Host posture is one; what are the other two?

6 Using the Host Credential Worksheet sample in Table 7-8, what posture is assigned to a Windows XP user with the following features:

Cisco Trust Agent version 2.1 is present and enabled.

Antivirus version 8.0 is present and enabled.

CSA version 4.5 is present but disabled.

a Healthy

b Checkup

c Quarantine

d Infected

7 Using the Host Credential Worksheet sample in Table 7-8, how many action(s) are assigned to a Windows XP user with the following features:

Cisco Trust Agent version 2.1 is present and enabled.

Antivirus version 8.0 is present and running patch version 11.

CSA version 4.5 is present and enabled.

    a Three: message notification, URL redirect, and enforcement ACL/VLAN

    b Two: message notification and enforcement ACL/VLAN

    c One: message notification only

    d None, business as usual

8 What is the default network access for users who fail authorization using NAC-L2-802.1X?

    a No access

    b No restriction

    c Access that is defined by ACL

    d Access that is defined by VLAN

9 Which NAC component allows configuration for NAH exemption using the MAC Authentication Bypass (MAB) feature?

    a Static list at any Layer 2 NAD

    b Static list at any Layer 3 NAD

    c Static centralized list at ACS

10 Which of the following timers takes precedence for revalidation?

    a Always the NAD-EoU timeout revalidation period

    b Always the ACS—Session Timeout period

    c The shorter time period of the two, regardless of NAD/ACS

    d The longer time period of the two, regardless of NAD/ACS

11 What happens when a host using a vendor's security application is attempting network access, but all the external policy server(s) are not reachable, so that specific vendor's host credential cannot be checked?

    a ACS will not use that specific credential when determining the system posture token.

    b The posture token for that credential will be assigned "unknown" by ACS.

    c The host fails authentication and uses the default network access, which could be no access.

12 What method(s) should be considered for increasing AAA availability, which is extremely important in NAC implementations?

    a Configuring IOS RADIUS failover

    b Using multiple external policy validation servers and configuring the primary and backup servers in ACS NAC policy

    c Configuring IOS server for load balancing among the ACS servers

    d Using load balancing and failover through the use of a Content Services Switch or module

    e All of the above

    f Only a, b, and c

13 Which of the following implementation tasks should be done last?

    a ACS policy enabled

    b External PVS policy enabled

    c NAD enabled for NAC

    d Host software (security application software and Cisco Trust Agent) pushed to all hosts

This chapter covers the following topics:

- Policing your information highway
- Begin by laying the framework
- Value is in the NAC partners
- Examples of admission control uses

CHAPTER 8

NAC Now and Future Proof for Tomorrow

Initial Network Admission Control (NAC) Framework implementations typically involve a solution that consists of partner NAC-enabled software that works with Cisco network infrastructure to limit security threats, such as worms and viruses, by focusing on validating host credentials and enforcing compliance. One of the many features NAC Framework provides is the capability to add the identity of both the user and host computer into the NAC enforcement decision mix.

This chapter describes additional capabilities that businesses can include with their future admission policies, requiring the network infrastructure to do the following:

- Use learned information about a host computer or user, or about where the computer or user resides on the network to determine rights and privileges that dictate resource authorization or access to certain data applications

- Detect company assets and enforce asset management policies by user or role

- Enforce regulatory compliance to protect client privacy and reduce the opportunity for leakage of business-sensitive data

- Automatically remediate noncompliant hosts and self-heal infected hosts

Policing Your Information Highway

Use NAC to police your information highway. NAC is analogous to a policeman who protects and enforces a variety of rules that users must abide by to have the privilege of traversing your information highway.

The traffic policeman's role and tools have evolved over time. During initial automobile use, policemen had fewer enforcement requirements and fewer tools to aid in their determination of compliance to the road rules. With increased automobile adoption, more rules and requirements were created to validate a minimum skill set for drivers as well as a minimum requirement for the automobile using the roads. Similarly, minimum compliance enforcement and identity verification are what many businesses will initially implement in their NAC deployments.

Compare the evolution of the modern traffic policeman's role and tools to NAC's protection and enforcement characteristics (noted in parentheses):

- The registration of the vehicle (host identity) by way of a vehicle identification number, or VIN (host serial number), the automobile license plate linked to the VIN (MAC address), an annual registration sticker to identify the tax paid for the privilege of driving the vehicle (accounting for billing to track who did what, where, and for how long).

- Vehicle inspection tag (host posture) that expires annually (host posture revalidation timer) to verify that the vehicle meets minimum standards to drive on the roads.

- Driver's license (user identity) that identifies that the driver has passed minimum driving skills. Sometimes a vehicle class (role or class of service) is assigned to indicate what type of vehicle a person can drive and to identify extra privileges. Physical characteristics are provided that identify the driver (user login) along with the expiration of the license (user identity revalidation timer).

- Police monitor the highway to ensure that drivers abide by road rules and do not exceed the maximum speed (posture compliance policy). Location can dictate a different set of rules (remote access versus LAN policy).

- When a violation occurs, the policeman assesses many criteria (credentials and policy). Besides the initial violation, he usually checks other database(s), such as outstanding arrest warrants, to determine compliance to other policies (external policy servers) before determining his action. For a minor violation, the driver might be warned but allowed to resume her journey without receiving a ticket (user notification stating out of compliance but network access allowed for now). Or, the policeman could determine that a more egregious violation, such as driving under the influence, or worse, such as a serious auto accident, occurred. The policeman can issue a ticket or tickets for the violation (application posture token for each posture credential).

- A driver might be required to appear in court (URL redirect) before a judge (policy server). The judge reviews the violations (application posture tokens) and sentences the driver based on the most severe violation (system posture token). In a simple case, the judge can issue a warning, fine, community service, or a temporary jail term (remediation in an attempt to make compliant). In severe cases, the judge can seize the driver's license, revoking her privilege to drive (no network access).

- The policeman (network access device [NAD]) enforces the judgment on the driver. The driver now has a record in a violation database; other police officers have access to the driver's history of violations (behavior trend).

Use NAC today to start policing your information highway. Start with a simple implementation, such as enforcing PC software compliance and validating user authentication. Over time, extend NAC's capability by adding more identity functionality to provide secure access to the ever-growing set of applications and system resources.

Begin by Laying the Framework

Businesses have two key areas of interest for their self-defending network: protecting their assets and thwarting misbehavior.

Asset Protection

Most businesses already have a software patch management process in place. Integrating software patch management processes with NAC can significantly improve the effectiveness of those processes. Before NAC, software compliance was not easily enforceable because host posturing did not exist. Users could stop updates from occurring or decide to update when they had time, which allows malware to spread even when software updates were made available to prevent such an outbreak. Being able to enforce software patch compliance is one of the initial major drivers for implementing NAC.

Cisco offers two network admission control choices: NAC Framework and NAC Appliance. Traditionally, businesses adopt one of the two models.

Many businesses initially adopt the NAC Appliance method, which provides a simpler approach to detection and enforcement of host software. NAC Appliance is an all-in-one solution that allows a rapid deployment model using a self-contained endpoint assessment, policy management, and remediation services. It provides similar operating system compliance checks and policy enforcement but can operate in a multivendor network infrastructure. It does not use an integrated approach with NAC partners that provide additional host posturing and enforcement functionality like NAC Framework. Also, at the time of this writing, identity enforcement is not available with NAC Appliance.

Others might want to add more admission checks, such as identity and corporate asset enforcement, migrating to an integrated environment as their deployments and requirements mature.

NAC Framework uses an integrated approach, leveraging infrastructure that is used as the policy enforcement point. NAC Framework also leverages existing security solutions from other vendors, such as antivirus, remediation, patching, and auditing services. The NAC Framework model allows a more flexible admission policy that is typically more complex than NAC Appliance deployments.

With NAC Framework, in addition to software compliance, you can add Identity-Based Networking Services (IBNS) to your admission policy decision when using NAC-L2-802.1X. Combining user and host authentication as part of the network admission decision is the strongest authorization model. With today's mobile workforces, you need to control who can gain access to different parts of the network. Your policy might need to differ based on a wired or wireless device. With identity as part of the admission policy, you can provide predetermined IP addresses only to valid users and devices that successfully authenticate and have been verified as being compliant.

Many NAC partners provide IBNS capabilities that can plug into the NAC Framework today. For example, some IBNS solutions assign rights to resources based on the identity of a user, specifying the user's network access, shared resource access to servers and printers, access for file read and/or write, and ability to use specific software applications.

You might need an admission policy that can assign the appropriate rights based on when a device is used, where a device or user is physically located, or a combination of when, where, and who. Examples include the following:

- Internal wired policy versus wireless policy.
- Geography-based policy to preserve confidentiality of data by enforcing whether it can be accessed and/or retrieved based on host location. Different policies might be needed for:
  - VPN access from a public area, such as the airport, hotel, or coffee shop.
  - VPN access from a more private place, such as a remote or home office.
  - Region-based access to limit remote users from accessing locally significant information, such as files not allowed for export.
  - Time-of-day and day-of-week policy to limit access to sensitive areas outside normal business hours.

You can determine how you plan to enforce compliance on devices that you don't manage or control. You can determine whether you are going to include the ability to exempt devices that cannot interwork with NAC so that they can use the network. Different methods exist to accomplish registering and exempting devices that can't communicate their credentials. You can use a dynamic auditing strategy to scan unmanaged devices, or you can statically maintain an exception table.

Use NAC Framework if your initial NAC deployment requires the following:

- Deep vendor integration for assessment and/or remediation
- 802.1X for initial NAC deployment
- Too many NAC appliance servers and overlay devices to satisfy admission control solution for a large enterprise

If a rapid deployment model is required or a simpler management method is desired, use the NAC Appliance. It uses the Cisco Clean Access product to provide out-of-the-box functionality with preinstalled support for antivirus and Microsoft updates.

NAC Appliance uses a turnkey approach versus the more complex feature-rich NAC Framework model. While many see the value of NAC Framework, some don't need all the other capabilities today and prefer a more simplistic approach.

Cisco plans to move forward with additional features in both models as well as to build a tighter integration between NAC Framework and NAC Appliance. Both architectures will be able to coexist and be centrally managed by a common management interface.

Detecting Misbehavior and Dealing with It

Other components of the self-defending network can be optionally implemented to detect and defend against malicious behavior. Misbehavior can exist in many forms. It can be intentional or nonintentional actions from users, failing or compromised devices, or external misbehavior from hackers. Examples include the following:

- **Using an intrusion protection system (IPS), such as a network-based IPS (NIPS) or host-based IPS (HIPS), to defend in depth against misbehavior on the network and individual hosts**—An example of a HIPS is Cisco Security Agent (CSA) running on hosts that function as PCs and servers. CSA can recognize application behavior that can lead to an attack and can prevent its malicious activity. You can create custom profiles for the different roles of servers and users, providing various levels of protection based on device use. For example, servers used as shared resources might require a fixed and hardened security policy, such as not allowing software applications to be installed, preventing system configuration files from being altered, and not opening TCP ports other than the ones needed for the server's applications. In contrast, hosts operated by some users might need to add software to perform their jobs, while other users are not allowed to add software. Any behavior attempted beyond the profile's acceptable policy is not allowed. Use NAC to enforce the use of the HIPS application by making sure that it is enabled and up to date before allowing the host to access the network. For example, with the integration of NAC and CSA, dynamic policy decisions can be made based on information provided from CSA.

- **Using Cisco Secure Monitoring, Analysis, and Response System (CS-MARS) to analyze, monitor, and detect all types of events on your network and present them in a single networkwide topology view**—CS-MARS can detect anomalies that could be caused by a host generating huge amounts of traffic because of a worm infection. CS-MARS can work with the policy server to automatically shut down the affected section of the network to reduce exposure to others, shun an offending device, or force device remediation. Beginning with version 4.1, CS-MARS can correlate and report on IOS-based 802.1X authentication events from IOS, CatOS, and Access Control Server (ACS) devices. As a result, CS-MARS can act as the centralized NAC reporting engine for security operators to monitor authentication and device posturing policies. CS-MARS has many predefined NAC reports that can be easily interpreted by a help desk operator, providing a quick summary in a graphical view. For example, compliance reports can identify healthy or unhealthy devices. If more information is needed, the operator can query for details about the host or user to diagnose the problem.

- **Using Cisco IOS NetFlow, which is available in routers, to provide visibility across the entire network, capturing traffic data to aid in understanding typical traffic trends**—Changes in network behavior can indicate denial of service (DoS) attacks or anomalies such as viruses and worms. NetFlow works by tracking packet flows between a given source and destination, which helps identify the path an attack is taking through the network. The NetFlow data can be exported and used by other applications or network management technologies such as CS-MARS.

These additional self-defending network technologies work in harmony with NAC and extend its capability by proactively protecting and defending the network, hosts, and users against misbehavior.

Value Is in the NAC Partners

One of the big challenges is that businesses typically use different technologies, often supplied by many vendors, to provide different methods of protection, and they often work independently of each other. Wouldn't it be nice to use a common framework that allows the many vendor technologies to plug in and interoperate with the networking infrastructure that controls access to only compliant hosts and valid users?

As the adoption of IBNS matures, businesses will want to increase their admission policy requirements to include more identity enforcement besides user authentication. It will involve using more applications and technologies to monitor and enforce acceptable use of their resources as well as to enforce acceptable behavior.

The value that NAC Framework provides over all other network admission methods comes from the many vendors who are NAC partners. Cisco believes in working with standards bodies such as the Internet Engineering Task Force (IETF) to make NAC available and work with many vendors.

From its inception, NAC Framework has allowed third-party vendor integration. It supports a variety of partner products and technologies using standards-based, flexible application program interfaces (APIs) that allow third parties to contribute solutions to a NAC Framework environment. Besides the options available today, a variety of new applications can be created as part of the NAC posturing process. Posture plug-ins can be created to allow communication between the vendor's client application and the Cisco Trust Agent. The Cisco Trust Agent can be customized to pass credentials for any type of characteristic by way of the Host Credentials Authorization Protocol (HCAP) or the Generic Authorization Message Exchange (GAME) Protocol to policy servers that decide the compliance level of a device or user. The policy server can send actions that are enforced by the NADs or even the vendor's client application.

NAC Framework uses the following security protocols:

- Standardized protocols such as Extensible Authentication Protocol (EAP), Protected EAP (PEAP), 802.1X, and RADIUS services are used for communications between network components and a variety of hosts.

EAP–Flexible Authentication via Secure Tunneling (EAP-FAST) is a Cisco-authored protocol that allows multiple credential types, such as user identity and posture credentials, to be chained together in a single authentication packet. This allows NAC-L2-802.1X to perform both user and machine identity authentication as well as posture validation.

- At the time of this writing, the following NAC protocols are Cisco proprietary. Some of these protocols are going through the formal process of becoming standardized and could be standard by the time you read this:

    — EAP–type-length value (EAP-TLV) is an EAP extension that carries posture credentials and posture notifications between the host computer's posture plug-in agent and the Cisco policy server.

    — GAME is a proprietary protocol used by partner audit servers to scan a host that has no Cisco Trust Agent installed to determine software compliance. An audit server uses GAME to communicate compliance directly to a Cisco Secure ACS, which in turn enforces the appropriate security policy on the host.

    — HCAP is available for NAC partners to allow their external policy servers to interoperate with the Cisco Secure ACS and to be part of the admission policy decision.

Cisco also provides an API for Cisco Trust Agent, HCAP, and GAME that is available to licensed vendors. NAC partner vendors can write custom applications using the API to evaluate almost anything for admission.

NAC is simply the conduit that allows your infrastructure to police your information highway with the requirements of your choice.

Examples of Admission Control Uses

Businesses might use the following examples as part of future security policies for NAC to enforce. Some of these capabilities exist today in partner vendor products, while others require some development. All are possible with the use of custom applications that can plug into the NAC framework:

- Track and manage company assets
- Enforce the use of corporate-approved software
- Enforce operating system access control
- Enforce physical identification for higher security clearance
- Enforce a business policy or rule
- Enforce regulatory compliance
- Enact roles-based provisioning

- Enforce data restriction when external media is detected
- Use customized shared resources

The following sections cover these uses.

Tracking and Managing Company Assets

When a device is detected by the network, the serial number is checked with a policy server and a back-end database for validation. Only company-owned assets are allowed access to the network. If the host is assigned to a user, only the assigned user can successfully log in to the host computer. In addition, the database can be updated to provide a general location of where the host is logged in or was last logged in. The location can be determined by the NAD servicing it.

Enforcing Use of Corporate-Approved Software

Ensure that the host is running corporate-approved software (for example, corporate image). This could be determined by the host identity, such as the serial number, or by user identity. Use NAC to limit network access to users whose hosts are not running corporate-sanctioned software or image, regardless of application.

Enforcing Operating System Access Control

Protect operating system integrity by prohibiting access or changes to sensitive system files, system binaries, and registry settings. An example is to allow basic actions required by the operating system process but to prevent file manipulation by users or applications from the Windows system directory. Enforce the host firewall or require the use of Windows IPsec filtering to control the type of traffic, such as a shared server or PC, that reaches a host. A HIPS such as CSA can provide this type of hardening capability today. Use NAC to enforce an OS-hardening policy before the host is allowed access to the network.

Enforcing Physical Identification for Higher Security Clearance

For an extra layer of defense, add a physical authentication requirement to associate a specific host to a specific user when the user attempts to access extremely confidential information. The technology could use a portable USB smart token or even a biometric device to perform physical identification verification (PIV). The PIV device could scan and verify a user's fingerprint, palm, or even eye. An example of physical identification enforcement is where an admission policy requires a portable USB secure token to be present in the host that is attempting network access. The secure token requires a valid personal identification number (PIN) to be entered by the user for the host's security application to initiate the NAC validation process. After being successfully authenticated with this physical identity credential, the user gets more privileges assigned with a higher security clearance from the policy server. This higher privilege remains active until the assigned time period expires or until the USB secure token is removed. NAC has configurable timers and/or uses EAP over LAN–Start (EAPoL-Start) with 802.1X to verify that the device is still compliant with the existing security policy. It can detect when a change occurs. Another option is to have the host application reinitiate the NAC process when it detects a change, such as removing the USB token, to lower the user's security clearance.

Enforcing a Business Policy or Rule

Your business might have rules for users that can be automated for a quick, consistent resolution. An example is a user that requires manager approval to access a certain server or file or to download company-provided software. The user who needs permission attempts access but is denied. However, the user can be automatically redirected to an application to submit the request. After the request is submitted, it is automatically routed electronically to the user's manager for approval and allows an expiration period to be assigned to this privilege. After approval is gained, the policy server raises the user's access privilege for a period of time and notifies the user by means of a pop-up or e-mail message that access to the server or file is now available.

Enforcing Regulatory Compliance

Some businesses must comply with industry or government regulations, such as the Gramm-Leach-Bliley Act (GLBA), the Sarbanes-Oxley (SOX) Act, and the Health Insurance Portability and Accountability Act (HIPAA). NAC can enforce features such as password control, identifying the user, and allowing only those users with the proper identity to access business- or client-sensitive information. You could enforce a user's PC to initiate the built-in screen saver after ten minutes of inactivity. You could even guarantee that a password setting is used to regain the display. Extra steps such as these can automatically ensure that the host is secure, even when the user steps away. Use NAC to enforce PC functions such as this by means of a custom API that detects the settings and sends credentials to a policy server that enforces compliance.

Enacting Roles-Based Provisioning

Policy based on job type or device type provides a consistent set of common rules or privileges organized by groups. Privileges can include network access rights, file read/write privileges, common use of software or web applications, work time, and day schedule. When changes are made to the role, it provides a quick and consistent policy change to a common group of users/hosts. Use NAC to enforce a policy to a user or host from a policy server that controls access to a variety of resources. If role privileges are changed, the policy server can initiate a revalidation of those users who require enforcement of the new policy.

Enforcing Data Restriction When External Media Is Detected

Controlling read/write access to sensitive information with removable media can prevent loss of business-sensitive information or client financial or health data. An example is an application on a host that detects whether an external storage device, such as USB flash drive or external drive, is present. The host initially authenticated successfully when the device was not present. A host's application detects a change and initiates a NAC revalidation with the policy server. New credentials are sent. The admission policy for the device has changed and does not allow removable USB storage devices. It denies the user access to certain areas of the network, or it can prevent the downloading of certain types of files tagged as confidential, such as patient records. The offending host is not allowed to access the restricted area or perform downloads while the external device is present. When the external storage device has been removed from the host, the application detects this and a revalidation reoccurs. The policy server now grants full read/write access to the host and user. NAC works with other software applications to enforce policy and report user activity (for example, if a user attempts to save files tagged confidential to his host's hard drive without the external device plugged in and then transfers the files to the storage device later). The security software application such as CSA can be programmed by a user's profile to prevent the transfer of files to the hard drive and/or report this type of event.

Using Customized Shared Resources

Some businesses have a 24/7 multiple-shift operation in which employees share common resources, including desks, host computers, and telephones. Each work shift, an employee picks a free desk and successfully logs in to a host, which is associated with a phone and a desk. The user's identity is associated with a virtual machine that has personal settings and assigned applications with access to his personal files. The IP phone is configured for extension mobility, allowing the user to log in and activate his personal extension, feature buttons, and voice-mail settings to that phone. The desk has been checked out to the user and is logged as being unavailable for others to use. During the employee's work shift, his desk devices are personalized for his use. An auditing system keeps track of where the employees work, the hours worked, and the resources they use. This can serve to track usage for department billing and accounting for payroll use, and serve as a measurement for historical trends reporting. At the end of his shift, the user logs off the host and phone, which restores him to a defaulted guest access state, waiting for the next shift. Use NAC to associate an authorized user, host, and applications together, especially for users who do not have dedicated devices. Enforce software compliance and secure file access in this virtual environment.

These examples are just a sample of what can become part of your admission policy decision to help you police your information highway. Advanced identity and compliance capabilities can exist by including NAC-enabled vendor applications. Even if you don't need these advanced capabilities today, be assured that when you implement the Cisco NAC Framework, it sets the foundation to flexibly add a variety of future enforcement decisions to your network admission policy.

Summary

Use NAC to police your information highway by enforcing admission control rules for hosts and users that traverse your network.

Begin by laying the framework to use learned information about a host, user, or user's location on the network to control network access based on the user's compliance to the admission policy. *Use posture + identity = best access control.*

NAC can leverage existing network infrastructure, security software services, and security policies to provide enforcement points to disperse locations.

For those network-attached devices that are not NAC capable, use other methods, such as an audit server, which can scan hosts and determine software compliance and then communicate the result to the policy server to determine their admission rights.

Don't limit NAC to just enforcing software compliance; NAC can do much more. It is simply the conduit to allow your infrastructure to police your information highway with the requirements of your choice. Integrate other applications, available from Cisco NAC partners, as part of the compliance checking and enforcement process. In addition, create applications using the API to detect and enforce any type of identity characteristic that is important for your business.

No two NAC Framework implementations will be alike. NAC Framework provides the most flexible and feature-rich network admission control solution, adaptable to your needs for today and in the future.

Answers to Review Questions

Chapter 1

1 Which NAC component(s) act(s) as the policy enforcement point? Choose all that apply.

a NAC-enabled Cisco router

b NAC-enabled Cisco switch

c NAC-enabled software application

d Cisco Trust Agent

e Cisco Secure ACS

Answer: a, b

2 Which NAC component(s) operate(s) as the policy decision point? Choose all that apply.

a NAC-enabled Cisco router

b NAC-enabled Cisco switch

c Cisco Secure ACS

d CiscoWorks VMS

e Supported NAC partner antivirus or identity server

Answer: c, e

3 Which NAC component(s) communicate(s) host credentials to the NAD? Choose all that apply.

   a Cisco Secure ACS

   b Cisco Trust Agent

   c Cisco Security Agent

   d NAC-enabled software application

Answer: b

4 What type of actions can the Cisco policy server specify to enforce on the device? Choose all that apply.

   a Display a message to the user

   b Redirect users to a remediation server

   c Permit or deny network access

   d Notify an administrator

   e Send a lock to the host computer

Answer: a, b, c

5 Guests frequent the campus and routinely use the public conference rooms. Many of the guest vendors use the Internet in meetings to demonstrate their services. You are responsible for enforcing the company security policy, which requires specific updates to an antivirus application and to host operating systems. What options do you have for guests that allow them access to the Internet while maintaining the security policy? Choose all that apply.

   a Use an audit server to scan hosts and determine their compliance state for policy enforcement. Guest network access can be determined by the compliance outcome.

   b No exceptions exist for nonconforming guests; network access is not allowed.

   c Configure a default access policy that only allows access to the Internet on the NAD supporting those conference rooms.

    d   Have the conference room NADs provide a pool of IPs that are assigned to a guest DHCP pool and configure those IP addresses to be exempted on the NAD.

    e   All of the above.

    f   Options a. and c.

Answer: f

Chapter 2

  1 Match the NAC protocol to its function:

    a   EoU

    b   HCAP

    c   GAME

    d   EAPo802.1X

    __ Uses IEEE MAC frame
    __ Uses port 21862
    __ Queries the PVS
    __ Queries an audit server

    Answer:
    d   Uses IEEE MAC frame
    a   Uses port 21862
    b   Queries the PVS
    c   Queries an audit server

  2 Which of the following are EAP packets types? Choose all that apply.

    a   Request and response

    b   Hello and acknowledge

    c   Request and acknowledge

    d   Success and failure

    Answer: a, d

3 Which protocol is available for communication of the host credentials to security vendor policy validation servers?

   a   GAME

   b   HCAP

   c   ACS

   d   RADIUS

   Answer: b

4 Which Cisco Trust Agent:Cisco:Host credential attributes can be evaluated by a NAC policy? Choose all that apply.

   a   Service packs

   b   Hot fixes

   c   OS-Version

   d   Protection-Enabled

   Answer: a, b

5 Which of the following methods can trigger the NAC process for a host connecting to a NAD that uses the NAC-L2-802.1X mode? Choose all that apply.

   a   Any IP traffic

   b   DHCP snooping

   c   EAPoL-Start

   d   Ethernet linkup signal from the host

   e   Dynamic ARP inspection

   Answer: c, d

6 Which two methods can trigger the NAC process for a host connecting to a NAD that uses the NAC-L2-IP mode?

a   Any IP traffic

b   DHCP snooping

c   EAPoL-Start

d   Ethernet linkup signal from the host

e   ARP inspection

Answer: b, e

7 Which method can trigger the NAC process for a host connecting to a NAD that uses the NAC-L3-IP mode?

a   Any IP traffic

b   DHCP snooping

c   EAPoL-Start

d   Ethernet linkup signal from the host

e   Dynamic ARP inspection

Answer: a

8 Which of the following defines the situation where the NAD challenges a host to make sure that nothing has changed since the validation process?

a   Revalidation

b   Status query

c   Posture validation

d   EAP identity response

Answer: b

9 Which techniques can be used to permit a network printer onto a NAC-protected subnet, even though it is not NAC capable? Choose all that apply.

a Include the printer's MAC in the NAD exception table.

b Include the printer's static IP address in the NAD exception table.

c Include the printer's device type "printer" in the NAD or ACS NAC exception table.

d Use an audit server to scan and validate the printer.

Answer: a, b

10 Which posture token is assigned to a host when it has not fully booted up and some services have not yet started?

a Checkup

b Unknown

c Transition

d Quarantine

Answer: c

11 Which of the following APTs does ACS decide to use as the SPT and take action against?

Quarantine—Cisco Trust Agent host from local ACS check

Healthy—Cisco Trust Agent PA from local ACS check

Checkup—CSA from local ACS check

Checkup—Antivirus client from vendor PVS

a Both checkup and quarantine actions

b Checkup actions, because two exist

c Quarantine action only

d ACS defers action to antivirus client's PVS

Answer: c

12 Which two methods can be used to audit an agentless host?

   a   Exception table

   b   MAC Authentication Bypass

   c   Network scan

   d   URL redirection to an audit server

Answer: c, d

13 Which NAC Framework component causes a user's browser to pop up with the URL redirect from the notification string?

   a   Posture plug-in agent

   b   NAD

   c   Cisco Trust Agent

   d   Audit server

Answer: c

14 Which of the following ACLs is used for enforcement by routers serving as NADs?

   a   VACL

   b   PACL

   c   RACL

   d   PBACL

Answer: c

Chapter 3

1 Cisco Trust Agent includes an 802.1X supplicant for which type of interfaces?

  a Any type of access interface

  b Only wired interfaces

  c Wired and wireless interfaces

  d All Layer 2 and Layer 3 interfaces

Answer: b

2 How is the protected EAP tunnel established between ACS and Cisco Trust Agent?

  a Both use a shared secret password only.

  b Choice of using either a shared secret password or certificate.

  c Cisco Trust Agent presents a certificate to ACS.

  d ACS presents a certificate to Cisco Trust Agent.

Answer: d

3 When evaluating identity and posture credentials, which EAP type must be used with 802.1X?

  a EAP-FAST

  b Protected EAP

  c EAP-TLS

  d EAP-GTC

Answer: a

4 Cisco Trust Agent communicates directly with which two NAC components?

  a NAD

  b ACS

  c NAC-enabled applications posture plug-in

  d Posture agents

Answer: a, c

5 Which type(s) of NAC vendor file is located in the host directory C:\Program Files\Common Files\PostureAgent\Plugins?

   a   .dll

   b   .log

   c   .exe

   d   .inf

   Answer: a, d

6 Which common filenames are assigned to the two posture agent plug-ins?

   a   ctapp.inf

   b   CiscoHostPP.inf

   c   CiscoHostPP.dll

   d   ctaapi.dll

   e   ctapp.dll

   Answer: a, b

7 Which of the following statements is false?

   a   A benefit of using CSA with NAC is that it can protect Cisco Trust Agent from being altered.

   b   CSA MC allows the ability to install Cisco Trust Agent and required certificates along with the CSA quiet install.

   c   CSA can discover and mark application traffic with DSCP values.

   d   CSA is a posture agent and does not require the use of Cisco Trust Agent.

   Answer: d

Chapter 4

1 Which ACS version 4.0 NAP window is used to configure MAC Authentication Bypass to be allowed?

a   Posture Validation

b   EAP Configuration

c   Authentication Protocols

d   External Posture Validation Servers

Answer: c

2 Which of the following can be used as external policy server(s) for NAC Framework? Choose all that apply.

a   Trend Micro OfficeScan

b   McAfee Policy Manager

c   QualysGuard

d   Altiris

Answer: a, b, d

3 Which of the following can be used as external audit server(s) for NAC Framework?

a   Trend Micro OfficeScan

b   QualysGuard

c   McAfee Policy Manager

d   Altiris

Answer: b

4 Which of the following policy server(s) can logically evaluate the received client's TLV information?

a   Cisco Secure ACS

b   Trend Micro OfficeScan

c   McAfee Policy Manager

d   QualysGuard

Answer: a

5 Refer to Figure 4-6. For the Trend-OSCE policy rules for ID 1, if only one condition matches the policy rules, which posture token is assigned?

   a Trend:AV:Healthy for that rule because one match is all that's needed

   b Cisco:PA:Healthy for that rule because one match is all that's needed

   c Trend:AV:Quarantine because the healthy state requires all rules to be matched 100 percent

   d Cisco:PA:Quarantine because the healthy state requires all rules to be matched 100 percent

   Answer: c

6 Which whitelist technique can be used for NAC-L2-802.1X implementations?

   a MAC wildcard for posturing hosts

   b IP wildcard for posturing hosts

   c MAB only

   d Any of the above

   Answer: c

7 Which enforcement actions are not available for NAC-L2-IP when using NAC Framework Phase 2 (at the time of this writing)?

   a VLAN assignment

   b URL redirection

   c Downloadable ACLs

   d Posture status queries

   Answer: a

Chapter 5

1 Choose additional benefit(s) that can be observed when combining 802.1X into the admission policy.

   a   Identity-based access control

   b   Traceability of users for auditing purposes

   c   Visibility of users

   d   All of the above

   Answer: d

2 Match the type with its function.

   ____ Requests service

   ____ Validates credentials

   ____ Enforces authorization policy

   a   Authentication server

   b   Authenticator

   c   Supplicant

   Answer:

   c   Requests service

   a   Validates credentials

   b   Enforces authorization policy

3 Which of the following is a response from a supplicant to an authentication server?

   a   RADIUS-Challenge-Request packet

   b   RADIUS-Access-Request packet

   c   EAPoL-Start packet

   d   EAP-Identity-Request packet

   Answer: b

4 Which three EAP tunneling modes can be used with 802.1X?

   a PEAP, EAP-TLS, EAP-FAST

   b EAP-TLS, EAP-TTLS, EAP-FAST

   c PEAP, EAP-TTLS, EAP-FAST

   d EAP-FAST, LEAP, PEAP

Answer: c

5 The main advantages of using 802.1X VLAN assignments are the ability to limit access by risk criteria and to assign access by a group, such as "guest" or "sales". True or false?

Answer: True

6 Which RADIUS attribute value pair (AVP) parameter specifies the link layer topology type to which a VLAN is applied for use with 802.1X?

   a Tunnel-type

   b Tunnel-medium-type

   c Tunnel-private-group-ID

   d Identity-type

Answer: b

7 What triggers a Guest-VLAN to be assigned to hosts that do not have an 802.1X supplicant?

   a By default after 30 seconds of no response from an authenticator's EAPoL-Identity-Request.

   b By default after the host has failed authentication from the authenticator.

   c By default after three retries of no response from an authenticator's EAPoL-Identity-Request.

   d By default, after 90 seconds of no response from an authenticators EAPoL-Identity-Request, the authenticator's port goes to a TRANSITION state.

Answer: c

8 When using a Cisco switch port that has been enabled for both IP telephony and 802.1X, the data port can never authenticate if the telephony device lacks an 802.1X supplicant. True or false?

Answer: False

9 Which switch-based Layer 2 technique provides network access to known devices that lack an 802.1X supplicant?

a   MAB

b   Guest-VLAN

c   By using Cisco Trust Agent

d   Exception table

Answer: a

10 Which RADIUS attribute(s) allow a host to reauthenticate passively, where the 802.1X state machine transitions to a CONNECTING state versus DISCONNECTED?

a   Session-Timeout + Termination-Action = "Default"

b   Session-Timeout = "RADIUS-Request" + Termination-Action = "NONE"

c   Session-Timeout + Termination-Action = "RADIUS-Request"

d   Session-Timeout = "Default"

Answer: c

Chapter 6

1 Which protocols should be allowed so that the EAPoUDP Layer 3 mechanism and control plane can operate?

a   DHCP

b   EAP port 21862

c   UDP port 21862

d   TCP port 443

Answer: a, c

2 The RADIUS Message-Authenticator attribute prevents attackers from subverting EAP by providing per-packet authentication and integrity protection. Which Message-Authenticator attribute found in Table 6-1 is used for HMAC-MD5 for a Catalyst switch?

   a Attribute No. 1

   b Attribute No. 29

   c Attribute No. 79

   d Attribute No. 80

   Answer: d

3 ACLs deployed to support NAC-L2-IP and NAC-L3-IP are assumed to be source-based ACLs that are used on a per-host basis and accomplished by what statement in an ACE?

   Answer: any

4 Which method(s) allow IP phones to be exempted from NAC?

   a Enabling Cisco Discovery Protocol

   b Static exemption using phone IP address

   c Static exemption using phone MAC address

   d All of the above

   Answer: d

5 Which Catalyst switch security features can prevent spoofing of EAPoUDP states?

   a EAP-Status-Query

   b IP-Source-Guard

   c ARP probing

   d Dynamic ARP Inspection

   Answer: b, d

Chapter 7

1 Which lifecycle phase should security administration and management roles and their responsibilities be defined?

    a   Operate

    b   Plan

    c   Prepare

    d   Design

Answer: c

2 You want to implement posture and identity to hosts connected to hubs. What are your options? Hint: Refer to the NAC Framework Phase 2 Implementation Decision Tree in Figures 7-4 and 7-5.

    a   You cannot use hubs for any type of NAC detection; replace hubs with Cisco switches.

    b   Only posture can be accomplished through the use of hubs.

    c   Use an 802.1X supplicant for this NAC method.

    d   Hubs work fine with NAC.

Answer: b

3 Match the following NADs to the NAC method.

    a   NAC-L2-802.1X

    b   NAC-L2-IP

    c   NAC-L3-IP

    d   Can't be done

    __ Router with posture and identity

    __ Router with posture only

    __ Switch with posture and identity

    __ Switch with posture only

Answer:

d   Router with posture and identity

c   Router with posture only

a   Switch with posture and identity

b   Switch with posture only

4   Match the definition with its NAC policy type.

   a   MAC exception

   b   Group membership

   c   Who, what, when, how

   d   Software update not current

   __ Identity definition

   __ Policy definition

   __ Credential definition

   __ NAH definition

Answer:

b   Identity definition

c   Policy definition

d   Credential definition

a   NAH definition

5   Three decision elements can determine who has network access. Host posture is one; what are the other two?

   Answer: User identity, host identity

6 Using the Host Credential Worksheet sample in Table 7-8, what posture is assigned to a Windows XP user with the following features:

Cisco Trust Agent version 2.1 is present and enabled.

Antivirus version 8.0 is present and enabled.

CSA version 4.5 is present but disabled.

a Healthy

b Checkup

c Quarantine

d Infected

Answer: d

7 Using the Host Credential Worksheet sample in Table 7-8, how many action(s) are assigned to a Windows XP user with the following features:

Cisco Trust Agent version 2.1 is present and enabled.

Antivirus version 8.0 is present and running patch version 11.

CSA version 4.5 is present and enabled.

a Three: message notification, URL redirect, and enforcement ACL/VLAN

b Two: message notification and enforcement ACL/VLAN

c One: message notification only

d None, business as usual

Answer: a

8 What is the default network access for users who fail authorization using NAC-L2-802.1X?

a No access

b No restriction

c Access that is defined by ACL

d Access that is defined by VLAN

Answer: a

9 Which NAC component allows configuration for NAH exemption using the MAC Authentication Bypass (MAB) feature?

   a Static list at any Layer 2 NAD

   b Static list at any Layer 3 NAD

   c Static centralized list at ACS

Answer: c

10 Which of the following timers takes precedence for revalidation?

   a Always the NAD-EoU timeout revalidation period

   b Always the ACS—Session Timeout period

   c The shorter time period of the two, regardless of NAD/ACS

   d The longer time period of the two, regardless of NAD/ACS

Answer: b

11 What happens when a host using a vendor's security application is attempting network access, but all the external policy server(s) are not reachable, so that specific vendor's host credential cannot be checked?

   a ACS will not use that specific credential when determining the system posture token.

   b The posture token for that credential will be assigned "unknown" by ACS.

   c The host fails authentication and uses the default network access, which could be no access.

Answer: c

12 What method(s) should be considered for increasing AAA availability, which is extremely important in NAC implementations?

   a   Configuring IOS RADIUS failover

   b   Using multiple external policy validation servers and configuring the primary and backup servers in ACS NAC policy

   c   Configuring IOS server for load balancing among the ACS servers

   d   Using load balancing and failover through the use of a Content Services Switch or module

   e   All of the above

   f   Only a, b, and c

Answer: e

13 Which of the following implementation tasks should be done last?

   a   ACS policy enabled

   b   External PVS policy enabled

   c   NAD enabled for NAC

   d   Host software (security application software and Cisco Trust Agent) pushed to all hosts

Answer: c

INDEX

Symbols

Numerics

A

B-C

**preparation phase of NAC Framework lifecycle,
145–149**
corporate security policy, defining
acceptable use policy, 147
incident-handling policy, 149
information security policy, 146
network access control policy, 147
security management policy, 148–149
corporate security policy, defining, 145–149
prioritizing NAC solution objectives, 150
progression of NAC technology, 4–5
protecting assets, 205–206
protocol messages for 802.1X EAP exchange, 98
PVID (Port VLAN Identifier), 135–136

Q-R

QualysGuard appliance, 82

RACLs (router access control lists), 48
**RADIUS (Remote Access Dial-In User
Service), 36**
attributes for 802.1X, 100, 102
authenticated identity, leveraging, 117–118
EAP
end-to-end, 103–104
negotiation, 102
EAPoUDP, 129–132
RADIUS-Access-Request packets, 100
RCAs (RADIUS Authorization Components), 87
redirection, 169
**regulatory compliance enforcement, example
NAC policy, 211**
remediation, 3
requirements
for NAC Framework adoption, 206
for NAC Framework solution, 10
Cisco Secure ACS support, 12–13
Cisco Trust Agent support, 13
router support, 10
switch support, 11
VPN concentrator support, 11
wireless support, 12
revalidation timers, 40, 44
**roles-based provisioning, example NAC
policy, 211**

S

**sample migration strategies for NAC Framework
deployment, 189–195**
**scalability considerations for NAC Framework
deployment, 180–183, 185**
ACS database replication and
synchronization, 183
calculations, performing, 184–185
dispersal of NADs/ACSs, 180
NAC timers, 182–183
number of hosts and users, 181
protocol authorization rates, 182
security management policy, defining, 148–149
selecting posture token, 83–84
self-defending network technologies, 207
server-side protocols, 36
services within Cisco Trust Agent, 57
software
compliance enforcement process, 13–16
cost of, estimating for NAC Framework
deployment, 161–162
specifying enforcement actions, 86–88
SPT (system posture token), 26–27
standard ACLs, 47
static exceptions, 49
static exemptions for NAHs, 31
supplicants, 94–97
NAC-enabled, 115
support strategy, defining, 160
surveying current network, 151–158

T-U

TLV file format, 132
Trend Micro OfficeScan solution, 81
trust agent disappearing, 136–137
Trusted QoS, 67–68

uncontrolled ports (802.1X), 96, 111
URL redirect, 133

V-W-X-Y-Z

THIS BOOK IS SAFARI ENABLED

INCLUDES FREE 45-DAY ACCESS TO THE ONLINE EDITION

The Safari® Enabled icon on the cover of your favorite technology book means the book is available through Safari Bookshelf. When you buy this book, you get free access to the online edition for 45 days.

Safari Bookshelf is an electronic reference library that lets you easily search thousands of technical books, find code samples, download chapters, and access technical information whenever and wherever you need it.

TO GAIN 45-DAY SAFARI ENABLED ACCESS TO THIS BOOK:

- Go to **http://www.ciscopress.com/safarienabled**

- Complete the brief registration form

- Enter the coupon code found in the front of this book before the "Contents at a Glance" page

If you have difficulty registering on Safari Bookshelf or accessing the online edition, please e-mail customer-service@safaribooksonline.com.

Learn more about
Cisco Network Admission Control

Volume 2 is now available from Cisco Press

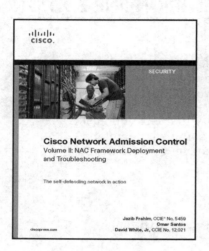

Cisco Network Admission Control,
Volume II: Deployment and Troubleshooting

Authors: Jazib Frahim, Omar Santos,
David White

ISBN: 1587052253

Published December 2006

Secure the network edge with the premier book on NAC deployment and management

Cisco Network Admission Control, Volume II provides a comprehensive guide on how to deploy and troubleshoot phase 2 of NAC to protect networks from attacks and threats and to ultimately create a self-defending network. By highlighting what protection NAC provides when a virus outbreak occurs, this book is a guide for any network professional who manages network security and monitors organizational infrastructure for day-zero threats. This first book on deploying and managing the Cisco NAC solution also addresses the security risks of remote and mobile computer users connecting to corporate networks.

Visit **www.ciscopress.com** to find out more about this and other Cisco Press titles.